Ernest L. Schusky

The Forgotten Sioux

An Ethnohistory of
the Lower Brule Reservation

Nelson-Hall nh Chicago

Library of Congress Cataloging in Publication Data

Schusky, Ernest Lester, 1931-
  The forgotten Sioux.

  Bibliography: p.
  Includes index.
  1. Brulé Indians—History. I. Title.
E99.B8S38   978'.004'97   75-503
ISBN 0-88229-138-6

for
The many generations of Lower Brule people
who have gone
and the many generations yet to come

Contents

Acknowledgment

This acknowledgment relates much of the history of the book as well as indicating my debt to others.

My interest in Indians, which began while I was in high school, was encouraged by my father. Later at Miami University, Professor George Fathauer widened this interest to all of mankind, revealing how study of one group could shed light on all peoples.

In graduate work in anthropology I must acknowledge the guidance of Professors Edward Spicer, Fred Eggan, and Sol Tax, who further encouraged my study of American Indians. I owe a special debt to Robert Thomas, a fellow student at the University of Chicago, who shared much of his knowledge and insight with me.

My first involvement with the Dakota began in 1958 when the Institute of Indian Studies at the University of South Dakota invited me to do fieldwork at the Lower Brule Sioux Reservation. They sponsored my research there for six months between March and September, 1958. For the next two years while I taught at South Dakota State College, I was able to continue research among the Dakota due to the kindness of Professor Vernon Malan, who shared his research project with me.

During this period, contemporary problems outweighed a pursuit of Lower Brule history. However, I began to appreciate the insights that a history gave, as I acquired more and more background. I began an intensive historical study in 1967 when a sociologist, Elliott Rudwick, finally persuaded me to do so, and another sociologist, Robert Campbell, prodded me with friendly encouragement. Only after I completed a first draft did I realize it was essential that I consult all available primary sources. This work began in the summer of 1968 at the State

Historical Society of South Dakota where the director, Dayton Canady, furnished me access to early Dakota Territory newspapers and scarce sources on the Dakota. He also directed me to the Federal Records Center in Kansas City, the depository for Bureau of Indian Affairs records.

The Federal Records Center personnel were most cooperative in furnishing me these valuable stored sources. Because of a lack of personnel the data are not indexed; in fact, most of the records remain in the boxes originally used to send them to the center. The records are mostly copies of the agents' correspondence. Letters to Washington were transferred into letterbooks, and many of them were obliterated because of dampness. The originals of these letters to the Commissioner of Indian Affairs are preserved in Washington in good condition, but much of the Indian agents' correspondence was distributed to a wide variety of offices. This correspondence is only available in the Records Center.

At the National Archives I was able to read the correspondence lost in the letterbooks, as well as letters from various correspondents other than Indian agents. Washington is the only source for the rare letters from Lower Brule Indians to the Bureau of Indian Affairs. The staff at the National Archives and the Records Center were most helpful in guiding my wife and me in our search of this material. I particularly want to thank Mr. Richard Maxwell of the National Archives.

My wife, Mary Sue, aided me in checking for sources at the Nebraska State Historical Society in Lincoln and the Colorado State Historical Society in Denver. Personnel were courteous and helpful with their source material for the Dakota, although data on Lower Brule were scarce. The Museum of the Friends of the Middle Border in Mitchell, South Dakota, was most cooperative in letting me search their picture files for photographs of Lower Brule. I owe much to this museum.

Some financial support for searching these primary sources came from the American Philosophical Society, the Research and Projects Office of the Graduate School and the

Anthropology Department of Southern Illinois University. Donna Rees, Roben Kelley and Ann Van Horn showed a remarkable interest as well as forbearance in typing the manuscript.

My major help in the research came from my wife, who, as reference librarian, found many an overlooked source. She also participated in dusting, lifting, and checking the twenty-pound record books at the National Archives while locating much of the data basic to Lower Brule history. In writing the history she provided editorial assistance along with my father-in-law, Irving Dilliard. Further assistance was given by personnel of the Missouri Historical Society, which published an earlier version of Chapter 2 of the present work.

Finally, my thanks must go to the people of Lower Brule whose friendship made my initial stay there so memorable. I am especially indebted to Andrew, Frank, Gensler, and John Estes, but all of the Lower Brule epitomized the Dakota value of hospitality. Hopefully, this history of their community will express something of my fondness for them.

Introduction

One day two men were out hunting buffalo when a strange light appeared. The light was like the one you see in pictures of Jesus. A woman came down the light. She was a good woman. In English she was something like a virgin. She brought a Pipe with her when she came. She told the two men to go back to their village and find a good man—it's hard to say in English—a man who never did any sins. They picked out such a man and took him to the woman. She gave the Pipe to that good man. Then she walked over the hill. At the top she turned sideways. When she did that she turned into a White Buffalo.

—Told by an elderly Lower Brule Indian in 1958.

God gave his Son to the White Man across the ocean. He gave the Peace Pipe to the Indian. I have a cousin who has made the trip to see the Peace Pipe a couple of times. Each time he goes, the Pipe is a little shorter. I think it keeps getting shorter because there are fewer Indians. It will disappear soon when the last Indian disappears.

—Told by a young Lower Brule Indian in 1958.

In contrast to Western mythology, the Dakota Indian legend assumes that Indians always existed. Instead, their myth concentrates on origins of the Pipe, relations with God, and involvement with other powerful forces. Obviously the Dakota were self-assured and proud; they felt no need to explain their own origins. They had always been.

However, by 1958, many Lower Brule had developed serious self-doubts that are reflected by their belief that the original Pipe was disappearing. This belief about an early end for the Indian was frequently expressed to me quite explicitly. Moreover, tribal members often acted as if their culture would end in a generation or two, and the tribal council made its decisions on the basis of such an assumption.

As an outside observer, I very soon had doubts about the validity of the assumption. I found that the man who believed the Pipe was disappearing was himself fasting and seeking visions. He sponsored visits of *Yuwipi*, or medicine men, to Lower Brule, and other Indians assumed he might one day become a *Yuwipi* himself. It is true that this man also officiated in Episcopal church services and several times explained Episcopalian dogma to me in sophisticated terms, but clearly Christianity was an addition, not a replacement, to his aboriginal religious beliefs. Frequently in talking with other Indians I heard them deplore the Indians' end and express regret that no one spoke Indian anymore. They were sure knowledge of the language would end with their generation. Yet while we were talking, they would break into their Indian tongue to admonish their small children, who obviously understand Siouan better than English. Clearly in everyday life the Lower Brule were perpetuating much of an Indian culture, even though they anticipated an end to their way of life.

I have argued elsewhere that we should expect the Lower Brule to continue indefinitely as an Indian community.[1] The Indians' belief that they are disappearing is largely a result of listening to too many whites who continually tell them Indians are and should become more like white men. However, many processes are at work to prevent such assimilation; perhaps one of the more important of these factors in retaining a difference is the Dakotas' deep sense of pride. Since 1960 that pride is much more consciously expressed, and the value of Indian identity has become explicitly recognized. Young Indian militants, who have formulated a philosophy of Indian identity sometimes expressed as Red Power, have contributed to a shift in the Indian consciousness,[2] but they likely only hastened an inevitable discovery.

Still many Lower Brule are unsure of their future. After all, they have been surrounded for more than a hundred years by whites who have insisted that Indian culture was inferior, and they "proved" their assertions by military conquest followed by economic and technological comparisons. The proof has convinced many whites as well as Indians of the superiority of the dominant culture. Logically it follows that Indians would be better off to join the superior culture.

It seems to me that the only person who can decide whether an Indian should assimilate or maintain a separate identity is an individual Indian himself. However, it is grossly unfair to have to make that choice when one's history is distorted by invidious comparisons. An objective look at the Dakota past shows them making the best of a situation when another people simply overwhelmed them in numbers. Unfortunately I do not feel qualified to make this point with many Dakota; but I do feel confident that some Indian will soon accomplish this end. I do hope my history will enlighten whites and that the people who surround Indian communities may come to see their relations with Indians as a part of this history. Although such a history will never be complete, it is far more helpful than the myth that Indians must disappear because Western culture is superior.

chap
Dakota be

The tw
counts for origins. work
concerned themselves wi
people, before God, who
concerns the beginnings

In the olden times it was
(especially the Teton band of S
during the year. This gathering
midsummer when everything loo
live to see nature at its best—tha
ceremony took place and vows wer
tribal gathering took place in the
condition, when wild fruits of all
on the trees and plants were the br
One reason why the people gat
as a whole might celebrate the victor
other good fortunes which had occurr
bands were scattered and each band w
ly. Another reason was that certain ru

1

head chiefs and other leaders of the tribe, by which each band of the tribe was governed. For instance, if a certain band got into trouble with some other tribe, such as the Crows, the Sioux tribe as a whole should be notified. Or if an enemy or enemies came on their hunting grounds the tribe should be notified at once. In this way the Teton band of Sioux was protected as to its territory and its hunting grounds.

After these gatherings there was a scattering of the various bands. On one such occasion the Sans Arc band started toward the west. They were moving from place to place, expecting to find buffalo and other game which they would lay up for their winter supply, but they failed to find anything. A council was called and two young men were selected to go in quest of buffalo and other game. They started on foot. When they were out of sight they each went in a different direction, but met again at a place which they had agreed upon. While they were planning and planning what to do, there appeared from the west a solitary object advancing toward them. It did not look like a buffalo; it looked more like a human being than anything else. They could not make out what it was, but it was coming rapidly. Both considered themselves brave, so they concluded that they would face whatever it might be. They stood still and gazed at it very eagerly. At last they saw that it was a beautiful young maiden. She wore a beautiful fringed buckskin dress, leggings, and moccasins. Her hair was hanging loose except at the left side, where was tied a tuft of shedded buffalo hair. In her right hand she carried a fan made of flat sage. Her face was painted with red vertical stripes. Not knowing what to do or say, they hesitated, saying nothing to her.

She spoke first, thus: "I am sent by the Buffalo tribe to visit the people you represent. You have been chosen to perform a difficult task. It is right that you should try to carry out the wishes of your people, and you must try to accomplish your purpose. Go home and tell the chief and headmen to put up a special lodge in the middle of the camp circle, with the door of the lodge and the entrance into the camp toward the direction where the sun rolls off the earth. Let them spread sage at the place of honor, and back of the fireplace let a small square place be prepared. Back of this and the sage let a certain frame, or economic and technological comparisons. The proof has convinced many whites as well as Indians of the superiority of the dominant culture. Logically it follows that Indians would be better off to join the superior culture.

It seems to me that the only person who can decide whether an Indian should assimilate or maintain a separate identity is an individual Indian himself. However, it is grossly unfair to have to make that choice when one's history is distorted by invidious comparisons. An objective look at the Dakota past shows them making the best of a situation when another people simply overwhelmed them in numbers. Unfortunately I do not feel qualified to make this point with many Dakota; but I do feel confident that some Indian will soon accomplish this end. I do hope my history will enlighten whites and that the people who surround Indian communities may come to see their relations with Indians as a part of this history. Although such a history will never be complete, it is far more helpful than the myth that Indians must disappear because Western culture is superior.

chapter 1
Dakota before the White Man

The two myths of the Pipe that introduce this work are abbreviations of a myth that accounts for origins. It is well to note that the Dakota have not concerned themselves with their own origin. They are a humble people, before God, who have always been. Their origin myth concerns the beginnings of religious symbols and values.

In the olden times it was a general custom for the Sioux tribe (especially the Teton band of Sioux) to assemble in a body once at least during the year. This gathering took place usually about that time of midsummer when everything looked beautiful and everybody rejoiced to live to see nature at its best—that was the season when the Sun Dance ceremony took place and vows were made and fulfilled. Sometimes the tribal gathering took place in the fall when wild game was in the best condition, when wild fruits of all kinds were ripe, and when the leaves on the trees and plants were the brightest.

One reason why the people gathered as they did was that the tribe as a whole might celebrate the victories, successes on the warpath, and other good fortunes which had occurred during the year while the bands were scattered and each band was acting somewhat independently. Another reason was that certain rules or laws were made by the head chiefs and other leaders of the tribe, by which each band of the tribe was governed. For instance, if a certain band got into trouble with some other tribe, such as the Crows, the Sioux tribe as a whole should be notified. Or if an enemy or enemies came on their hunting grounds the tribe should be notified at once. In this way the Teton band of Sioux was protected as to its territory and its hunting grounds.

After these gatherings there was a scattering of the various bands. On one such occasion the Sans Arc band started toward the west. They were moving from place to place, expecting to find buffalo and other game which they would lay up for their winter supply, but they failed to find anything. A council was called and two young men were selected to go in quest of buffalo and other game. They started on foot. When they were out of sight they each went in a different direction, but met again at a place which they had agreed upon. While they were planning and planning what to do, there appeared from the west a solitary object advancing toward them. It did not look like a buffalo; it looked more like a human being than anything else. They could not make out what it was, but it was coming rapidly. Both considered themselves brave, so they concluded that they would face whatever it might be. They stood still and gazed at it very eagerly. At last they saw that it was a beautiful young maiden. She wore a beautiful fringed buckskin dress, leggings, and moccasins. Her hair was hanging loose except at the left side, where was tied a tuft of shedded buffalo hair. In her right hand she carried a fan made of flat sage. Her face was painted with red vertical stripes. Not knowing what to do or say, they hesitated, saying nothing to her.

She spoke first, thus: "I am sent by the Buffalo tribe to visit the people you represent. You have been chosen to perform a difficult task. It is right that you should try to carry out the wishes of your people, and you must try to accomplish your purpose. Go home and tell the chief and headmen to put up a special lodge in the middle of the camp circle, with the door of the lodge and the entrance into the camp toward the direction where the sun rolls off the earth. Let them spread sage at the place of honor, and back of the fireplace let a small square place be prepared. Back of this and the sage let a certain frame, or rack, be made. *Right in front of the rack a buffalo skull should be placed. I have something of importance to present to the tribe, which will have a great deal to do with their future welfare. I shall be in the camp about sunrise."*

While she was thus speaking to the young men one of them had impure thoughts. A cloud came down and enveloped this young man. When the cloud left the earth the young man was left there—only a skeleton. The Maiden commanded the other young man to turn his back toward her and face the direction of the camp, then to start for home. He was ordered not to look back.

When the young man came in sight of the camp he ran in a zigzag course, this being a signal required of such parties on returning home from a searching or scouting expedition. The people in the camp were on the alert for the signal, and preparations were begun at once to escort the party home. Just outside the council lodge, in front of the door, an old man qualified to perform the ceremony was waiting anxiously for the party. He knelt in the direction of the coming of the party to receive the report of the expedition. A row of old men were kneeling behind him. The young man arrived at the lodge. Great curiosity was shown by the people on account of the missing member of the party. The report was made, and the people received it with enthusiasm.

The special lodge was made, and the other requirements were carried out. The crier announced in the whole camp what was to take place on the following morning. Great preparations were made for the occasion. Early the next morning, at daybreak, men, women, and children assembled around the special lodge. Young men who were known to bear unblemished characters were chosen to escort the Maiden into the camp. Promptly at sunrise she was in sight. Everybody was anxious. All eyes were fixed on the Maiden. Slowly she walked into the camp. She was dressed as when she first appeared to the two young men except that instead of the sage fan she carried a pipe—the stem was carried with her right hand and the bowl with the left.

The chief, who was qualified and authorized to receive the guest in behalf of the Sioux tribe, sat outside, right in front of the door of the lodge, facing the direction of the coming of the Maiden. When she was at the door, the chief stepped aside and made room for her to enter. She entered the lodge, went to the left of the door, and was seated at the place of honor.

The chief made a speech welcoming the Maiden, as follows:

"My dear relatives: This day Wakan'tanka has again looked down and smiled upon us by sending us this young Maiden, whom we shall recognize and consider as a sister. She has come to our rescue just as we are in great need. Wakan'tanka wishes us to live. This day we lift up our eyes to the sun, the giver of light, that opens our eyes and gives us this beautiful day to see our visiting sister. Sister, we are glad that you have come to us, and trust that whatever message you have brought we may be able to abide by it. We are poor, but we have a great respect to visitors, especially relatives. It is our custom to serve our guests with some special food. We are at present needy and all we have to offer you is water that falls from the clouds. Take it, drink it, and remember that we are very poor."

Then braided sweet grass was dipped into a buffalo horn containing rain water and was offered to the Maiden. The chief said, "Sister, we are now ready to hear the good message you have brought." The pipe, which was in the hands of the Maiden, was lowered and placed on the rack. Then the Maiden sipped the water from the sweet grass.

Then, taking up the pipe again, she arose and said:

"My relatives, brothers, and sisters: Wakan'tanka has looked down and smiles upon us this day because we have met as belonging to one family. The best thing in a family is good feeling toward every member of the family. I am proud to become a member of your family —a sister to you all. The sun is your grandfather, and he is the same to me. Your tribe has the distinction of being always very faithful to promises, and of possessing great respect and reverence toward sacred things. It is known also that nothing but good feeling prevails in the tribe, and that whenever any member has been found guilty of committing any wrong, that member has been cast out and not allowed to mingle with the other members of the tribe. For all these good qualities in the tribe you have been chosen as worthy and deserving of all good gifts. I represent the Buffalo tribe, who have sent you this pipe. You are to receive this pipe in the name of all the common people [Indi-

ans]. Take it, and use it according to my directions. The bowl of the pipe is red stone—a stone not very common and found only at a certain place. This pipe shall be used as a peacemaker. The time will come when you shall cease hostilities against other nations. Whenever peace is agreed upon between two tribes or parties this pipe shall be a binding instrument. By this pipe the medicine-men shall be called to administer help to the sick."

Turning to the women, she said:

"My dear sisters, the women: You have a hard life to live in this world, yet without you this life would not be what it is. Wakan'tanka intends that you shall bear much sorrow—comfort others in time of sorrow. By your hands the family moves. You have been given the knowledge of making clothing and of feeding the family. Wakan'tanka is with you in your sorrows and joins you the great gift of kindness toward every living creature on earth. You he has chosen to have a feeling for the dead who are gone. He knows that you remember the dead longer than do the men. He knows that you love your children dearly."

Then turning to the children:

"My little brothers and sisters: Your parents were once little children like you, but in the course of time they became men and women. All living creatures were once small, but if no one took care of them they would never grow up. Your parents love you and have made many sacrifices for your sake in order that Wakan'tanka may listen to them, and that nothing but good may come to you as you grow up. I have brought this pipe for them, and you shall reap some benefit from it. Learn to respect and reverence this pipe, and above all, lead pure lives. Wakan'tanka is your great grandfather."

Turning to the men:

"Now my dear brothers: In giving you this pipe, you are expected to use it for nothing but good purposes. The tribe as a whole shall depend upon it for their necessary needs. You realize that all your necessities of life come from the earth below, the sky above, and the four winds. Whenever you do anything wrong against these elements, they will always take some revenge upon you. You should reverence them. Offer sacrifices through this pipe. When you are in need of buffalo

meat, smoke this pipe and ask for what you need and it shall be grant-
ed you. On you it depends to be a strong help to the women in the
raising of children. Share the women's sorrow. Wakan'tanka smiles on
the man who has a kind feeling for a woman, because the woman is
weak. Take this pipe, and offer it to Wakan'tanka daily. Be good and
kind to the little children."

   Turning to the chief:
   "My older brother: You have been chosen by these people to re-
ceive this pipe in the name of the whole Sioux tribe. Wakan'tanka is
pleased and glad this day because you have done what it is required
and expected that every good leader should do. By this pipe the tribe
shall live. It is your duty to see that this pipe is respected and rever-
enced. I am proud to be called a sister. May Wakan'tanka look down
on us and take pity on us and provide us with what we need. Now we
shall smoke the pipe."

   Then she took the buffalo chip which lay on the ground, lighted
the pipe, and pointing to the sky with the stem of the pipe, she said, "I
offer this to Wakan'tanka for all the good that comes from above."
(Pointing to the earth), "I offer this to the earth, whence come all
good gifts." (Pointing to the east, west, north, and south), "I offer
this to the four winds, whence come all good things." Then she took a
puff of the pipe, passed it to the chief, and said, "Now my dear broth-
ers and sisters, I have done the work for which I was sent here and
now I will go, but I do not wish any escort. I only ask that the way
be cleared for me."

   Then, rising, she started, leaving the pipe with the chief, who or-
dered that the people be quiet until their sister was out of sight. She
came out of the tent on the left side, walking very slowly; as soon as
she was outside the entrance, she turned into a white buffalo calf.[1]

   This myth in its various forms has long served the Dakota
as an explanation for their origin. In the early days of contact,
whites were often puzzled at how Indians could simply accept
an on-going existence of their people and explain the origin of
their religious beliefs. They probably would have been shocked
if the Dakota ever had asked them how they could simply accept

a prior existence of God and concentrate on an explanation of origin by special creation.

Like other whites, neither historians nor scientists were satisfied with the Dakota explanations. As early as 1883, one researcher described seven Dakota gods and found counterparts to them among Greek and Roman gods. In good anthropological fashion he concluded, "We would say that tradition, similarity of race, and mythology, shows a very strong case in favor of the Dakota coming from Europe."[2] More than twenty-five years later, scientific speculation had advanced to the point where one researcher sought Dakota origins in the myths of other Siouan speakers. Hidatsa and Mandan stories ". . . make it clearly evident that at one time they had their home on the South Atlantic seaboard, where Siouan tribes are known to have lived well within the eighteenth century, and where the remnant of the Catawba still lives. . . . it is safe to assume the plains Sioux (Dakota) came from the same general locality. Sioux tradition, borne out by that of other tribes and by knowledge of their earliest history, is convincing that in their Western migration, the Sioux passed north of the Great Lakes. This being so, and their origin on the South Atlantic being traditionally clear, their migration has been an exceedingly long one, probably following the line of the Atlantic coast. The very length of their journeying may reasonably account for the lack of a definite migration tradition."[3]

Careful examination of this Western explanation will show it has some characteristics of myth. For instance, Curtis arbitrarily asserts Siouan speakers migrated from the South Atlantic seaboard; he does not consider that some Siouan groups may have migrated there instead. Initially he claimed Dakota legends were no help in historical reconstruction, but he later contradicts himself and says their tradition indicates a journey north of the Great Lakes, without citing the tradition. Finally, no evidence is offered that a long migration should account for the absence of a tradition; indeed just the opposite conclusion seems more rational. Surely the Dakota myth that opens this chapter is just as reasonable as the explanation offered by Western minds at the turn of the century. Therefore, in another fifty years the present scientific explanation of Dakota origins may seem as myth-like as one that takes them along the East Coast and across Canada above the Great Lakes.

Where historical records are lacking, anthropologists must rely upon evidence from language and biology. Closely related languages indicate common origins for their speakers; physical or genetic resemblances likewise indicate a common origin. No doubt the assumption is sound in theory but difficult to apply in practice. Objective techniques for measuring "closeness" or "distance" of physical relation are not yet available. Physically Indians resemble most closely northern Asian peoples, but in blood genotypes, the populations do not appear to be closely related. Among Indians themselves one population of prehistoric Dakota bones seems more closely related to a bone sample from the Aleutian Islands rather than to Eastern Indians. This one study suggests a West Coast origin.[4] Generally anthropological guesswork improves with the addition of archeological evidence, but the conclusions of archeology often leave much to be desired. In sum, the current scientific explanation of Dakota origins may be no more adequate than the Dakota one, but to Western minds it is more reasonable and to be expected in any work on Dakota history.

Actually anthropologists have limited themselves to speculate on a location for the Dakota at about 1500 A.D. Their opinion on this location is based largely on linguistic evidence, and they would be ready to admit their answers are still open to question. A detailed knowledge of linguistics is not necessary in order to understand this linguistic argument. The first step in such a linguistic analysis is to find which languages are related and make some estimate about how close the relation is. For instance, if an English speaker heard German he would note some resemblances and conclude German and English were related. He would have to listen to Russian much longer before noting similarities, but eventually he would discover a few. He could listen to Chinese forever without noting any similarity. His conclusion would be that English, German, and Russian were all related, with German being more closely related to English than Russian. The second step in analysis would be to study the distribution of related languages. The location of English, German, and Russian does not tell much about their origin, but then many other related languages such as Italian and Persian have not been included. If instead one were only to map the dialects of English, one would know much about the colonization from England simply on the basis of the languages spoken in Australia, South Asia, South Africa, and North America.

The first step in the analysis of the Siouan language is provided by C. F. Voegelin.[5] He discovered a number of rules to demonstrate how linguistic changes occurred and why various groups formed. His four major categories of Siouan are designated by geographic terms, although present-day speakers are not necessarily located in those areas. He calls one group Eastern, which includes the Catawba language. A second group is Ohio Valley, represented by Biloxi; a third is Missouri River, which includes Hidatsa; and the fourth group is Mississippi Valley, including Dakota. On the basis of similarities in language, the groupings may be summarized as follows:[6]

Eastern	Ohio	Missouri	Mississippi
Catawba	Ofo	Hidatsa	Iowa-Oto-Missouri
	Biloxi	Crow	Winnebago
(probably the	Tutelo		Dakota
Carolina Siouan			Mandan
such as Cheraw,	(probably the		
Keyauwee, Eno,	Virginian Siouan		Omaha-Kansa-Osage-
Waxhaw,	such as Moneton,		Quapaw-Ponca*
Wateree, and	Saponi, Monacan,		
Sissipahaw)	and Nahyssan)		

*hyphens indicate closely related terms

The second step of the linguist is to locate these tribes on a map. The tribes of the Eastern grouping are mostly reported in the vicinity of North and South Carolina. Early Spanish colonists and tribes such as the Cherokee and Creek caused considerable dislocation among them, and their prehistory is the most vague of the Siouan speakers. Of the Ohio group, the Ofo and Biloxi are located along the Gulf coast well to the south of other Siouans. The Tutelo and other Virginian tribes were to the north of the Catawba. These Eastern and Ohio groups represent Siouan speakers east and south of the Ohio River. Most of these tribes rapidly became extinct in the conflict with the Spanish in Florida and the English as well as intertribal wars. Most of the languages are not very well-recorded, but it is clear that Tutelo is more like Siouan languages in the West rather than Catawba.

In the West, Hidatsa and Mandan would be located closely together on the Missouri River as representatives of early horticultural people on the Plains. Most of the other Siouan speakers would also be located there. The major dwellers in the Mississippi Valley would be the Dakota and Winnebago. The difference in these locations will become significant later. Presently the distribution simply shows a large number of Siouan speakers west and north of the Ohio River. The only Siouan speakers to the west and south would be the Quapaw.

Four explanations are possible for this distribution. Although unlikely, it is possible that a large group of Siouan speakers in the middle somehow disappeared. Second, the western Siouans migrated from the East, or third, the eastern Siouans migrated from the West. The fourth, and most apparent, is that for some reason Siouan speakers in the Ohio Valley split and migrated east and west, with a few groups, such as Biloxi, going south. Of course the greater diversity of Catawba suggests they may have broken off earliest, or they may have been a marginal group even before 1500. Strong Algonkin or even Iroquois expansions are possible forces for driving the Siouan speakers from the Ohio Valley.

Such an analysis leaves much to be desired, but often an anthropologist has only data such as these. In defense, it is better than no data at all. However, in this case some other bits of evidence are available from tribal legends and place names.[7] J. O. Dorsey reports that "Omaha" is a Siouan phrase for "to go against the stream," and it applies to Ponca, Osage, and Omaha who came down the Ohio River and then went up the Mississippi. On the other hand, the Quapaw, those who "float down stream," separated at the Ohio mouth and headed down river. Dorsey further reports that some Omaha had a tradition that the tribe once lived near St. Louis.[8] Alice Fletcher and Francis La Flesche confirm Dorsey's meanings of Omaha and Quapaw, and they report traditions about how the Quapaw were cut off from the others at the mouth of the Ohio and unintentionally went downstream.[9] Although they agree on an Ohio Valley location, they suggest the sojourn there was relatively brief, perhaps simply part of a migration from the East. An important Omaha myth relates how the Indians were first near a large body of water which Fletcher and La Flesche interpret as the Atlantic Ocean, and they postulate an earlier East Coast origin.[10]

Anthropologists have no certain way of determining the relation between myth or legend and actual history, but the oral history of many of the western Siouan speakers strongly suggests they came from the Ohio Valley. Ironically, an Ohio Valley origin was suggested by George Catlin as early as 1851. He speculated that the Mandan might be the descendants of a Welsh colony that had sailed up the Mississippi and into the Ohio in the fourteenth century.[11] A Welsh colony there would explain the "civilized" fortifications attributed to the mound builders. Catlin argued this view at length in a later appendix to his very popular book. In the best anthropological tradition, he supported his argument with linguistic, biological, and cultural evidence.[12] The belief that the Welsh or some other European group had influenced the Indians before Columbus was a popular conviction that occasionally occurs even today.

The present interpretation, which still agrees that the Ohio Valley was a former homeland, began with the discovery that the Tutelo in the East were Siouan speakers. Horatio Hale surprised the scientific community in 1870 when he pointed out that the Tutelo and other tribes in the Southeast spoke languages closely related to the familiar Mandan and Dakota.[13] Scholars poured over the puzzle of the distribution of Siouan with little comprehensive explanation until 1936, when Swanton offered his theory on a dispersal from the Ohio Valley. Although his reasoning is supported by most of the linguistic evidence, the archeological data suggest another interpretation. An expert on the area, James Griffin, believes the Ohio Valley prehistory cannot be connected with Siouan speakers, and he has questioned some of Swanton's ethnohistorical interpretations.[14] Swanton's reply to Griffin still has not provided the final answer, but it does make clear that the Siouan speakers must once have been located east of the Mississippi.[15] A complex and intriguing history must have scattered them over a wide area. Possibly some groups such as Catawba left the main group before 1500, but most of the others probably dispersed in the seventeenth century.

In this Siouan Diaspora the Dakota are first recorded historically in the Upper Mississippi Valley. The first reports are from French explorers and missionaries whose knowledge frequently was derived from the Ojibwa, also known as Chippewa. The Ojibwa called the Dakota "Nadouessi" or "Naduwessioux," meaning "snake" or "enemy." The word "Sioux" is probably a derivative from that term.[16] Several documents cite the Dakota in the Mille Lacs area of Minnesota between 1650 and 1700. As early as 1695, a Dakota Indian visited Montreal in the company of Charles Le Sueur. The French worked at length to initiate peace between the Dakota and Ojibwa because they wanted nothing to interfere with their fur trade. However, the Ojibwa were closest to the French; they had the earliest contact; and in the end they managed to outmaneuver the Dakota. Through trade, they acquired guns earlier and in greater numbers. Eventually it was the Dakota who left the area. Although the migration was forced in part, it seems likely the Dakota were also attracted westward by an abundance of bison there. Doane Robinson believes one group, the Teton, left about 1700; most of the others followed before 1750.

This migration may have been a small-scale version of the previous Siouan exodus from the Ohio Valley. What were probably minor differences in language and culture among the Dakota in Minnesota became magnified as the groups left the lake country at various times and moved to different locales. The splitting led to a complexity of groups that have been designated bands, sub-tribes, or even councils. Linguistic differences further complicate attempts to classify the groups. Three major divisions may be made on the basis of dialect differences. Indians, themselves, note "D" speakers that comprise the Eastern Dakota or Santee of James Howard's classification.[17] A group of Middle Dakota are called "N" speakers or Nakota. The Western Dakota or Teton are called "L" speakers or Lakota.

The D-speakers were spread over much of Minnesota and into the eastern parts of North and South Dakota. Their life resembled the Ojibwa with wild rice and some horticulture basic to subsistence. The group was so scattered that various subdivisions were recognized. Howard designates these subdivisions as the Mdewakanton, Wahpekute, Wahpeton, and Sisseton bands. The N-speakers, sometimes referred to as the Wichiyela, were divided into the Yankton and Yanktonai bands. The Teton or "L" speakers were called simply the seventh band. A number of legends that refer to the Seven Council Fires of the Dakota specify the four groups of Santee, the two of Wichiyela, and the Teton. However, the Teton were probably the largest of the dialect groups. They spread over a large area in the Missouri Valley and westward and entered various relations with other tribes. As a result, the Teton themselves subdivided. These sub-bands also numbered seven and are often confused with the Seven Council Fires. The fission occurred rapidly, because the Teton were in Minnesota late in the seventeenth century; they reached eastern South Dakota early in the eighteenth century, but probably did not occupy the Missouri Valley continuously much before 1750. These various groupings can be summarized as follows:

Eastern or Santee	Middle or Wichiyela	Western or Teton
Bands: Mdewankanton	Bands: Yankton	Band: Teton
Wahpekute	Yanktonai	Sub-bands: Hunkpapa
Wahpeton		Miniconjou
Sisseton		Blackfoot
		Two-Kettle
		Sansarc
		Brule
		Oglala

For a variety of reasons, particularly war and other violence, some bands and sub-bands became much better known than others. The forgotten Sioux are the remnants of groups that generally had peaceful relations with whites and have become relatively obscure. For this history, the forgotten Sioux are part of the Brule band, known as Lower Brule, who broke off from their more warlike cousins, the Upper or Rosebud Brule, and settled peacefully along the Missouri.

The history of the Lower Brule begins before they were even a separate group, and it is useful to establish some picture of the general Dakota way of life before they entered the Plains. Unfortunately the historical sources are scant on the Dakota at this point, but they must have been much like other tribes in the area.[18] Moreover, the Eastern Dakota, who occupied the lake lands continuously, must also represent original Dakota life near the Mississippi. Since this group serves as a prototype for all Dakota in the seventeenth century, it is fortunate that an ethnography of them is now available.[19]

In the Mississippi Valley, the Dakota showed only a marginal interest in bison. Likely an early spring hunt was important when other food sources were low. A later summer hunt could be productive, and the dried meat was easily stored. According to Landes, such hunting on the prairie required an unusual effort devoted to protection because the Dakota needed much defensive strength on the prairies. It seems likely that larger groups would also be more successful at hunting, because the usual technique was to drive the bison over cliffs or into surrounds before killing. This method required the cooperation of numerous hunters.

The bison hunt also required cooperation between the sexes. The hunt was exhausting as well as time-consuming, and men took no part in the butchering. The women followed the men, moved in quickly after a kill, and began skinning and quartering. Food had to be prepared for curing and packed, while at the same time prepared for that day's meal. Children accompanied the women, and the whole group was on constant lookout for enemy raids. Eventually horses made the routine fairly easy, but while dogs were the major pack animal, the women must have had nearly superhuman chores. To process two bison, a woman would have had to butcher about 5000 pounds of meat while holding off half a dozen hungry dogs and watching after a small child or two. She had to have the foresight to package the meat in such a way as to be carried by her dogs; set aside some choice pieces for the day's meal; get two heavy skins in position for packing; and save the parts that provided sinew for thread, intestines for tripe, and horn for spoons. Virtually every part of the bison was fit for some use, and a good woman would conserve all of it.

By fall the Dakota were back in the woodlands ready for deer hunting. The hunting groups were smaller, often composed of extended family members. People had to travel to hunting grounds, but they left the elderly and very young in more or less permanent camps. The rest of the band accompanied the hunters and camped near the hunting areas. An occasional elk or moose might be taken, but venison made the bulk of the winter's food supply. Yet even deer were not abundant, and a good hunter might kill only one or two a month. Small game added only a little to the supply.

By January the hunters had to return to their permanent

village. If they had been lucky in the fall hunt, venison plus some dried bison would provide meat through the winter until the first bison of spring. It seems likely that the meat supply was generally short, so late February, March, and part of April may have been meatless months. Certainly the Santee expressed considerable anxiety about building a winter's supply of food. Shaman were consulted at length in the deer hunt, considerable ritual surrounded the activity, and a number of taboos were observed carefully.

The meat provided by the men was well-supplemented by the women's food-gathering. Wild rice was a basic staple for all the tribes in the area, and for the Santee at least, it had ceremonial significance as well. Jenks has evaluated the importance of wild rice at length.[20] It seems likely to have been the major food of Indians in the area, although in years of drought or plant disease no rice could be gathered. In the rice harvest, men and women first filled a canoe with the husks, and then used specialized techniques for further processing. Collecting and processing maple sugar was equally complex. The sugar was an important food source in the early spring. Between the spring sugar-making and the fall rice-gathering, women collected a variety of berries, cherries, and wild plums. Several root crops were also harvested. Possibly the Dakota planted some corn and beans; the Santee are known to have farmed a little in the early nineteenth century. Clearly, however, most food came from the hunt, especially of forest animals, and the gathering of wild plants. Also throughout the year some fishing occurred and could be depended upon for minimal support in lean times. Certainly the Dakota had adapted well to the environment of the Upper Mississippi Valley. Their dependence on wild rice and maple sugar indicates a fairly specialized adaptation; it is doubtful they would have left the region except for compelling reasons.

These compelling reasons are obvious. On the one hand, the Ojibwa were acquiring guns in much greater numbers than the Dakota. The two tribes were traditional enemies, and consistently the Dakota began to experience the worst in battle. Prior to the advantage gained from fire power, it is likely the Dakota had the edge. They seemed more capable of organizing larger forces for longer periods of time than the Ojibwa, but one can only speculate on the pre-contact period. At that time, the French and later the English favored the Ojibwa in the fur trade. As that tribe built up fire power, they made life in the wooded marshes difficult for the Dakota. On the other hand, the prairies with their bison became a more and more attractive place with the appearance of horses. The coming of the horse is a story unto itself.[21]

Horses, not indigenous to the Western Hemisphere but brought to Mexico by the Spanish, did not arrive in significant numbers in the north until well into the eighteenth century. Once they were available by theft or by catching runaways and breeding them, Plains life was most attractive because bison could be killed in great numbers and the meat and by-products easily transported. Later as guns were also obtained by the Dakota, the combination of rifle and horse made possible an entirely new way of life.

Few people seem to appreciate fully the remarkable cultural change that the Dakota underwent in the migration west. Although Doane Robinson commented on it early, he could not change the frontier attitude that Indians were fixed permanently to a stable way of life.[22]

> *The removal from homes in the timber to the life in the open prairie country wrought some radical changes in the habits and customs of these people, who by this immigration exchanged a ration of wild rice, berries, fish and timber game for a very nearly exclusive diet of buffalo beef; who gave up a canoe for the pony and exchanged the residence of poles, earth, and bark for the light and transportable tipi of skins.*

This change in Dakota culture was certainly more revolutionary than the one that was to occur only slightly later on the

East Coast. And whereas the American Revolution would be limited largely to political change, the Dakota revolution involved radical change in their total way of life. Yet in less than a century, that is, three to four generations, the Dakota became the most powerful tribe in the Northern Plains, so well-adapted to their new environment that they have come to be the stereotype of all North American Indians. George Catlin was particularly impressed with the adaptation and one of the first to credit the Dakota for exploiting the region so thoroughly. "There are no parts of the great plains of America which are more abundantly stocked with buffaloes and wild horses, nor any people more bold in destroying the one for food, and appropriating the other to their use."[23]

The remarkable, radical change that the Dakota accomplished has often been dismissed as simply a reflection of adaptation to bison hunting. Certainly the bison was central to the way of life most Plains Indians worked out, but their adjustment to the High Plains required many ingenious discoveries. A wholly new ecological adjustment had to be made by the Dakota, and they accomplished it in an unusually brief time. The Teton Dakota in particular exemplify the rapid change, and since the Lower Brule are some of the descendants of this group, only the Teton way of life need be considered here. The middle and eastern Dakota, who seldom crossed the Missouri River, made many similar adjustments, although in some instances important differences occurred.

For the Teton it was essential to develop two different lifestyles. Efficient bison hunting required large-scale group efforts. Organized groups could not only kill larger numbers of bison per person but also were essential in defense against other Plains Indians. However, large numbers of people simply could not exist together in the winter, and the Dakota had to learn a pattern of scattering to occupy wooded stream and river beds. These areas provided essential fuel, protection, and forage for the pony herds.

Snow came to the High Plains as early as September. It seems likely the Dakota sought their winter campsites in late October and November. Parties of hunters went out in search of antelope, deer, and elk for intensive fall hunting and intermittent winter hunting. This pattern resembled the old one of Minnesota, but the hunting expeditions were on a smaller scale. Many of the Dakota wintered in the Black Hills, and men would not need to go far in search of game. Instead of the bark wigwam of the forest, the Indians occupied bison-hide tipis throughout the winter. Sometimes they would revert to bark housing during spring rains in order to preserve the hides, but the tipi was an adequate winter as well as summer dwelling. Its sides could be pegged or weighted securely, and a fire in a pit hole provided sufficient warmth. Bison robes supplemented deerskin clothing in severe weather. Meat from winter hunting was augmented by caches of seeds and dried fruits. Bison meat that had been dried and pounded with a berry mixture, a kind of pemmican, added further to the diet.

Winter was probably the time of greatest craft activity. The weather was simply too severe to ride on the Plains, so warfare was impossible and seldom could bison be hunted. Men worked on bows and arrows; a few prepared winter counts, a mnemonic calendar. It was likely at this time that women did most of their porcupine quill decorating. In addition to skirts, leggings, and moccasins, colorful decorations and designs flourished on a variety of storage bags and later, even trappings for the horses.

Just as in Minnesota, February and March could be times of near starvation for unlucky bands. The deprivation was almost always faced by small groups of closely related kin. An unusual leader might hold a larger number of families together under unusual circumstances, but most winter sites were comprised of only four or five families with consanguine ties. No strict rules governed the composition of the group, so generally they must have gathered in part on the basis of teamwork and the nature of the location. Such adaptation seems essential given the difficulty of Plains life in the winter with its limited food supply.

Spring comes late in the Northern Plains, and in March and April, the Dakota were still in their winter camps, more or less permanent seasonal bases. Once the deep snow melted, the men could hunt more extensively, so April usually marked the end of greatest deprivation. Hassrick reports that the box elder tree was tapped for its sap at this time, following the Minnesota custom, but it could not have provided anything like the product of the sugar maple.[24] When the rains were heavy, the people might have made use of bark shelters, again as done in the east, to preserve their skin tipis. Likely the tipis were repaired and worn skins replaced. The used skins could be converted to a variety of uses, such as making moccasins. Where the wooded areas provided spring berries and other vegetation, the Dakota stayed encamped until as late as May.

However, early summer saw the scattered families coming together again in larger and larger numbers. Always tribes had to be on the defensive and cooperate in the hunt, but in the early summer the congregating might be a slow process while young men gathered in small war parties to raid the Pawnee or Crow or visit the Cheyenne and Arapaho. An occasional bison was taken, but the animals were still lean from the winter. Usually the Dakota waited for them to fatten before killing them in large numbers. Meanwhile men might fast in preparation for the Vision Quest. No doubt four days of fasting and self-torture produced numerous visions. Their visions were patterned with their interpretations providing the dreamer with a guardian spirit, usually in the form of an animal. The animal or a part of it was often worn. The guardian spirit continued to appear to a man in his dreams throughout his life. While some young men approached the supernatural individually, groups of Dakota performed a number of rituals for the benefit of all. On many of these occasions a man gave away ritually all his possessions to demonstrate his sincerity. This part of ritual became institutionalized or standardized and was known as the give-away.

By mid-summer, the tribes reached their peak of population density and considerable organization became necessary. Frequent moves were required in pursuit of bison, in reaction to other tribes, and in relation to supplies of wood and water. People held regular places in the camp circle and fell into the moving processions accordingly. Associations of men regulated activities, and some of these associations became very much like a police force. Strict order was essential in large-scale hunts, and a minimum of social authority became a requisite part of the large camp circle. The associations also were a key to the organization of ritual and religious practice.

At the height of the summer were large-scale bison hunts and the Sun Dance. At its peak, the bison hunt was a communal affair involving all the men and boys. Most often the young men encircled the bison and began driving them by setting fires or waving blankets. If a bluff were handy, bison could be driven over it to die in awesome numbers. More frequently they had to be driven into narrow confines where men set to kill them as quickly as they could, with only a few escaping. The organization used in the drive frequently involved ingenuity as well as complexity. Cries of lost calves were imitated, wolves were impersonated, herds were stalked and slowly moved by men dressed in bison robes. Ritual was also employed, and the shaman played an essential role in large hunts. Once the bison were killed, the women and young started butchering, and the men lent a hand in time of need. Failure in the hunt or in preserving the meat meant extreme hardship and even starvation.

In addition to food, the bison provided much of material life.[25] Eight to twelve skins were necessary for one tipi cover. Tanned robes were made into winter cloaks as well as bed coverings. The rawhide was exploited in a variety of ways. Its shrinking and thickening property was helpful in making covers for hammer heads and handles to produce a rigid warclub, pemmican maul, and a variety of hammer-like tools. A wooden-skin pack saddle was similarly fashioned. The *parfleche* or storage bag was designed like an envelope so that one skin served as container. Another type of skin container was used for cooking; water could be boiled by dropping red hot stones into it. The light, flexible skin was far more advantageous than pottery utensils because of their need for mobility. The bison horn was also used as a storage item; it was even more useful as a spoon. The skins for clothing came from deer or elk because of their lighter weight, but tanned bison could substitute and was useful in making moccasins. The well-worked and decorated clothing is exhibited by most museums; it is illustrated in old photos by John Anderson.[26] Bison sinew was useful as thread in the heavier sewing and various bones provided other tools and decorations. Most of the bison's internal organs were eaten immediately, but the brains were often used in the tanning process. Of course, the Indians had had several centuries to work out the individual techniques of using the bison parts because they depended upon them in part while dwelling in the Upper Mississippi. Yet to learn to adapt to such a heavy dependence upon the bison in such a short period of time remains a remarkable adjustment.

In less than a century, the Teton Dakota had adapted to a different environment by a major ecological change of transhumance. In Minnesota, subsistence activities changed by season, and Indians had had to shift their residence accordingly. However, the shifting was minor, and a village of Indians not only remained close to an area but also resided together throughout the year. On the Plains, a totally new social organization had to be worked out for the different seasons. New kinship behavior must have occurred along with change in political and religious organization.

Although kinship was the basic foundation for all of Dakota organization, it was flexile enough to allow social organization to differ considerably between winter and summer. It would be naive to describe the summer organization simply as a coming together of the scattered families of winter. In the summer, a new kind of organization sprung up that was more than the sum of the parts of families. Although both summer and winter forms operated through the idiom of kinship, they differed in fundamental ways.

The Dakota called the members of a winter camp a *tiyospaye*. This group, or *tiyospaye*, has often been described as a band. Unfortunately, band is often equated with tribe, and it will be clearest simply to use *tiyospaye*. The *tiyospaye* included from five to twenty related families.[27] Actually the group was quite flexible and could take in non-kin, who were soon regarded as relatives. It seems most likely that a prominent man was at the head of a *tiyospaye*. He and several wives formed a core; their grown sons with their wives added to the nucleus. Other families might include a brother of one of the wives or nephews of the elder. Although most people preferred patrilocal residence, where wives came to their husbands' homes, a daughter might stay with her father after marriage. In short, rules for *tiyospaye* membership were not hard and fast. The popularity of the elder or even the convenience of the winter camp probably influenced the choice of who would dwell with whom. Such freedom of choice would have been critical in an environment which could support only a limited number of people.

The kinship system itself further provided a wide flexibility. The terminological system is known technically as an Iroquois or bifurcate merging type.[28] Essentially the terms equate the father's brother with father and the mother's sister with mother; consequently, the children of the father's brother and mother's sister are called by the same term as brother and sister.[29]

This terminology simply reflects appropriate behavior between kin. For instance, brothers and sisters were expected to show restraint in their relationship. Each was to respect the other throughout life. From adolescence on they should never be together except in a group; a woman did her best quill or beadwork for her brother; she was a chief mourner at his death; a brother was to show concern for his sister's virtue throughout life. This pattern meant that as adults, brothers and sisters were seldom together. Of course the division of labor further contributed to this separation. As a result the children of a brother and sister seldom came in contact, and the distance of relationship between them was emphasized. Possibly such cousins once were expected to marry each other. Today the Dakota do not remember such a practice, and it is not allowed. On the other hand, brothers were close companions who hunted and went to war together. In everyday life their children, who frequently accompanied them, were thrown into close contact. They all saw each other as brothers rather than cousins. Similarly the children of sisters were often together, especially while young, and came to regard themselves all as brothers and sisters. When they matured, these relatives—termed parallel cousins by anthropologists—continued to think of themselves as brothers and sisters. As a result, when the *tiyospaye* is described as a core of brothers, it is in Dakota terms. Thus the potential number of brothers is high. It is important to understand how an individual Dakota was likely to have numerous close relatives, because throughout his life almost anything he did was done in terms of kinship. Relatives were fundamental in everything from sharing food at the daily meal to participating in the Sun Dance.[30]

Still the organization of kin was one thing during the winter and another during the summer. As suggested above, the winter camp or *tiyospaye* was a close kinship group where leadership was exerted by the eldest male relative, whose power was limited to moral persuasion and example. This leader had to have proved himself in war and had to be generous with his wealth. He could not use these virtues to coerce others. When leaders attempted coercion, followers quickly left for another *tiyospaye* since almost anyone could claim kinship connections to numerous other *tiyospaye.*

As larger numbers came together in the summer, the *tiyospaye* was absorbed into the camp circle. Close relatives continued to live near each other and shared much in common, but the elder of such small groups was subordinate to camp leadership. Camp leaders could coerce not only their related followers but also the non-kin included within their following. This leadership itself was complex and divided into different parts. Typically the political structure varied among divisions such as the Oglala, Brule, and Hunkpapa; such variation probably accounts in part for the Dakota success in adapting to changing conditions.

Clark Wissler has described one form of this political organization which suggests the general pattern,[31] but it is likely that even this one structure varied for the particular group over time. Much power rested in a rather diffuse body called the chiefs' society. Most *tiyospaye* leaders were members but not because they were leaders of that group. Rather all the respected men over forty were included in the society because of their wisdom, war deeds, and generosity. The power of this group focused on seven chiefs who were selected by the society. These chiefs held office for life, and the position tended to be hereditary. At least younger brothers or sons of chiefs were commonly selected by the society. These chiefs in turn delegated power. Wissler reports a rather complicated delegation of authority which must have been more ideal than real. He records that the seven chiefs selected four shirtwearers who served as major councilors. They were responsible for finding good hunting and healthful campsites; in short they provided for the general welfare. Four other men were appointed by the chiefs and shirtwearers as *wakicun,* who were responsible for maintaining internal order. The *wakicun* were reorganized annually. In turn, they gathered an administrative staff of messengers, heralds, and *akicita* or police chiefs. The *akicita* either recruited police or selected one of the men's associations to serve as such. Although the details on selection of these police are often vague, most Plains Indians had such a force during the summer. It exerted much authority and could render serious punishment in the form of beating or property destruction. The police exercised most of their discipline in the bison hunt to ensure maximum kills. They were also essential in regulating war parties and in enforcing decisions of the chiefs and shirtwearers. In later conflict with cavalry, this group developed important tactical functions. Likewise, conflict with the whites seems to have concentrated power in exceptional chiefs who became the spokesmen for a tribe. This development is almost surely a late one and distorted an earlier, much more democratic form of political organization.

Power in the early form was not only diffuse among governmental rulers but was spread further among various associations. These groups were important for all Plains Indians; their powers ranged from ritual control to military and police activity. Lowie notes that among the Dakota, the men's associations had both private and public functions.[32] They provided for a social life of eating, dancing, and singing together on the one hand while policing or fighting for the general welfare on the other. It is possible that the association, much like a fraternal organization, grew out of war parties. Whatever their origin, the Teton had numerous specialized associations. Wissler reported more than a dozen such men's groups with functions relating to the public order. Still other associations were organized primarily as feasting or dancing groups, but even common craft interests brought people together. Finally, common dreams led people into a cult or association-like grouping. These latter associations were of course devoted to nonpolitical activity, but on occasion they must have served as special interest groups.

Somehow these associations continued over time even though their membership was broken up and scattered every winter. Indeed, many employed some spring ritual to mark their revival. Still, if membership in the winter and summer encampments was fluid, as it seems to be, association membership likewise must have been flexible. In short, the lack of rigidity in the Dakota associations seems essential for the kind of life required on the Plains. The nature of their associations may account for their fairly rapid disappearance under reservation conditions. Apparently many of them quickly dissolved, but possibly some of the groups simply re-formed around the new Christian churches. For instance, a variety of men's and women's associations flourish within the Catholic and Episcopal denominations.

The former religious organization paralleled the rest of Dakota society. The winter months saw a religious activity that occurred within the *tiyospaye*. It operated within a context of kinship wherein individuals were given the support of their close kin. In the summer, however, the associations were the foundation for much of religion, and the tribe as a whole engaged in some ritual such as the Sun Dance. One interpretation of this difference in religious organization is that the individual emphasis was a pattern borrowed from the Algonkin Indians when the Siouan speakers were east of the Mississippi. Ritual by the group was supposedly an old Hokan-Siouan pattern as exemplified by Cherokee or Creek. That is, the Teton religion can be interpreted as a compromise of two traditions. However, most anthropologists see Teton religion as a patterned whole instead, and the differences in organization can best be traced to the ecological adjustment.

Certainly Teton belief, myth, cosmology, and tradition indicate a well-integrated whole. *Wakan'tanka*, often translated as God, was a superior force that could be placated either by an individual or group approach. The Sun, a father, and the Earth, a mother, were major deities complemented by a host of lesser figures such as Thunder. Again, individual Dakota had access to each of these powers while the religious associations generally had special ties to one or more of them also.

Although some cures were accomplished simply by herbalists in a secular way, Dakota medicine men largely cured by religious means frequently complemented with herbs in a *yuwipi* ceremony. The aroma of sage and the smoke of tobacco also were common aspects of healing, and the sweat lodge was a preventive form of medicine as well as a cure. In addition the medicine man, known as a *yuwipi* by the Lower Brule, employed psychosomatic methods for curing. To prove his control of supernatural forces, a *yuwipi* might pick up red hot rocks through psychosomatic controls over his own body, or he might practice sleight-of-hand trickery. Many *yuwipi* were most impressive escape artists; the term itself is sometimes translated as "tied up." *Yuwipis* also used tent shaking and other feats to demonstrate their power.[33]

Men of supernatural power were also important in other crises, and the people expected them to anticipate danger by foretelling the future. A *yuwipi* accompanied most war parties to warn of ambushes, to judge the size of an enemy camp, and to avert other dangers. They were equally important in judging the behavior of bison and locating herds. As these functions diminished in importance, the *yuwipi* turned to locating lost items, and on the reservation today he may be asked to find stolen property or to determine who has committed crimes. Formerly a *yuwipi* may have had some control over animals as well as forecasting their behavior. For instance, one *yuwipi* was believed to know songs that made horses dance; he could also communicate by telepathy with rattlesnakes.[34]

In many of their performances, *yuwipi* worked very much as individuals directing their powers toward individual ends, such as curing or recovering lost goods, but always to help others before themselves.[35] Likewise each Dakota male sought his own special access to the supernatural through a vision quest. In his first vision quest a young man fasted, sometimes tortured himself, and eventually fell into a trance-like state. He reported his dreams or hallucinations to a wise elder who interpreted them. Commonly the vision provided the youth with a guardian spirit which would protect him throughout life. In later vision quests a man communicated further with his guardian spirit. Yet as summer began, ritual and religious activity found outlet largely through the voluntary associations or groups of people. The group effort peaked in the Sun Dance when on occasion large numbers of Brule might join temporarily with Oglala. J. R. Walker provides the earliest source of this ceremony in which he notes the importance of individual initiative but also the need for direction by a yuwipi and other assistants.[36] As the ritual preceding the Sun Dance progressed, numerous individuals participated, and the ceremony culminated in total tribal involvement. Still, individuals stood out as some endured unusual acts of self-punishment—generally, however, for the well-being of others.

This Dakota religious organization clearly reflects adaptation to the different seasons on the Plains. In addition to this variation, a further flexibility was allowed in both the individual and group performances. Prayers, songs, rituals, and interpretations of dreams in the vision quest demonstrate the variation in individual accomplishment.[37] The wide range of variability allowed in the Sun Dance so impressed one anthropologist that he devoted a thesis to the topic.[38]

Given the relatively short period of time the Dakota had to adapt to the Plains environment, it is not surprising that their institutions lacked firm or rigid structures. And whether or not fixed and regular procedures would have developed in any case is a moot question. The Dakota took up residence west of the Missouri River only briefly before the first white men visited the area. Shortly after 1800, explorers began to document the country for the rest of the world, and a fur trade began to flourish. This new development required further extensive change, and it appears that the Dakota were among those tribes best able to handle it. The river-dwelling tribes, such as Arikara, Hidatsa, Missouri, and Oto, had lived on the Plains longer and appear to have worked out more fixed routines. Contact with whites meant quick extinction of their ways and drastic declines in population. On the other hand, the Dakota prospered for some time as a result of contact and probably did not reach their zenith as Plains Indians until about 1870.

The Dakota seem to have managed this feat because variability was accepted as a way of life, based on a value of extreme respect for the individual's right to make decisions for himself.[39] In effect the Dakota were adept at trial and error, and they rapidly found techniques that allowed them to adapt to the Plains. Soon after this adaptation they were faced with another major one—working out relations with whites.

These relationships are the major subject of the chapters to follow. Almost all the initial contacts with whites were friendly, and soon the Dakota had replaced their skin cooking containers with brass kettles. Guns augmented bows and arrows; beadwork nearly replaced quillwork; woven cloth supplemented skins. A variety of foods were added, such as flour, but coffee, sugar, and alcohol were more common items. Only beaver and other fur skins were necessary to trade for these goods, so the exchange did little to upset the Plains way of life.

However, toward the middle of the nineteenth century, government agents and fur traders were followed by settlers. The increasing contacts between Indians and these whites were much more important. As a result of the introduction of new diseases the Indians who were settled more or less permanently in the Missouri Valley were nearly wiped out, but the adaptable Dakota soon learned to combat smallpox or measles by scattering themselves just as they did in the winter. As the other tribes diminished in numbers, the Dakota became ever more dominant.

After 1850 contacts between Indian and white were often hostile. Again Dakota institutions showed their flexibility and individual chiefs came to prominence. Some of the best known, such as Sitting Bull or Crazy Horse, were essentially war leaders, and their exploits against whites made them famous. Many other chiefs, however, became prominent because of their bargaining and negotiating ability. These men, such as Red Cloud, seemed reluctant to seize power but stepped forward in order to protect their land and people. Once a leader was found who negotiated well, he was asked to serve others. The endurance of these men in preserving the reservations against white encroachment has been told vividly by George Hyde.[40]

By the turn of the century, the political force of such chiefs had finally been subverted, but other Dakota institutions remained. When Indians were forced to take up individual land assignments, many families managed to string out along a creek bed in the old *tiyospaye* organization. As ranching operations began, brothers often worked together along old cooperative lines. Under reservation conditions that produced a high mobility of young people, grandparents were ensured a viable role in rearing children. Hassrick reports that this "adaptation of old devices keeps order where there might be chaos. The existence of the system as it now functions promotes conservatism. It helps to keep the Indian an Indian. . . ."[41]

All these adaptations apply generally to the Teton, and some of them are characteristic of other Plains tribes as well as other Dakota. But it must be noted that even among the Teton there was a range of variation in the adaptation, especially in the military-political sphere. The most prominent chiefs in American history were men who led their people in resistance against the federal government. Some of these chiefs made their mark through strategy and tactics, others through such political machinations as gaining eastern support, subverting local agents, or frustrating government intentions through a variety of ingenious tricks. The leaders of such resistence far overshadowed various small groups of Dakota who were attempting peaceful cooperation with the whites.

A few Dakota who remained behind in Minnesota after a bloody uprising there in 1862 are scarcely mentioned today. Another small group who homesteaded and bought land at Flandreau, South Dakota, are hardly ever considered in a discussion of Sioux Indians. Much larger numbers of Dakota, who settled along the Missouri and maintained a fairly constant, peaceful contact with whites, are also generally overlooked as Sioux. The Lower Brule Sioux are one among these forgotten Sioux. Perhaps their history will inspire histories of their other tribesmen who chose peaceful cooperation with whites rather than warfare.

chapter 2
Prelude to Reservation Days

It is almost certain that the Brule and Oglala bands of the Teton led the westward migration of the Dakota and were among the first to occupy hunting grounds across the Missouri River. While the Oglala spread largely along the Bad River and into the Black Hills, the Brule hunted along the White River. Both groups, however, found an abundance of bison along the Platte as well, and their hunting range soon covered northern Nebraska as well as the western part of the Dakotas. Occasionally the Brule would return to the lake and prairie country of eastern South Dakota where they may have received their name.[1]

However, the White River country provided a more certain supply of bison and other game. In addition, the valley with its tributaries gave winter shelter and pasture for the pony herds as well as firewood and tipi lodge poles. Furthermore, the White River met the Missouri at a point convenient for French traders from St. Louis. Soon after entry into the country, the beaver fur trade became an important part of Dakota life.[2] Winter counts of the Teton document trade in 1794 and 1795, and the appearance of white traders is noted as often as wars against neighboring tribes.[3] These initial contacts with the Dakota were highly irregular because the traders' primary interests were with the Mandan and the other village dwellers along the Missouri. The La Vérendrye expeditions illustrate the French intent. In 1738 the Sieur de La Vérendrye set out from Lake Winnipeg in search of a westward passage to the Pacific. He briefly wintered among the Mandans at the later site of Fort Berthold Reservation before returning to Canada. His two sons returned in the spring of 1742 and spent fifteen months exploring the northern Plains.[4] Unfortunately the details of this expedition are vague; it is noteworthy today because near Pierre, South Dakota, the explorers buried a leaden plate which was not discovered until 1913.

Although a few contacts like the La Vérendryes continued between Canada and the Upper Missouri, the growth of the St. Louis beaver trade pushed explorers and traders ever further up the Missouri River. In 1790 a St. Louis trader, licensed by the Spanish, visited the Mandan and found English-Canadians still occupying what was then considered Spanish territory. However, between 1794 and 1797 the Missouri Company, formed by St. Louis merchants, sent out regular expeditions to the Upper Missouri. In addition to seeking a western passage, the explorers secured trade with the Indians. By 1800 St. Louis was preeminent as a trading center because of its unique location, where the Missouri converged with the Mississippi. This area was to be returned to France briefly before being sold to the United States as part of the Louisiana Purchase in 1803.

The turn of the century saw a fur post established near the Big Bend of the Missouri River, the eventual site of the Lower Brule Reservation.[5] Most trade, however, was still conducted farther east where the Teton frequented the James River and occasionally the Minnesota River with their beaver pelts. In much of the trade, the Dakota of the east served as middlemen passing on the goods of the white man, but an annual spring trade fair often brought direct contact between Teton and whites with their guns, ammunition, and liquor.

The first major American interest in the area was marked by the Lewis and Clark expedition commissioned by President Jefferson after the Louisiana Purchase. Like early French and Spanish explorers, the ostensible purpose of their trip was exploration, mapping, and discovery of a route to the West, but Lewis and Clark also were concerned with reconnoitering the fur trade, locating other resources, and establishing American dominance in trade with the Indian tribes. On August 30, 1804, the party first met with Dakota, probably Yankton, near the present town of Yankton, South Dakota. These Indians asked that traders be sent among them and appeared quite friendly. In late September, however, a large party of Teton apparently planned to block the expedition just above the Big Bend. Lewis and Clark nearly came in open conflict with them. The event must have been as impressive to the Teton as it was to the Americans. It seems to have been recorded in one of their winter counts.[6]

At this time the Indians were able to gain many advantages from contact with the white man. It is likely the Teton soon reached a peak of prosperity. In Hyde's opinion: "The Sioux were probably never as prosperous and happy again as they were during the period 1780–1820, when they crossed the Missouri, acquired horses, and occupied the fine hunting grounds to the west."[7] In their own version of Teton history, the winter counts record smallpox as the major incident of 1780–1781; otherwise, war and glorious hunting feats stand out between 1782 and 1800. Victories or skirmishes occurred with the Mandan, Arikara, Crow, Omaha, Gros Ventre, and Ponca. But the winter count of 1794–1795 notes that three white men came to trade and promised to return with weapons. By 1800 "nine white men came to trade," and the Indian record for the next twenty years increases proportionately in trade to war incidents. As long as the power lay clearly with the Indians, the traders led a harassed and exploited life. A prime example lies in Loisel's account of the indignities and the subordination he suffered in 1803 while trading with Brule near the White River.[8]

They virtually kidnapped him when they insisted he stay among them much longer than he planned.

Of course the balance of power was soon to shift, but during the early 1800s the Teton had little to fear from the white men. Rather, they enjoyed the immediate and obvious profits from acquiring guns, ammunition, cookware, blankets, and trinkets. Although the effects of liquor, smallpox, and other diseases were already at work, the Indians could scarcely understand their consequences. Neither did they understand that trade was making them dependent on the white world while it began to work its subtle changes on their general lifestyle.

The consequences of trade remained negligible until about 1820. While the events of the War of 1812 had shifted the federal government's emphasis westward, focus sharpened when the bison robe became a popular trade item. Ironically only the tongue of the bison had been considered important for awhile, but the eventual demand for bison skins led to the growth of more than a hundred trading posts in the Dakota territory. Most of these posts were in the Missouri Valley.[9] Although the early trade was dominated by the Missouri Fur Company, the Columbia Fur Company established a post at Fort Lookout on a site that eventually became the southern edge of the Lower Brule Reservation. After 1830, the American Fur Company dominated the fur trade. Its only serious opposition in the vicinity of the Big Bend came in 1842 when the Fox, Livingston & Company of New York established Fort George. This post was located on the present day northern edge of the Lower Brule Reservation.[10]

The fur trade of the early part of the century provisioned the Dakota with sufficient guns and ammunition to intensify warfare with their neighboring tribes. The Teton virtually eliminated the Arikara in 1823 when they joined with whites in a punitive expedition; they were also continually at war with the Pawnee, who became their traditional enemies. Events had given the Dakota a superiority among Plains tribes, and their population spread. Those Brule who had frequented the upper reaches of the White River shifted toward the Platte. Partly the chance to raid the Pawnee attracted them; partly the attraction was an abundance of game. The bands on the Platte gradually separated from the other Brule although interchange between them must have been frequent. The part of the band that continued to hunt along the White River and descend it to trade along the Missouri River probably became the Lower Brule.[11]

During this time, the ancestors of the Lower Brule were coming in contact with a number of whites other than traders. Some early scientists and a few of the curious—perhaps the first tourists among the Dakota—began visits as early as 1811. In 1823 Prince Paul of Wurtenberg visited Dakota along the Missouri and spent some time with Joshua Pilcher, who operated a fur post near the present town of Lower Brule. Another scientist, Maximilian, an aging German prince, traveled through the area in 1833 and left a description of the fur post at Fort Pierre. Other foreign visitors included the French scientist, Nicholas Nicollet. He was accompanied by John C. Frémont, who later explored beyond the Rockies. George Catlin and John Audubon likewise traveled through the country. Of course, a number of missionaries were also spending time among the Dakota. Stephen Riggs was to become one of the best known missionaries among the Indians, particularly for his Dakota dictionary. Father Pierre DeSmet first visited at this time and later acquired fame for a life's work after returning in 1850.[12]

However, the most lasting and profound influence was to be the federal government although it hardly existed for the Indians at this time. In March, 1819, the Upper Missouri Agency was authorized by an act of Congress, expressed in one sentence designating the annual salary of the agent.[13] The agency fell under the jurisdiction of former explorer William Clark, who was superintendent of Indian Affairs for the Northwest. Stationed in St. Louis, Clark was so occupied with regulating trade and maintaining peace with Indian tribes on the Upper Mississippi that several years lapsed before an agent was even appointed for the Upper Missouri Agency.[14] The initial responsibility for this agency rested in the hands of Agent Benjamin O'Fallon, who reported to Superintendent Clark in St. Louis. The first agents worked to keep the peace in order to insure profitable trade. Often they spent only a few months of the year at their agency. Politics and patronage brought a rapid change of agents on the upper Missouri, but William Clark continued to serve as superintendent until his death in 1839. Little is known of the early agents, but it is clear that most of them spent a minimum of time fulfilling government obligations to the tribes, sending for vaccine during epidemics, and attempting to prevent warfare. O'Fallon's major accomplishment was to participate with Henry Atkinson in negotiating the first treaties with Ponca, Blackfeet, Cheyenne, Arikara, Hidatsa, Mandan, Crow, Oto, Missouri, and five bands of Dakota, one identified as Teton probably being Brule. All of the Indians were along or close to the Missouri River.[15] One of O'Fallon's first letters on record is a request for leave of absence. The request is coupled with this expression of paternalism: " . . .knowing that absence from my station will produce much disappointment to my charges, and greatly interfere in progressing in improving the character and disposition of my Indians which I had flattered myself I had much improved but much was left to be done."[16]

Actually the government was little interested in changing Indian culture at this time. It was much more anxious simply to keep the peace and promote the fur trade. Commanders of army posts, unlike the agents, had to remain at their posts, and they reported regularly on the condition of the tribes. These men often assumed the responsibility for preventing intertribal warfare that should have been borne by an absent agent. Initially the Upper Missouri Agency existed only on paper. No physical facility existed although the agent was assumed to reside at Council Bluffs. O'Fallon was soon joined by two sub-agents, but the three maneuvered to spend much time at Fort Leavenworth, St. Louis, or Washington. They even had excuses to visit as far away as Virginia and Pennsylvania.

Agents frequently started with a zeal that lasted as long as a year. However, Dakota winters were formidable, lack of quarters brought an embarrassing dependence on the fur traders, and life was lonely. Early in 1826, O'Fallon resigned. In his long correspondence he had enumerated at length the difficulties of life while fulfilling bureaucratic obligations; rarely did he mention Indians.

Peter Wilson replaced O'Fallon. He visited the Mandan, Hidatsa, Arikara, and Sioux and counselled with Ponca, Oto, Osage, and others. Wilson took a noticeable interest in his work based on a long frontier experience with Indians, but he soon died in office. For several years, the various sub-agents acted autonomously.

Then John Dougherty attempted to monopolize communications with Clark. An able politician, he exploited his contacts to the fullest. In 1827, after a trip to Washington, Dougherty returned to Council Bluffs as a leading sub-agent. Shortly afterward, the Osage raided the Oto, and he found himself amidst many traditionally hostile tribes. However, he optimistically planned a number of councils to bring peace. His attempts at a Pawnee and Kansa reconciliation met with some success. He then attempted to persuade the government to enter major negotiations. He argued that to achieve peace, the government would have to show great force or distribute gifts. Since it was in no position to show force, a large amount of gifts would be required. Dougherty's rationale for gift-giving anticipates the arguments of the later proponents of the peace policy by more than twenty-five years.

Dougherty's vision provided numerous solutions and policy suggestions. In 1829 he proposed a scheme much like the Allotment Act that did not become policy until more than fifty years later. His advice reveals something of his attitude as well as his politics. He advised a senator on how to "promote the benevolent views of our excellent government in relation to the vagrant and wretched savages," and he described as "utterly impossible" the presidential policy "to bring the Indians under the form of civil government." Dougherty advocated instead that the tribes be located on tracts of land that are " ... good for farming but destitute of game ... in order to wean the Indian from his favorite pursuit and thereby gradually prepare his mind to encounter the laborious duties of domestic life."[17] Once the Indians had learned to subsist through farming, Dougherty would introduce school masters, mechanics, letters, law, and religion, but only after they had learned farming would they be ready for such civilized pursuits.

Dougherty's autocracy is ironical since he himself would not comply with William Clark's numerous orders to reside at Council Bluffs in proximity to the tribes composing the Upper Missouri Agency. Instead Dougherty spent most of his time at Leavenworth or elsewhere. In the fall of 1828 he was accused of being in Missouri campaigning against Andrew Jackson. Despite the various charges, Dougherty was appointed to head the Upper Missouri Agency in 1830. The promotion embittered F. A. Sanford, a sub-agent who served on the edge of the frontier at the Mandan villages, and who lived more than a thousand miles up the river from Dougherty. He claimed Dougherty had "no more connection with me or my Indians than the Governor of Vermont has." Sanford described Dougherty as nothing more than an interpreter.

Meanwhile other political bickering continued full scale. In 1832 fur trader Joshua Pilcher, at the request of Superintendent Clark, drafted a lengthy evaluation of Dougherty. He criticized the agent's residence at Leavenworth as preventing any useful contact with Indians and charged that Dougherty spent only a month of each year at Council Bluffs; on one occasion he had Pawnee brought to him rather than visiting them. Pilcher also charged that the Indians were given annuity goods when they wanted money and implied that Dougherty had profited from buying annuities. Most early treaties stipulated an annual payment of goods for a certain number of years. These annuities were always a potential area for graft, and Indians regularly misunderstood the values of the goods compared to cash, and that the annuities would be paid only for a limited time. Finally Pilcher accused Dougherty of forgeries in transactions with the tribes. Overall the agent's reluctance to leave the comforts of Leavenworth had led to much misunderstanding on the frontier.[18]

Despite the obvious hostility between Pilcher and Dougherty, the former secured a sub-agent's appointment in 1835. His initiation as agent foretold the experience of many later agents. Although Pilcher was formerly an experienced fur trader and had an exceptional knowledge of Indians, his work started in confusion and frustration. Usually agents purchased annuities and accompanied them up river in the spring. In 1835 luck accompanied Pilcher. Dry goods and hardware were available at reasonable prices, and the steamboat made the passage with little trouble. Pilcher met the boat at Council Bluffs, and when it reached Big Bend, the Indians were anxiously awaiting distribution. However, Pilcher was missing an important participant. Because of past scandals in the Indian service, Congress required the presence of a military officer at all annuity distributions. Any agent who distributed annuities solely by himself was automatically suspect. Pilcher judged that his greatest problem was the immediate one of Indians near starvation, and he issued the goods two weeks before the arrival of an army officer. In his account, he argued that he had given sufficient notice but implied that his correspondence had been deliberately delayed at Leavenworth, where Dougherty may have interfered with it.

The political fighting among the agents took up so much of their correspondence that warfare among the tribes sometimes received little attention. The agents were still faced with the difficulties of settling Prairie tribes among Plains Indians. The Sac and Fox, for instance, attacked the Wahpeton Dakota in June, 1835. The traditional animosities between the settled river tribes and Dakota also continued. In the same year, the Yankton waged war against the Mandan and Gros Ventre. The bickering between Pilcher and Dougherty occasionally subsided while they grappled with this warfare and the problem of devastating diseases.

A smallpox epidemic in 1837 made an earlier distemper epidemic mild by comparison. By the time the disease was through, the country was "converted into one great grave yard." Pilcher reported: "The Mandans, consisting of 1600 souls, had been reduced by the first of October last to 31 persons—the Gros Ventres or Minitaries, a tribe of about 1000, took the disease a month later —one half had perished and the disease was still raging—many were also committing suicide."[19] He further estimated that 4000 Assiniboine, 8000 Blackfeet and 3000 Cree were virtually wiped out, while the Yankton and Santee were severely hit. Pilcher urged the Brule and other Dakota to flee westward and spend the year away from the river. The Lower Brule appear to have joined other Teton near the Black Hills.

Probably few people on the frontier realized it, but by 1840 relations between the tribes and the government had changed dramatically. Disease had reduced most of the river tribes to helplessness and near starvation. Only the Dakota managed to remain strong. They had acquired a monopoly on the beaver and bison fur trade although the trade itself would not continue long. They further harassed the other tribes in numerous ways. Proportionally the United States government also had grown greatly in strength. In the 1820s, an agent briefly visited the upper Missouri tribes during the summer and handed over presents in hope of maintaining peace. Twenty years later, sub-agents had created fairly stable posts at Council Bluffs, Yankton, Fort Pierre, and in the Mandan villages. Soon the government would have an additional post on the Yellowstone, and its influence throughout the Missouri Valley would be complete.

These government outposts had also become permanent. Even if a sub-agent found excuses to visit elsewhere, a few employees generally remained on duty. In an annual report

Pilcher gave a glimpse of the background of the employees comprising the Yankton Agency in 1838. Zephier Rencontre was a Dakota interpreter born at Prairie du Chien, Wisconsin; A. Primeau, the Ponca interpreter, was born in Canada; Antoinie Chenie, the blacksmith, was born on the Mississippi River; and James Hayes, laborer, was born in Ireland. Pilcher's dedication led him to the superintendency of Indian affairs in September, 1838, upon the death of William Clark. He served as superintendent only until September, 1841, but his experience with Indians was considerably longer than most of the agents who would follow. William Clark and Joshua Pilcher had set admirable records for their work among Indians. Generally, relations between whites and Indians had been peaceful and both sides had prospered in the fur trade.

The 1840s saw a rapid turnover of several superintendents and even more agents. One agent lasted less than a year. An exception was David Mitchell, who had been a veteran fur trader before assuming the superintendency. He served at the Upper Missouri Agency from 1841 until 1853, although he spent several of these years in the war with Mexico over Texas, which then included parts of present-day Colorado, Kansas, New Mexico, Oklahoma, and Wyoming.[20] Mitchell and his fellow agents had to contend with an extensive liquor trade introduced by Spanish traders along the Santa Fe Trail that began in Independence, Missouri, and extended some 780 miles to Santa Fe, New Mexico. A detour from the trail to points along the Platte River brought a quick profit to the Spanish and introduced considerable whiskey to the Brule. The movement to the Platte brought the Brule into close contact with Pawnee, old enemies of the Dakota. During the 1840s and into the 1850s, the feuding between the two tribes was fairly constant. In between killing each other, several dozen whites were slain by the Pawnee and Dakota as well.

These killings, and an expanding frontier, brought federal troops to the upper Missouri Valley. In addition, the strength of the tribes was seriously threatened by a steady decline in the number of bison. Whites led a wholesale slaughter of the animals, and with guns and horses, Indians could kill many more bison. Some whites on the frontier realized Indians would have to submit to white domination once their subsistence was destroyed, so they encouraged the destruction of the bison. The superintendent of Indian Affairs at St. Louis seriously warned of the difficulties that would follow the reduction of the herds. The annuities, first received by the Indians simply as compensation for rights to cross their land, came to be regarded as necessities for their survival. Indeed by 1850 guns and powder were essential for hunting the scarce game, and the annuities were important in their provision.

However, the growing Indian dependence upon the government was no guarantee of peace. In fact, the decade of the 1850s was a period of hostile dependency and more serious warfare than ever. Several events set in motion this increased contact with the army. Creation of Kansas and Nebraska Territory in 1854 foresaw a diminishing Indian land base. The emigrant trails to California and Oregon required posts if not settlements along the way and sowed the seeds for the transcontinental railroad. As settlers filled Nebraska, the lands along the Missouri River became suitable homesteads. The spread of settlement resulted in the founding of Sioux City in 1855.

The Oregon Trail along the Platte River in Nebraska and the gradual settlement of lands brought important military posts close to the Dakota. Fort Laramie was established in 1849 and Fort Riley in 1853. In 1851 the United States concluded a treaty of peace and friendship with most of the Teton in order to allow whites movement through their territory, but at the end of summer in 1854 a small military force, on a punitive expedition over the killing of a Mormon emigrant's cow, was wiped out by a party of Upper Brule.[21] The Gratton Massacre or incident marks the first open violence between the Teton and the United States government.[22] Although thirty white soldiers were killed, the Brule sought revenge for the death of one of their chiefs, possibly the only Indian killed. In November, they killed three more whites in an attack on a mail stage, while Uncpapa and Yanktonai Dakota along the Missouri destroyed annuity goods and defied the Indian agent.

The trouble led Washington to organize a major expedition against the Dakota. In 1855 General William Harney set out with more than one thousand troops. He routed a Brule camp in northern Nebraska, killing nearly a hundred Indians and capturing many women and children. Harney scouted through the White River country and wintered at Fort Pierre. In the spring he relocated at Fort Randall. This site marked the firm establishment of the military among the Dakota. In 1856 Harney negotiated a major treaty. From his position of strength, he directed that all Indian murderers of whites would be delivered up for trial, that travelers along the western trails would be undisturbed, and that each band would choose a chief to be responsible for the conduct of the band. In return the United States was to protect Indians from white impositions and provide agricultural implements whenever they were desired. The latter provision seems surely to have been some white man's idea. Finally General Harney restored the annuity payments that his expedition initially had curtailed. Ironically the Senate failed to confirm this treaty, which would have been so advantageous to the government. The effects of Harney's campaign, however, lasted for many years. For example, in 1856, Alfred Vaughn was acting as an agent for the Upper Missouri. He was intimidated on numerous occasions, even when making annuity distributions. On one occasion a Yanktonai had grabbed Vaughn's glasses and put them on in order "to see" the small amount of goods he was getting. Vaughn reported: "General Harney has produced more terror and dismay among those hostile Sioux and renegade white men than anyone could have imagined." He concluded that the Yanktonai needed a similar lesson.[23]

Vaughn's correspondence indicates a paradox for him that probably many others in the government faced. On the one hand, the fate of the Yankton appeared to be the logical outgrowth of government policy. No longer able to hunt or roam, and in a destitute condition, they were "much pleased to receive their pork and rice" and listened attentively when Vaughn exhorted the virtues of farming. They were planting, but only "with luck would they have a good crop."[24] On the other hand, Vaughn was now well enough acquainted with Indians to appreciate their resentment of white encroachment. A few months after his report praising the destitute Yankton, he was sympathizing with the Blackfeet and excusing their raid on a party of whites who were wantonly killing buffalo.

In addition to the paradox, a major misunderstanding was developing on the frontier. Whites and Indians differed totally in their conception of the presents and annuities distributed by the Indian agents. In the early 1800s explorers, traders, and government officials had feasted Indians and given them gifts simply as a means of establishing contact for trade. Later the agents saw the gift-giving as a measure of good will. The extent of Indian reciprocity is not well-documented, but the Indians must have returned the favors to some extent. This initial exchange was modified later by the government as regular trails that cut across Indian country were opened. The annual gifts became payment for rights to cross Indian land, and soon the government was using the annuity system as a means to acquire Indian lands permanently.

Although the system was initiated by whites, well familiar with such a contractual obligation, many of them came to misunderstand it. The Indians erred often in interpreting the distributions as tribute or else failed to understand that they were permanently ceding land. Many whites likewise distorted the meaning of the treaties. Even agents occasionally expressed a belief that the annuities were due more to governmental largess than to a contractual obligation. But the greatest blunder was an assumption that the Indians would soon disappear either by dying off, as many had in previous epidemics, or by becoming assimilated into white culture. Therefore a specification of annuities for a ten- or twenty-year period was assumed to provide for the Indians until they disappeared.

By the late 1850s, many of the tribes had ceded to the government all of their land except some small area around the various agencies. It was this remaining land that came to be known as a reservation. In 1858 a major land treaty with the Yankton was signed which allowed settlers into the Missouri Valley west of Sioux City. While settlers began occupying the Missouri Valley between present-day Vermillion and Yankton, the Yankton Dakota were placed on a reservation centered around the Greenwood Agency. This reservation served the Lower Brule for several years as a partial buffer from white contact. Although the Lower Brule were fairly well settled near the mouth of the White River, their contacts with whites were limited almost solely to trade.

However, the end of their isolation was marked clearly by the move for territorial organization. Political factions among the whites so distorted petitions and election results, that population size for 1860 is unknown. But early in 1861 a fairly accurate petition, with nearly 500 signatures, sufficiently impressed Congress so that Dakota Territory was created on March 2, 1861. The Yankton Reservation could no longer keep the Lower Brule from intensive contact with the white man and his culture.

The opening of the Yankton lands allowed the solid establishment of a territorial base. Political and economic power began shifting northward. T. B. S. Todd, an early sutler near Yankton, was soon outbidding Pierre Chouteau of St. Louis for delivery of annuity goods, and the territorial governor replaced the St. Louis superintendency. With the establishment of a newspaper in Yankton, advertisements for settlers appeared, and Dakota Territory began receiving a wide variety of immigrants. Many of these settlers held little respect for Indians. Newspaper comment illustrates the condescension felt for them.

Hail to the Chief! Our dusky old friend, the veritable "Smutty Bear," second chief of the Yancton, made us a friendly call last week. The old cub was as loquacious as ever. A few years ago Smutty visited

Washington and mixed in the most refined circles. . . . Than he, no one is better versed in the wiles of gallantry, and the fine act of playing the agreeable.[25]

While most whites looked toward a land boom, the Indian agents of the Upper Missouri manipulated Indian affairs for their own ends. Sammuel Latta saw his future with the frontiersmen and favored them with contracts. Chouteau's American Fur Company had its friends, too, and a power struggle ensued, implicating finally even the missionary, Father DeSmet. In the end Latta and the Dakotans won most of the government contracts. Controlling Indian affairs, however, was not without problems. For instance, in 1861 Major Burleigh, agent for the Yankton, found the $30,000 annuities for that year had sunk with the steamboat, *J. G. Marrow.* To recover the loss he had to press charges against the owners. He "represented that the loss took place through gross neglect on the part of the officers of the boat, but more immediately through the conduct of the pilot, who was much intoxicated during the entire trip, and wholly incapacitated on the day of the casualty."[26]

In summary, the late 1850s saw the establishment of strong white power among the Dakota Indians. When Indians were considered at all, they were seen primarily as a nuisance. The military had been summoned to ensure the protection of travelers; many had stayed to open a new frontier and settle the land. In the conflict between military and Indians, the former established a clear superiority. Certainly General Harney's expedition had served to do much more than simply provide safe passage on the Oregon Trail. Of even more significance was the arrival of pioneers and their extensive settlement in the Missouri Valley above Sioux City. These whites continually worked for further expansion at the expense of the Indians. Their ambitions for statehood, real estate speculation, and foreign immigration brought overwhelming pressure on the Indian lands. The 1858 treaty with the Yankton alienated most of the land east of the Missouri River; it was only the first of many with the Dakota that eventually took virtually everything.

However, the steady encroachment of whites was upset in the first half of the next decade. The Civil War drew federal troops away from the West, and serious hostilities between whites and Indians occurred from Montana to Arizona. Although few of the outbreaks were in the Missouri Valley, the western migration was substantially reduced. A Santee uprising in the summer of 1862 in Minnesota was the most notable conflict among the Dakota.[27] The Santee killed nearly 400 settlers and 100 soldiers, but the Indians had to flee, and 39 Indians were later executed in a mass hanging in the fall. Because of the conflict serious depopulation occurred in western Minnesota, and many Dakota settlements were temporarily abandoned. Yanktonai in the Upper James Valley followed the lead of the Santee and attacked several settlements including Sioux Falls. The panic following the outbreak is well-illustrated by the front page of the Yankton paper.

> *Owing to the confusion we were thrown into by the recent Indian excitment—women and children taking possession of our office—we have found it impossible to issue our paper for the past two weeks.*
> ### THE INDIAN TROUBLES
> *For the past two weeks the people of Dakota have been suffering from unusual excitement caused by the fear of an Indian invasion. The recent outbreak in Minnesota caused some alarm, but not until the news reached here of the murder of Judge Midon and his son, at Sioux Falls, did the excitement commence to show itself.[28]*

The "excitement" was more like panic. Yankton was filled with refugees from Sioux Falls and settlers further up the Missouri; Vermillion was abandoned as people fled to Sioux City. Much of Sioux Falls was burned. Yankton claimed to be the only point in Dakota Territory that held out during the trouble. Although probably never in any serious trouble, its citizens began erecting a large block house. The newspaper called on General Pope for 15,000 men to destroy the Santee: "We are decidedly for the 'wiping out' policy" as suggested by the *Sioux City Register*.[29] The paper also urged further investigation into a St. Paul press allegation that secession agents from Missouri may have promoted the outbreak. Finally the paper saw that the outbreak could be made an instrument for further expansion.

> There is no longer any doubt but that the frontier settlements are marked as the prey of several large tribes of Indians, who by recent acts of murder and pillage, have severed whatever bonds of friendship and rights to protection and assistance, which have been guaranteed . . . by treaty stipulation.[30]

The logic of this argument was expanded a few months later in order to indicate explicitly that land rights should be included.

> It has been urged by those most experienced in Indian Affairs, that all Indians hereafter should be made to understand that they have no right or title to the soil. It is unquestionably the true ground to occupy toward the Indian, and the Government is now sufficiently powerful to enforce that policy . . . .
> The Indians will soon learn that they have no control over their sovereignity and they will peacefully yield to the inevitable fate of their race, and it may be, as these last remnants totter "toward the evening sun," they may gracefully assume the habits and customs of civilized life, and eke out the balance of their existence as a race, in the quiet enjoyment of an "enlightened age."[31]

This hard line against Indians seldom lasted long. In less than five months the *Dakotian* was welcoming the settlement of the Santee who had been in the Minnesota uprising. Their virtual imprisonment on the Missouri River demanded the presence of a garrison of perhaps 2000 troops, which was no small market at that time. The paper only regretted that the annuities for these Indians had been redirected to white survivors of the uprising; thus they would not be spent in Dakota Territory. By July the press was even blaming the Minnesota newspapers for the Indian scare. It noted that $300,000 came into the territory in annuities; furthermore, no Indians had ever attacked whites in all of Dakota history, except for two killed at Sioux Falls.

This ambivalence of the press toward Indians continued for years. On the one hand, any Indian outbreak was major news, and difficulties between Indians and whites were immediately featured. On the other hand, the newspapers stood to gain by boom times and never wanted to frighten away settlers. A feature column in *the Dakotian*, "Town and Territory" illustrates this point on May 17, 1864: "Everyday brings us fresh arrivals of New Yorkers. Let them come . . . they are generally pleased with Dakota. It is reported that at least one thousand families, from different parts of the East, are at the present time, on their way to Dakota. Who's afraid of Indians?"[32]

Obviously the people of Yankton had feared Indians in the late summer of 1862 when Sioux Falls was burnt. The territory also faced much more real danger again in 1863. Indians had heard of successes against the militia in Colorado and elsewhere; moreover, they were being confined to closer quarters. Those east of the Missouri River saw an expanding white population on their south as settlers from the Missouri moved northward along tributaries such as the Big Sioux and James rivers. Settlers in Minnesota and an army seeking revenge pushed in from the east. Yanktonai, mostly along the James Valley, raided some homesteads and attempted to prevent further settlement.

These disturbances finally brought government response. In May 1863 Iowa volunteers, who had enlisted for the Civil War, entered Dakota Territory on a punitive expedition. Under the command of General Alfred Sully about 600 cavalry rode up the Missouri River to make a base camp a few miles above Fort Pierre. In July the command set out after Dakota toward the northeast.[33] In early September they finally encountered a band of more than 1000 hostile Dakota near present-day Ellendale, North Dakota. The engagement became known as the Battle of White Stone Hill. The Indians lost several hundred warriors; less than a score of whites were killed. The Indians were probably mostly Yanktonai with remnants of Santee. Doubtless some Brule were also among them.

General Sully continued the campaign against the Dakota for the next two years, pursuing them west of the Missouri River in 1864 and 1865. A colorfully written account gives much insight into frontier attitudes toward Indians.[34] The author, J. R. Drips, and most of his fellow soldiers were from Iowa. While encamped along the White River, he gave one of the first accounts of the Lower Brule Reservation country, although few Dakota then occupied it. Drips' work is much like a diary, and he continually reported on the availability of grass, water, and wood. Rarely were all three available; often only one of them was satisfactory. Drips frequently commented: "The same dry, barren country as heretofore." The force established itself near Pierre; frequent mail trips between Fort Pierre and Fort Randall provide further accounts of the region.

The first conflict with Indians occurred in July when eight were taken prisoner. Although Drips was not present, he reported what happened when the officer in charge left. "The soldiers said the prisoners attempted to escape and the soldiers fired on them, killing all but one and he died shortly afterwards."[35] The lack of discipline among the troops was most vividly illustrated by an encounter with bison a few weeks later. The troops became so excited killing bison that several of them shot their own horses by mistake. The lack of discipline among the volunteers does not account for all the brutality of the campaign. In 1864 on the west side of the Missouri River, a captain was killed by three Dakota. In response, "The general [Sully] started a party out with orders to bring in the Indians' heads. This was done and then he ordered them stuck upon poles to warn other Indians. We had a good camp here, having plenty of wood, water and grass."[36] This viewpoint of Indians as something less than human was made explicit by Sergeant Hobbs in an account appended to Drips' book. In his description of Indians, he facetiously began:

Poor dear creatures! As though Indians possessed the attributes of humanity or the affectionate instinct of the higher order of brutes! As

though their fiendish hearts were susceptible of one spark of the an-
guish they so gloatingly inflict upon others! They are devoid of every
embling emotion of the human heart, instinctively brutal, preternatu-
rally degraded, essentially heartless, vindictive and remorseless. Their
stately pride and mobility of character exists only in the ideal fancies of
imaginative flash novel writers.[37]

Such an attitude was not confined to troops in combat with
the Indians. The Yankton press expressed a similar view in
August, 1864. For instance,

The government is and always has been, too generous, too mag-
nanimous and scientific in its dealings with the savages. We do not
shoot an Indian on sight, but we shake hands with him, and ask him
if he is friendly, while his comrade is launching a deadly arrow into
our side . . . .
The Indians are aware that our armies are strong, but they
laugh at our manner of fighting. Their *mode of warfare is* indis-
criminate, of all ages and sexes. *Ours should be the same.*[38]

While newspapers called for a program of near genocide
and Sully nearly practiced it, other forces were at work. Mahlon
Wilkinson, the Upper Missouri agent, had urged a new treaty;
additional pressure in Washington for a peaceful solution led
to appointment of a major peace commission. The commission
was also charged to determine what lands the Indians would
cede. This commission was the first to negotiate with the Lower
Brule at length and recognize them as a distinct tribal group.
The commission was composed of two generals, H. H. Sibley
and S. R. Curtis, as well as four civilians: Newton Edmunds,
Orrin Guernsey, Henry Reed, and Edward Taylor. Taylor was
superintendent of Indian Affairs for the North; Newton Edmunds was a Dakota politician who served as territorial governor between 1863 and 1866.

The commission planned its first meeting with the Dakota
in the spring of 1865, but many details delayed the commission.

Meanwhile a series of events augured failure. Even the distribution of annuities that year had gone wrong. Agent Wilkinson failed to accompany the steamboat to the Yellowstone, and the Crow, Mandan, and Assiniboine annuities were distributed to the wrong tribes in the wrong proportions.[39] Appointment of replacements for commissioners who refused appointments was delayed, and even a meeting postponed until fall was nearly cancelled. Commission members were outspoken in their pessimism about the outcome. Several times Newton Edmunds forecast the bleakest of prospects. He predicted that General Sully's 1865 expedition, which never should have started, had been such a failure that few Indians would appear.[40] The day before the commission left, Edmunds again predicted few Indians would appear because they would be hunting bison. But, politician that he was, Edmunds claimed he would make every effort to carry out his assignment despite the odds against him. Even the weather frowned on the commission, and low water halted the boat at Crow Creek. The commissioners had to request General Sully to send wagons for the remainder of their trip to Fort Sully.

While the peace commission was preparing in its halting way for a meeting with the Indians, Sully and his cavalry had been busy. Soldiers had attacked Indians near the Black Hills in the summer of 1865, and some bands had turned away from meeting in a peace council. The troops themselves were in a near mutinous condition, many demanding to be mustered out. Their anger could easily have exploded upon the Indians. Major General Pope, commanding the department of the Missouri, urged agents to withhold annuities that year because he believed the Indians construed the distribution as a bribe made out of fear, and "Their belief simply leads to a renewal of hostilities in the hope of more presents."[41]

Sully confused matters even more by calling a council of his own and further claimed to have made a treaty with two-thirds of the Indians, at no expense to the government. The general, of course, was only interested in keeping the peace and ensur-

ing settlers safe passage across the Plains. He did not understand the commitment of the frontiersmen, represented by Edmunds, to expand a territory. Thus General Sully reported on
his council:

> *There is one thing the Indians are very tenacious about, and that
> is the taking of their lands from them. In all their councils they have
> spoken about this, and I have assured them such is not the wish of our
> government for their land is worth nothing to us. All we ask, and we
> must have it, is, the right of way through their lands, west of them.*[42]

Sully recognized that many Dakota were not committed by
the treaty he had made. He suggested continued war with the
hostile bands, payment for their scalps, and a punitive expedition against half-breeds from Canada who traded with them.

Of course these recommendations were contrary to the
stated policy of the peace commission. Its aim was to provide
the Indians with sufficient goods so as to make war unnecessary.
Their "peace policy" was justified on the basis of its being much
more economical than warfare, but more importantly perhaps,
the commission wanted to define boundaries for some agencies
and reduce the Sioux Nation to lands west of the Missouri. Even
the western land was being allocated in part for "reservations"
although few people yet had much interest in the future of these
tracts.[43]

The treaty made in the fall of 1865 barely began the process
of land alienation. The commission had given up hope of meeting with enough Indians to guarantee any commitments. Some
bands which had settled near the forts and trading posts
showed an interest in the treaty, but the commissioners were
interested in those Indians who roamed the Plains and did the
fighting. Few of these groups had reported to Fort Sully. Nor
was it wise to expect many of them to come into the headquarters of the general who had been fighting them for the past
three years. Under these conditions, three of the commissioners left believing their mission was futile; Edmunds, Guernsey,

and Curtis were to await the next steamboat. The next day several bands of nomadic Dakota showed up as vanguards, and within a week, the three commissioners had negotiated with a fair representation of the Dakota on the Missouri. The emphasis of the agreement was upon peace, but in the process the commissioners managed to commit the Indians to further talks. Initially the Indians were so hostile to any discussion of ceding land that the topic was largely ignored. Land, however, was certainly Edmunds' major concern, and he simply postponed negotiations in that realm.

The settled Dakota had become almost totally dependent on whites by this time. In the winter of 1866, Indians at Crow Creek were reduced to near starvation. Annuity goods were held up, to be added to the treaty distributions. The army had been ordered to withhold all provisions from Indians. By late May, food was virtually gone. A visitor at Crow Creek indicated conditions by pointing up the remarkable honesty of Santee prisoners there. "They will run like chickens to gather the fall from the slop buckets that are carried from the garrison kitchens while they pass without touching a pile of corn and hundreds of loose cattle."[44]

Although the Crow Creek Indians were attempting some farming under these conditions, the Lower Brule had refrained. Food supplies for them must have been almost as low, and they cooperated in the treaty-making of 1866. Little Pheasant, a band leader, complained of annuity thefts and asserted his people were starving. Iron Nation, a prominent Lower Brule chief, stated: "Look at us! You see we are starving, we are thankful to that man [apparently, J. R. Hanson] that we are alive, but he has told us he has no more to spare and I believe it." Iron Nation went on to ask that annuities be delivered at the point selected for their farming (near White River) although he made no promise to plant.[45] The destitute condition of the Lower Brule was confirmed by J. R. Hanson, who had been appointed agent for the Upper Missouri Sioux Agency. (Apparently, it had become the "Sioux" agency because the other tribes had disappeared or had settled on small reservations with separate agents.) Hanson reported: "Misery seems the predestined lot of these Indians, and I really wonder that so many adhere to their allegiance to the Government."[46]

In sum, the Dakota along the Missouri River had become highly dependent upon white goods, either through trade or through the government annuities. Even the more militant Dakota to the west were sharply reducing their raids, and many of the Brule along the Platte evidenced a much greater dependence upon the government.[47] At the Big Bend, a smallpox epidemic once more struck. Agent Hanson appointed Dr. Henry Livingstone to help temporarily; the doctor stayed much longer, finally becoming an agent himself. Hanson, though seemingly sympathetic to the suffering Crow Creek and Lower Brule, proposed to divert some of their annuities from immediate relief to a different scheme. He laid plans for extensive building and advertised for ground-breaking at the mouth of White River. Further, about $1500 was withheld from Lower Brule annuities for plowing; probably that was the first done for the Lower Brule. It may also have been the first in Dakota Territory west of the Missouri.[48] Another favorite tactic of the agents, a trip to Washington, had also been imposed on the Indians. Hanson guided a delegation of Crow Creek and Lower Brule, among them Iron Nation, to the Capitol in 1867 to impress them with governmental strength. In short, the Indians along the Missouri were meant to recognize that they had little or no bargaining strength in 1868 when major treaty-making began.

That the Lower Brule did not lose many of their rights in 1868 seems due more to the strength of hostile Indians under leaders such as Red Cloud and Sitting Bull rather than to governmental largess. In the main the treaty called for peace. It further guaranteed annuities to the Indians for a number of years while white pioneers and settlers were to have safe passage along specified trails. The government recognized that the land west of the Missouri River within the Dakota Territory was

**Iron Nation at Fort Laramie in 1868, photographed by Alexander
Gardner. Photo from the South Dakota State Historical Society.**

the great Sioux Nation, although it guaranteed to the Lower Brule certain lands within that area. Some aspects of the 1868 treaty were confusing because they entailed provisions carried over from or amended from previous treaties. For instance, one provision stipulated that any future treaty required ratification by three-quarters of the Dakota adult males, a virtually impossible accomplishment. Another agreement was to the effect that the Dakota could claim unused federal land anywhere in the nation if they would relinquish their claims to lands outside the Sioux Nation. Both of these provisions more than likely originated with whites to use either as shrewd bargaining devices or possibly included as humanitarian measures prompted by easterners.[49] Ironically those provisions allow today's Indians to press a serious claim to the Black Hills, Alcatraz Island, and other government-owned lands.

The Lower Brule reservation was firmly established by the 1868 treaty. Previous treaties had not made it clear where they were to settle nor had they designated precisely their relation to the government. Now the Lower Brule were put on a separate reservation within a greater Dakota reserve. They were guaranteed an agency at the mouth of the White River and their reservation would extend twenty miles in length and ten miles in depth (14 Stat. 699). Twenty-two years later the reservation was shifted northward. Agency headquarters were frequently relocated; several times headquarters were transferred to Crow Creek.

The Lower Brule, with minor exceptions, abided by the Peace Treaty of 1868. They remained reluctant to begin farming, but only a few minor cases of violence ever occurred between them and whites. Yet the peace treaty was greeted with contempt by many whites on the frontier. A Yankton editor colorfully assessed the Indians' peaceful intent: "Our faith is not of the proportions of a grain of mustard seed." He then proceeded to report rumors about a trader "near Pierre" who was killed only a day after the treaty was signed. Those who expected trouble would have little trouble finding it, although they had to look among hostile Indians who had never participated in the treaty-making.

On the reservation, it seems that the Lower Brule settled in several scattered locations. The records give only the slightest clues to everyday life, but it appears that nine groups comprised the reservation population. Several early agents reported nine bands. Nine chiefs and head men signed the 1868 treaty: Iron Nation, Medicine Bull, One Who Kills the White Buffalo Cow, Little Pheasant, White Buffalo Cow that Walks, Brave Heart, Wounded Man, Gourd Ear Rings, and Iron White. It is likely these men headed *tiyospaye* or extended families, with the groups settling along creeks or small rivers or around the agency. The core of the *tiyospaye* generally would be several brothers with their parents, wives, and children. Other combinations of relatives also occurred, because the Dakota readily accommodated any grouping of relatives that cooperated well.[50] Leadership of a group probably fluctuated except where an unusually able man led. Such a man would begin to exert some influence among other *tiyospaye* whose members were also related to him, even if more remotely. Iron Nation and Medicine Bull exerted such leadership, and whites often designated them as the "chiefs" of the Lower Brule. Their power was limited, however, to exemplary behavior; they would have been backed by little or no coercive force.[51]

Settlement or residence at the reservation was also a relative matter. In the fall of 1868, agent Hanson urged the Lower Brule to move westward to hunt because he could not begin to feed them until winter, having enough beef for only four months. Hanson was also in trouble because of the vagueness of his appointment. As Sioux agent for the Upper Missouri, he had charge of employees at Cheyenne River, but he was seldom able to leave the Crow Creek and Lower Brule reservations. Furthermore, General Harney was at a U.S. Army Post near Cheyenne River and was actually taking charge. Hanson was happy to delegate any responsibility he might have had, and he noted that the general, with his unlimited supplies, could much better feed the Indians.[52]

The instability of settlement on the reservation makes any population estimate for the Lower Brule mostly guesswork. An 1867 estimate of two hundred "lodges" became the standard guess for several years. The agents based total population on six persons to a lodge, so the Lower Brule population was reported as between 1200 and 1400. Generally the Indians objected to being counted; later when they discovered their rations were based on population, they insisted on submitting their own numbers.

Since agent Hanson had a full-time job on his hands at Crow Creek, he could spend little time among the Lower Brule. In the initial years after the reservation was formed, contacts with other whites were also kept to a minimum. Still, the Lower Brule saw that the bison were disappearing and recognized that a new way of life would have to be found. Undoubtedly they realized subsistence from whites would be necessary. From their perspective, they probably thought they deserved support in return for being peaceful.

At this time sentiment in the East coincided with such a view. Abolitionists like Lydia M. Child and Wendell Phillips of Boston turned their attention to Indians after 1865, and espoused a humane treatment of Indians based on a belief in equality among all races. Henry Ward Beecher offered a similar view in his lectures given in East Coast cities. Their individual efforts eventuated in a number of organizations, and the efforts helped the Grant administration in formulating a peace policy. The new policy had little effect on Lower Brule except to guarantee the Indians enough food and clothing for subsistence. On the frontier, however, few plainsmen sympathized with such policy. The nineteenth-century philosophy of social Darwinism was readily adapted to a world where whites wanted and intended to have Indian land. Progress was not to be retarded by humanitarian idealists. Thus a Yankton editorial warned on

February 2, 1867, that when civil authority replaced the military, it could not be lenient:

> *If the end arrived at is the civilization of the Indian—to wean him from his barbarous pursuits, and make him a useful member of society, then we contend that the government must literally lay its hands upon him, and compel him to work and learn—or die.*[53]

The writer assumed that the Indians would lose most of their land because by nature and heredity they were not suited to agriculture. He concluded that the government should encourage mechanical and vocational training. This position of the Yankton paper appears almost sympathetic compared to one in Sioux City:

> *Peace Commissions, so far as dealing with Indians is concerned, are played out. The name of Harney has far more terror for the Indians and . . . is more potent for good, than the visitation of all the latter day peace commissioners.*[54]

The frontiersmen very much opposed allowing the Dakota to retain so much land, but they overtly based much of their argument on the Indians' need for civilization. The Yankton paper doubted that Indians could stay within imaginary lines, but even if they could,

> *. . . it is not only a poor way to civilize the Indian but it is doing him a positive wrong. If the Indian cannot endure the contact of civilization and adopt the habits of civilized life, let him pass away and the sooner the better. But we maintain the Indian is capable of civilization, and it is only necessary to adopt the proper means and policy to prove it.*[55]

A local historian of the time presented a similar view but with a somewhat different rationalization:

The people of Dakota dislike to have to see so large and important a portion of their Territory set apart for an Indian Reservation, but if it must be so for awhile, they will cheerfully submit to it and make the most of it. If it deprives us of the Black Hills and their products, we get in exchange one of the best local markets in the Northwest, for these Agencies and Military Posts require an immense quantity of Beef, Pork, Flour and Vegetables which the farmers of Dakota are expected to furnish.[56]

The Lower Brule Reservation was founded, then, at a time when whites assumed Indian culture was a temporary necessity. Indians and their culture would soon conveniently disappear as part of an evolutionary scheme. Certainly change in the Plains Indian culture had been rapid. In less than fifty years, the function of the Upper Missouri Indian Agency had been transformed from attempts at peace-keeping through gift-giving to nearly total control of the Indians by providing subsistence. In 1819 only a few trading posts had existed among numerous tribes along the Missouri. By 1868 most of these tribes had been reduced to virtual nonentities or sent to Indian territory, the present state of Oklahoma. Only the Dakota retained any strength, but they were faced with an overwhelming, powerful frontier population that demanded further land cessions and a conformity to their values. The Lower Brule could not have understood all the consequences of being located on a reservation or anticipated what major changes would occur. The reservation posed many new problems. Dakota ingenuity allowed an accommodation, but it could scarcely provide a multitude of solutions. Still, the Dakota had undergone revolutionary change less than a hundred years before when they adapted to the Plains. They had not lost their identity as Dakota then, and they were not ready to lose it in 1868. Indeed, many of them had no intention of giving up their way of life without a fight.

chapter 3
Years of Struggle – 1868-1876

When the Treaty of 1868 established a reservation for the Lower Brule, their contacts with white men were still limited. Even their agent, J. R. Hanson, did not see them often. He resided at Crow Creek and was expected to administer from across the river. For a few months in winter, when the Missouri River was frozen over, the two reservations were readily accessible to each other. For the rest of the year, agency headquarters were cut off from Lower Brule. Crossing in a boat was always hazardous and nearly impossible with high water. A ferry and eventually a bridge at Chamberlain allowed passage, but such a trip was far from convenient.

It would appear that bureaucrats in Washington generally failed to appreciate how much of a barrier the Missouri River was. Whenever separate agencies were established, someone a few years later would think the government could save money by consolidating Crow Creek and Lower Brule agencies. Yet in addition to geography, social distinctions between the Yankton at Crow Creek and the Teton at Lower Brule contributed to differences between the reservations. However, the Bureau of Indian Affairs had maintained one headquarters for the two agencies much of the time, and in 1869 the Lower Brule retained much of their independence because of this governmental policy.

Meanwhile the reformers in the East had become influential lobbyists. They sought to end the Indian wars immediately and eventually to assimilate the Indians. When U. S. Grant became president in 1869, he laid out a peace policy. Major features of Grant's policy were the appointment of a Board of Indian Commissioners and a call on the various religious denominations to nominate Indian agents from the clergy.[1] These two steps were taken to end the widespread graft and corruption which had made the Bureau of Indian Affairs notorious. The corruption was probably reduced although many shrewd businessmen continued to bill naive Indian agents who knew little of accounting procedures and even less about Indians. The major feature of Indian policy affecting the Lower Brule was the intent to feed them instead of fighting them. Thus the Lower Brule found a subsistence at their reservation, but otherwise they were left alone for a few more years.

Grant's peace policy had many unanticipated consequences.[2] It was established by men and women who believed they had the interests of the Indian at heart in applying their Christian principles. Some were missionaries, but others were people like Sammuel Tappan, a Boston abolitionist. Tappan had moved to Denver in 1860 and served as a correspondent for Horace Greeley. He maintained his liberal Republican philosophy in framing Indian policy. These proponents were hated by frontiersmen, and western newspapers reserved their most acrimonious comment for the benefactors of "Mr. Lo," a nickname derived from Alexander Pope: "Lo! the poor Indian, whose untutor'd mind sees God in clouds or hears Him in the wind." This newspaper epithet was intended to irritate easterners. One of the most difficult consequences for the peace proponents to defend was that peaceful Indians received comparatively little from the federal government. To achieve peace, the bulk of rations had to go to hostile tribes like many of the Dakota. Although the difference in treatment simply followed pragmatic administration, some elaborate justifications were presented. It is worth examining in some detail a defense of the policy provided by the Commissioner of Indian Affairs, Francis A. Walker:

> The Indian policy, so called, of the government is a policy, and it is not a policy, or rather it consists of two policies, entirely distinct, seeming, indeed, to be mutually inconsistent and to reflect each upon the other: The one regulating the treatment of the tribes which are potentially hostile, that is, whose hostility is only repressed just so long as, and so far as, they are supported in idleness by the government; the other regulating the treatment of those tribes which, from traditional friendship, from numerical weakness, or by the force of their location are either indisposed toward, or incapable of, resistance to the demands of the government. The treatment of the feeble Poncas and of the friendly Arrickarees [sic], Mandans, and Gros Ventres of the North is an example of the latter; while the treatment of their insolent and semihostile neighbors, the Sioux, furnishes an example of the former.
>
> It is hardly less than absurd, that delegations from tribes that have frequently defied an authority and fought our troops and have never yielded more than a partial obedience to the most reasonable requirements of the government, should be entertained at the national capital, feasted, and loaded with presents. There could be no better subject for the lively paragraphist or the heavy editorial writer on a dull news day.... And yet, the government is right and its critics wrong; and the "Indian policy" is sound, sensible, and beneficient because it reduces to the minimum the loss of life and property upon our frontier and allows the freest development of our settlements and railroads....
>
> Especially has the absence of Indian hostilities been of the highest value, in directing and determining to the extreme frontier the immigrants arriving in such vast numbers....
>
> The fact that Americans are more daring and adventurous in the presence of a danger more familiar to them only constitutes a stronger reason for maintaining the immunizing which has been secured by the feeding process. There are innumerable little rifts of agricultural or

mining settlements all over the western country which, if unmolested, will in a few years become self-protecting. . . .

In addition to his purely expedient arguments, Walker overwhelmingly commits himself to the manifest destiny of the United States. The argument also was surely meant to mollify the western criticism of the Bureau of Indian Affairs.

No one certainly will rejoice more heartily than the present commissioner when the Indians of this country cease to be in a position to dictate to the government; when in fact, the last hostile tribe becomes reduced to the condition of suppliants for charity. This is, indeed, the only hope of salvation for the aborigines of this continent. If they stand up against the progress of civilization and industry, they must be relentlessly crushed, the westward course of population is neither to be denied nor delayed for the sake of all the Indians that ever called this country their home. They must yield or perish. . . .[3]

It was in this atmosphere, where whites saw Indians as destined to disappear, that the Lower Brule Reservation was established. Some frontiersmen were ready to speed up the process, and in critical times a few newspapers went so far as to advocate genocide. A view close to genocide was expressed even at the fairly high level of territorial secretary. After granting that "savage life in the open air" increased the Indians' power of perception, he commented that "every other trait of civilization, and faculty of intelligent races, vanished or degenerated." In his next paragraph he discarded the views of his enemies in the East: "The immense consideration given to the so-called rights of the Indian by some of his Eastern sympathizers, would seem to indicate a belief in some of their absurd legends—that the Indians derived their grant of rights directly from a Higher power." The solution, of course, was known on the frontier, not in the East.

Western men, with a better knowledge of facts and Indian charac-

ter, and with a great deal more genuine sympathy for the Indian, think they have derived some rights by purchase, and that they would be justified in obtaining more if necessary, by conquest in the name, and for the sake of Christianity, civilization and progress of an intelligent race.

The real red man of the forest is lazy, cruel, treacherous and cowardly; and the Indian maiden, upon occasions, shows greater fiendishness than the men, especially towards prisoners. Efforts to civilize them are vain, absolutely futile; those converted by missionaries grow more inert and degraded than in the wild state, and it has been proven that children taken young and educated by pale-faces and at maturity returned to their native tribes, have in a few days thrown off all habits of civilization, and become the worst among bad Indians.[4]

Official government policy never accepted such an extreme position, but it ended similarly. Indians would be absorbed into the larger population while Indian cultures gave way to a superior civilization. The process was not expected to take long. Feeding the Indians while they lasted was expedient and economical as well as humane. The westerners could make fun of the policy, but they could not change it. The peace policy had been construed to satisfy too many different groups.

The assumption that Indian cultures would soon end caused a lack of any long-range planning for reservation life. Congress avoided the problem in 1869 by entrusting Indian affairs to the prominent men appointed to the nonpolitical Board of Indian Commissioners and to the religious denominations. The denominations, which divided the reservations among themselves, assigned the Missouri River Indians in the following way: Roman Catholics, Standing Rock; Congregational Church, Fort Berthold; Methodist, the Montana agencies; Episcopal, Cheyenne River, Crow Creek, Lower Brule, Whetstone; Society of Friends, the Nebraska agencies. For the most part, the churches avoided sending the traditional type of missionary to administer a reservation. They did seek men of outstanding character who could be assumed to set a Christian example and of course men who agreed with the peace policy. Obviously they seldom looked to the frontier for such men. Therefore few Indian agents ever had much experience among Indians, even when military officers were recruited.

Thus an agent often arrived at his post totally ignorant of Indian culture. Since the Indians themselves were adjusting to a new way of life, there was little chance in the situation for anything but confusion if not chaos. The agents and missionaries presented a version of white culture that contrasted sharply with the one offered by most of the frontiersmen. In addition, Indians saw that the more hostile groups were better treated than those who docilely cooperated. The confusion that resulted has been very well documented by one of these early agents whose detachment matches that of an anthropologist. Although not at Lower Brule, he was at the neighboring agency of Whetstone, temporarily established a few miles down river.

Major DeWitt C. Poole was stationed in Atlanta in the spring of 1869 when he received orders to report to a newly created agency on the Missouri. He was surprised at the assignment since he lacked any experience with Indians and had never shown any special interest in them. Perhaps these qualities contributed to his abilities as observer. His arrival at Whetstone initiated him into the hectic life of an early reservation.

Since Poole had been told that Whetstone was planned as a major agency for the Dakota, he anticipated a large facility. Upon leaving the steamboat he found instead: "There were no houses or churches at Whetstone. . . . My predecessor did ask me to receipt for a schoolhouse when receiving the government property on my arrival, but upon inspection, I found that it existed only in imagination."[5]

Poole had barely settled when he found that the Indians were expecting their annuities. In fact payment and distribution were overdue, but the agent had no idea of their whereabouts. By ignoring regulations, he was able to borrow from the annuities in transit for Crow Creek and Lower Brule. These tactics made it possible to keep the peace, but the Dakota at all three agencies were in an ugly mood. One Indian became so angry that he fired three shots into Poole's cabin one night, afterwards fleeing safely to Montana. Poole began to hope for a calm atmosphere at the end of his first month when he experienced one trouble-free week, but barely a month after his arrival, the Pawnee attacked a hunting party of Brule. The Dakota immediately began preparations for war, which the agent met head on. Somehow he managed to pacify them, but the army chose that moment to return some Brule women who had been captured by the Pawnee. Poole then recognized that he had no chance of stopping the ensuing preparations for war. Just as he gave up hope, however, a small Brule raiding party returned with five Pawnee scalps that served as adequate revenge. Poole was unaware that the group had even left. He would, of course, have been obliged to stop them; now their return satisfied the Brule need for revenge. Although it had been a hectic time for Poole, he enjoyed reporting the irony of the situation.

The pace of troublesome events continued through much of Poole's tenure in office. A few months later an eclipse occurred that probably would have gone unnoticed except that the agency physician decided to capitalize upon it. The doctor was much irritated with the Dakota medicine men and wanted to end their influence with the Indians. To show his much greater power the doctor threatened to obliterate the sun. The Dakota paid little attention to him until the peak of the eclipse, when they did panic. They began firing their guns rapidly toward the sun. When the sun reappeared, they concluded that whatever force threatened the sun could be frightened away by gunfire.

Much more troublesome for Poole were developments among the Indians themselves. Many different bands had come to the agency either to draw the rations provided by terms of the peace policy or to receive treaty annuities. These bands had experienced a great degree of autonomy formerly; even within a band a man was quite independent and joined another group whenever he differed with a leader. Whites generally assumed that large groups of Indians were led by one chief, and they would have liked to deal with large numbers through a handful of chiefs. Under agency conditions, such as control over annuities' distribution, the Indian band leaders were put into a competitive situation to become *the chief*. Not only did the leaders compete, they also disagreed about the kind of cooperation to be extended to whites and the treatment to be offered the hostile Dakota who refused rations.

This factionalism led to a murder in October 1869, less than six months after agent Poole's arrival. Big Mouth was rising to become an important Brule chief. His influence derived primarily from the friendly Indians known as Loafers, ones who became totally dependent upon rations. Big Mouth was killed by Spotted Tail, who was one of the most influential Brule leaders at the time.[6] Although Spotted Tail had come to the Whetstone agency, he kept his followers some distance off to isolate them from the whiskey trade and other contacts with whites. On the night of the murder, the Brule were on the verge of an intensive intratribal war between the Loafers and the followers of Spotted Tail, who believed in resisting white influence. The affair eventually was dropped in the lap of Poole, who actually had no authority over murder nor any precedent to judge such matters. The account of that night is the epitome of the harrowing life of an Indian agent.

A crowd of frantic Sioux had snatched up weapons and were preparing to fight. The wagon train boss ran to the agent's office, shouting that the Sioux were fighting; and Captain Poole, awakened from sleep, came and opened the door. "Here they come!" shouted the wagon master and ran into the office to hide. The Sioux came pouring in all yelling and brandishing weapons. They pushed Poole through the office and into the council room, where he was dumped into a chair, and Spotted Tail sat down on the floor beside him, his blanket drawn closely about him, alert and cool. Big Mouth's brother, Blue Horse, started a violent harangue. He had a rifle in one hand and a strung bow in the other, and when he dropped his blanket, two navy Colts and a big scalping knife could be seen. He was in a raving fury, leaping and bounding about the room as he hurled accusations and threats at Spotted Tail. The head chief seemed calm, but he was watching Blue Horse intently. He now had a rifle, and at one point in the violent harangue he cocked the gun. Agent Poole was frozen to the chair. The room was thronged with enraged Sioux, all armed and ardently itching for a fight. If they started shooting, Poole was in a wonderful position to field most of the bullets and arrows.[7]

Poole's modesty prevents a full exploration of the ingenuity used in solving this crisis. In the end he negotiated a settlement by payment of ten ponies to the Loafers, keeping in line with customary Dakota practices for resolving conflict. Although there were a number of "squawmen," whites married to Indians, who could have advised Poole on appropriate procedure, not many of the early agents listened to them. Probably Poole did. He had the sense to observe very early:

I noticed at this time one fact which was later confirmed, that those who had been sometime associated with Indians assumed to know little of their character, and usually had no plans for their management . . . .

But a newly appointed attaché of the Indian Bureau, born and raised in the New England states, will unhesitatingly mark out a course to pursue, which will transform a savage into an enlightened citizen, surely within the period of his administration.[8]

Actually Poole himself arrived fairly quickly at his own course to pursue, although it consisted largely of common sense advocated before by sensible men. The Great Plains simply could not be cultivated successfully with nineteenth-century technology. Rainfall was hardly ever sufficient for the varieties of corn or wheat then known, and when the rain was adequate, the crop was most likely destined for grasshoppers. Easterners who insisted that the Dakota farm for a livelihood were misled by some limited successes in farming by Indians on the prairie; they did not understand that conditions change rapidly west of the Missouri River, despite the many maps that labeled the area the Great American Desert.

Poole had arrived at Whetstone to find a wide variety of farming tools. The administration was so certain of agricultural success that it also had sent a grist mill and a saw mill. Huge log carts further indicated how little the Washington office understood conditions along the Missouri River. Watching all this equipment going to waste, Poole concluded in one of his reports that Dakota men were not lazy. In hunting or herding, that is, in jobs they considered male work, the Dakota exhibited endurance and persistence. They would not carry supplies, unload a steamboat, or farm because it was not appropriate for an Indian man. But they did care for their pony herds and they did thoroughly understand bison and the hunt. Thus Poole asks:

Why endeavor to make of poor material unwilling agriculturists, in place of leading them to a pastoral life, for which they show considerable inclination, and which has always come first in the regular state of advancement from barbarism to civilization?[9]

The frustrations of having Washington continually ignore his recommendations and requests, plus the constant harassment from the Indians, led Poole, like most capable agents, to seek another assignment. His book indicates great interest in meeting the challenge of agency life, but his analysis of the overwhelming frustration is classic:

Without the boundaries of civilization, isolated from the association and comforts of a home, pestered and tormented by some of the worst specimens of white humanity, seeing the credulity of the Indians imposed upon, and the good effects of honorable dealing neutralized, often traduced and villified by men whom he may have thwarted in some nefarious scheme, made to share the consequences of deficiency in supplies over which he never had control, and made responsible by the public for any outbreak among the untamed savages under his charge, his lines are not cast in pleasant places.[10]

Unfortunately no agent has left a comparable record for the initial years of the Lower Brule Reservation, which must have been similar to Whetstone. As early as 1866, treaty provisions established an agency for the Lower Brule, but Newton Edmunds undermined its establishment by insisting the Crow Creek agent could serve the Lower Brule. As territorial governor, Edmunds was ex officio superintendent of Indian affairs, and his interests were primarily in seeing that expenditures for Indians were made in South Dakota. The merger of Crow Creek and Lower Brule agencies was simply expedient administration. Even though the Lower Brule insisted on a separate agency, they had to depend initially on an agent who resided across the river at Crow Creek.

However, the persistence of the Lower Brule did result in establishment of their own reservation under the Treaty of 1868. It is fairly clear from the treaty that a separate agency was intended also, but its establishment was postponed. During this period the Lower Brule were far from a settled people, but their behavior toward whites is not clear. One observer, for instance, reported most unfavorably:

> *The Lower Brule have a reservation and cultivate at White River; draw rations at Fort Thompson. They acknowledge no chief; are perfect Ishmaelites, wandering in small bands thousands of miles over the prairies; are treacherous beyond all other Sioux and commit most of the rascalities which occur in this district.[11]*

Certainly the Lower Brule were not wandering over thousands of miles, nor is it likely they were the most treacherous Indians in the territory. Another military officer, stationed at Fort Randall, implies they might have been cool but not hostile: "I had a talk with Little Pheasant, Medicine Bull and several other of the Lower Brule and find them dissatisfied about being called to council at this post. They want to meet where they are to farm at White River and ask that their seed, tools and whatever goods is brought for them be delivered there."[12] The man who probably knew them best, agent J. R. Hanson, seems to have been favorably impressed.

Although from New Hampshire, he was one of the few Easterners who did not immediately plan the Indians' destiny. Hanson, as mentioned before, apparently arrived at Crow Creek late in 1866. His appointment was as Upper Missouri agent, but his responsibilities were primarily for the Crow Creek and Lower Brule. The Yankton and Santee had their own agents; General Harney was in command at Cheyenne River. Hanson does not reveal much of himself in his correspondence with Governor Faulk, who followed Edmunds, nor in his letters to the commissioner of Indian affairs. Neither did he write at any length about Indians. From Faulk's correspondence to Washington, it is obvious that Hanson's life was every bit as complex and difficult as Poole's. The doctor who had been serving the agency was about to leave because he had gone eighteen months without pay. Inflation had halved the amount of annuity goods delivered to the Indians, who failed to appreciate that the Civil War should deprive them of half their treaty goods. At the approach of each winter, there were never enough cattle to last until spring, and flour and bacon supplies frequently had to be shuffled among various agencies. On several occasions, General Sherman wrote directly to agents giving them orders contradictory to those of Governor Faulk. Sherman either did not understand the territorial governor was ex officio superintendent or else he believed himself superior as commander of the military district. In between coping with such problems, the agents were called upon to secure a bow and arrows as a gift to the queen of Portugal.[13] Hanson's major task, however, was to create some semblance of an agency at Lower Brule and initiate the Indians to farming. In the summer of 1868 he contracted for the erection of several agency buildings just above the mouth of White River and managed to have built a few log homes for Indian families as well.[14] A Yankton paper announced that the Lower Brule treaty provisions were fulfilled that year. They allowed a farmer and blacksmith to be employed plus payment of a $6000 annuity. The farmer, Judson Lamoure, served as sub-agent for Lower Brule. He broke nearly 150 acres and was about to harvest a good crop when grasshoppers devoured nearly three-quarters of it.[15]

As the winter of 1868–1869 set in, Hanson's overriding problem was lack of supplies. The summer crop had been a failure even at Crow Creek, where some farming was done on a regular basis. Many of Hanson's letters, begging for supplies, went unanswered. Contractors had been unable to provide enough cattle in the fall, in large part because the Dakota agencies were a new market for them. By January, Hanson was pleading to be ordered to Washington to seek special funds. A new territorial governor, John Burbank, was sympathetic but slow to respond as he gradually learned his duties as ex officio superintendent.

In effect, the peace policy had been inaugurated largely at an idealistic level; the logistics were far from complete. The result was near starvation for the Lower Brule and many other Indians. At a few agencies, Indians killed their work oxen in desperation, and some casual white observers concluded that it was the beginning of hostilities. Hanson started a correspondence with the Yankton paper assuring people that the Indians did not mean trouble. In addition to near starvation, he reported that he had been without funds for months, and his employees were threatening to quit. The agencies' rations were far behind schedule; even small game had disappeared. Nevertheless he assured people, "The general disposition of the Indian is one of friendship."[16] Further, he believed that relief would soon be forthcoming from the nearby military garrisons. What he did not relate publicly was that he had previously offered his resignation, to be effective with the arrival of his replacement. Although he minimized his difficulties to the press, he was pleading for relief to Washington. In a long letter explaining how he has just divided up scant rations among far too many Indians, he concludes: "Where in God's name is my successor? I want to get out of this country *immediately* for I can't stand these appeals of starving people much longer, and I won't."[17] Still Hanson persisted a while longer and by mid-summer was engaged in encouraging agriculture and planning fall logistics. He estimated a need of fall rations for 140 lodges or 840 individuals. Through winter and spring another 60 lodges could be expected. In short, 1200 people would have to be fed for more than six months. This figure of 1200 became a standard one, though Hanson estimated that there were more Lower Brule than that; some lodges had gone to other agencies where they were better supplied.[18] While Hanson struggled with the mundane problem of feeding these 1200 mouths, frontiersmen called for a grand solution. "Make no more treaties. But say to the Indians that everyone of them who will abandon his tribal relations and who will settle upon and improve 160 acres of land. That he shall have the land . . . . Every Indian who accepts this proposition is then disposed of." The others could be disposed of by vocational training because "many have a natural faculty for the mechanic arts."[19]

Hanson's replacement finally arrived in late August. Lt. William H. French was one of the strangest agents the Lower Brule ever experienced. At best French could be described as highly idiosyncratic when he arrived; certainly when he left he was in a state of mental collapse. He owed his appointment in part to an influential father who was a colonel in the Regular Army. He became much more intimately involved with the Lower Brule than most agents, but he probably made more enemies than friends. Only a few months after arriving he began a feud with Governor Burbank over payment for a sawmill.[20] French also found it easier to correspond directly with Washington, and Burbank expressed frequent anger over being continually by-passed. Otherwise French's first winter seems to have passed without notable incident.

Spring, however, brought trouble. The Indians interpreted

fate quite differently from whites, as agent French soon discovered in his first major difficulty with the Lower Brule.

> *On the first instance, while taking beef across the river [the Missouri], one of the boats upset and one of the Indians was drowned. The Indians said the white man put bad medicine into the water for the purpose of killing them and that they would have to kill a white man, whereupon an Indian tried to shoot the superintendent of farming.*[21]

Alex Rencountre, a long-time employee of the agency, came to French's aid and pacified the Indians temporarily. Later, however, they broke into their provisions stored by the agency and took several weeks' advance rations. A large number of Indians then left the reservation, apparently to join hostiles in the Black Hills. As if these troubles were not enough, French became engaged at the same time in a bitter squabble with white settlers near Crow Creek. French accused them of squatting on Indian land and threatened to drive them off. Although they were there illegally, they had settled as a result of a confusing situation, and most of the settlers sincerely believed they could acquire legal title. Burbank, of course, was glad to back up frontiersmen any time but especially at the expense of agent French.

In response, French leaned even more toward the Indians. He made an unusual request for leave time in order to hunt with Little Pheasant and three or four friends west of the Missouri.[22] Before he could take leave, however, he became embroiled with the military. General D. S. Stanley, commander of Fort Sully, formally charged French with being unfit although the report probably originated with Guido Ilges, commander of another military post near Lower Brule. Ilges claimed that French's "mind was affected," and he was no longer capable of managing the Indians. The rumor of a Lower Brule outbreak probably spread among the military, who usually saw more hostility than was actually present.

Governor Burbank had visited Lower Brule that summer

and found agent French with an Indian mistress. The governor also charged the agent with drunkenness and other offenses. Further, Burbank recommended removal of the agency, which was only "a few small log huts, covered with dirt roofs ... and styled an agency." The governor chose a new site just above Crow Creek Island. He urged that a saw mill first be built there to provide lumber for the agency. Since the mill would be only ten miles below the Crow Creek Agency, it could serve that agency as well.

The military helped in preparation for the relocation. Given their presence and the state of French's mind, some Indian hostility must have existed. The Lower Brule were still conducting some raids against other Indians; Medicine Bull had supposedly taken a Pawnee scalp as late as May. Such inter-tribal fighting never reassured whites who failed to distinguish it from their own form of warfare. The army's report, from their headquarters near Lower Brule, certainly portrays considerable unrest on July 31, 1870:

I have the honor to report that on the 28 inst., the removal of the agency from the old site to this point was completed.

The chief farmer and the interpreter informs me (Capt. French, the agent being absent at Yankton) that before leaving the Indians, particularly the bands of Little Pheasant and Medicine Bull, behaved in a most insulting manner, firing pistols and guns around them, frightening Little Pheasant from the reservation and threatening the lives of Medicine Bull and Iron Nation. The latter with his band has removed to this place and is camped within a mile of this point. As they were leaving the Agency, some Indians fired at the buildings with the exception of the house of Little Pheasant. (It is believed that Little Pheasant's band did it.)

The cause of this outbreak is as yet unknown, but the supposition is that the removal of the agency was taken as a pretext to avenge themselves for a recent reconstruction of the bands, made by the agent, when he reduced three chiefs. These chiefs had been appointed by him last winter to assist the principal chiefs in controlling their bands. Little Pheasant's reason (he was absent at the time of the burning) is that news had reached the Indians of a fight near Fort Laramie, in which some relatives had been killed, but I take it that the whole reason can be found in the fact that they are a bad lot of Indians.

Mr. Fielder [a sub-agent who spoke Dakota] tells me that he only considers 28 lodges in Iron Nation's band of 118 as peacably disposed.²³

Some of the contradictions of this report confuse the picture more than clarify it. The report does indicate that French had added to his troubles considerably by mixing into tribal politics. Many agents were tempted to appoint chiefs favorably disposed toward them, but such tactics generally increased dissension and in the end decreased the agent's influence. In less than a year, it appears that agent French had antagonized most of the Lower Brule, neighboring whites, the military commanders of the region, and especially his immediate superior, Governor Burbank. If a mental illness had not brought on most of this trouble, then the trouble brought on French's collapse. Early in the fall the agent was relieved of his duties despite his protests.

French's replacement was Henry Livingstone. Livingstone was formerly a physician at Crow Creek and one of the few men who seems to have managed an amiable relation with French. Livingstone thus had some experience at the agency before becoming its chief administrator. He also enjoyed the full confidence of the prestigious Board of Indian Commissioners who endorsed his appointment. Although Livingstone had inherited a complex set of problems from his predecessor, he managed to serve as agent for the next six years.

In his initial year he was visited by William Welsh, an influential member of the Board of Indian Commissioners and one of the most active of the "Indian friends." Welsh submitted to commissioner Delano a recommendation, urged by French, that Lower Brule be made a separate agency. Welsh praised Livingstone's ability but noted that administering Crow Creek was a full-time job in itself. Furthermore:

> *The Lower Brule are more numerous, more important and less civilized than the Yanktonnais, who reside near Crow Creek, the site of the present agency.*
>
> *Second, the ferriage across the Missouri river at this point is so tedious that the cost of transporting stores is very great and the agent is unable to visit the Brule frequently or to encourage them to become farmers.*
>
> *Third, the Brule are very much dissatisfied at not being under the supervision of an Agent having authority. The young men mostly congregate at what is called a hostile camp.*[24]

It took some years, however, before a separate agency was established. In the meantime Livingstone continued to be responsible for both groups. Certainly during this period problems increased in rationing, encouraging farming, and administering a growing staff. Special problems, such as construction of a telegraph line in 1871, were additional headaches. As a conservation measure, Livingstone had put a stop to rafting logs from the reservation to Fort Randall in the spring, but later the Missouri Telegraph Company requested poles for a line to Pierre following the east bank of the Missouri. Construction of the line would mean a station located at Crow Creek with much better access to the outside world. The Crow Creek Indians were very much opposed to the idea because they believed that the telegraph was always followed by a railroad line. They demanded a very high price for their trees hoping to discourage construction. Livingstone's report on the matter indicates his opinion: "I think that these Indians have been influenced by half-breeds who have a great deal of gratuitous advice. When the Indians find that they cannot prevent the construction of the line, they will consent to sell the poles at a fair price."[25]

Eventually enough pressure was applied to convince the Crow Creek to sell, but then it was discovered they did not really have enough timber, and cedar poles had to be acquired from the Lower Brule. The Lower Brule were even more reluctant to sell than the Crow Creek. Once they were persuaded and the line was finally finished, hostile Indians occasionally shot off insulators while other Indians helped themselves to sections of wire whenever it was needed. Livingstone tended to defend the Indians in this matter implying the telegraph company tended to exaggerate its claims for damage.

The agent's major problem was to redirect the Indians' efforts at subsistence. His agency was at a point in the Dakota Territory where annual rainfall was marginal. Not far to the east crops could be reliably grown, and some years provided a more than adequate amount of rain in the Missouri Valley itself. However, periods of drought, combined with grasshoppers, made farming highly unreliable. Since Livingstone had lived in the area long enough to realize the futility of farming, he continually requested that the government replace farming with ranching. He further realized the Dakota would show much more interest in cattle herding. In an annual report, he argued: "If they can be induced to care for cows as faithfully as they do their ponies, they would in a very short time become successful stock growers."[26]

The request had little effect in Washington. The very next year the commissioner recommended at length a farming policy that was meant to end the rationing system. The threat of ending rationing was coupled with the loss of annuities for the Lower Brule because they were due to expire five years after the Treaty of 1868. In short, the Lower Brule unknowingly faced dire economic straits.

Apparently Livingstone anticipated the difficulties and knew how serious they would be, but many other problems demanded his attention. Almost daily a wide variety of minor crises presented themselves. Livingstone's diary records a number of these events, although it generally reports a rather drab and boring existence. "Spent the day trying to cross cattle at Dry Point. Drowned 12 head and crossed 4. Have had a tedious day."[27] Another type of problem arose from special agents such as one in 1871 who "discovered" that neither a church nor a school had been built at Crow Creek and found conditions at Lower Brule even worse. Livingstone was expected to remedy the situation. Actually a missionary was present at Crow Creek at least part of the year; at Lower Brule Mr. Walter Hall and Miss Leigh began visits there as early as 1870. They operated from an Episcopal mission based in Yankton. In 1872 the Reverend H. Burt settled at Crow Creek and William Cleveland, from a Scranton, Pennsylvania parish, joined Hall and Leigh.[28] A Santee Dakota, Luke Walker, became active at Yankton; later he would become prominent at Lower Brule.

The increase in missionary effort at Lower Brule reflected a broad Episcopal movement under way among the Dakota. In the fall of 1872 all Dakota missions were transferred from the Nebraska Bishop to a new Bishop of Niobrara. A young minister, who had quickly risen to become secretary of the Foreign Committee of the Band of Missions, was elected Missionary Bishop of Niobrara. Bishop William Hare was to spend most of the remainder of his life among the Dakota. Bishop Hare's reminiscences gave writer Mark Howe an opportunity to reconstruct a life that sheds much light on frontier conditions and the Indians' view of a new religion.[29] For instance, a Dakota winter is graphically recalled by Hare, who arrived at Yankton early in 1873.

> *My arrival occurred just after one of the most memorable storms that Dakota has ever known, and the effects of it were plainly to be seen in the carcasses of cattle which had perished in it, and in huge banks of snow which lay still unmelted. The storm had overtaken Custer's celebrated cavalry, while they were encamped about a mile or two outside of Yankton, and brave men, who never quailed before the foe, had fled in complete rout before the tempest, and taken shelter in any house where they could find a shelter, leaving all their camp equipment and horses to their fate.[30]*

The northern climate bothered Bishop Hare throughout his life, but he immediately dedicated his energies to expanding the mission effort. Lower Brule proselytism was part of that effort, and Hare frequently visited the reservation throughout his life. The new position and reorganization reflected a view that Indian Episcopalian churches were a distinct entity. They would be kept separate from neighboring white churches for many years. The energy and enthusiasm of young William Hare certainly stimulated the missionary effort among the Dakota, but it probably contributed to this separateness of the Indian churches.

While pressure built for further civilizing influences at Lower Brule, a much more significant event occurred throughout the surrounding area. Rumors of gold in the Black Hills became more and more persistent. In the spring of 1872 the acting governor of Dakota Territory assured the commissioner of Indian affairs that a rumored invasion of the Black Hills was simply talk in Sioux City; nevertheless he had issued a proclamation prohibiting exploration in the Black Hills. Yet in 1873 the territorial delegate in Congress was attempting to initiate legislation that would open up the Black Hills for exploration. The outcome from this action was the appointment of another commission, instructed to determine what would be necessary to acquire the land from the Indians. The Lower Brule were involved marginally in these meetings because leadership of the Indians centered in the western groups at the Red Cloud and the Spotted Tail agencies.

The commission was headed by Felix Brunot, chairman of the board of Indian commissioners. Although the commission seemed sympathetic toward the Indians, it recognized the value of the Black Hills. Still it could not decide just how the government could begin acquisition. Brunot probably presented a fairly accurate summary of the Indians' feelings when he reported:

In the speeches made by the Indians at this council the subject of the boundaries of their territory was voluntarily brought forward by

*nearly every speaker, and the sensitiveness which is felt by these tribes
to the relinquishment of any portion of the country at present held by
them was impressed upon your Commission in many ways and under a
variety of exaggerated claims. Similar tenacity of purpose and jealous
regard for their stipulated privileges was shown in connection with the
subject of hunting.[31]*

Limiting the Dakotas' right to hunt became an initial major
task; the secretary of the interior found an excuse for it a few
months after the commission's report. "The Sioux having vi-
olated provisions of the treaty which guaranteed their right to
hunt on the Republican Fork, by their recent attack on the
Pawnees, have given the Department the opportunity to comply
with the request of the Governor [of Nebraska], and to exercise
its authority to the extent of taking from them their privileges
[to hunt]."[32] However, even the secretary of the interior could
not rationalize away the guarantees to land secured by the
Dakota in the Treaty of 1868. Their unity in holding this land
made any cessions seemingly impossible.

The pressure from the public for acquiring the Black Hills
was overwhelming. Early in 1873 the army was arguing strenu-
ously for a reduction in territory for the Sioux Nation. One
general pointed out that his intelligence showed only one Indian for every twenty square miles; clearly there was "no way they
could hold it." More importantly, he saw Dakota Territory as
being greater in wealth than Montana and believed the Black
Hills' gold many times more valuable than Montana's. Finally he
appealed to destiny: "It must come some day, and why post-
pone it any longer to favor a people who are practically and
professedly assassins, and nothing but assassins."[33] William T.
Sherman strongly endorsed the recommendations in forward-
ing the letter to the Department of War.

In 1874 the army pushed matters further. Lt. Colonel
George Armstrong Custer was ordered to proceed toward the
Black Hills to reconnoiter the territory. The expedition had
caught the romantic fancy of many men. John Brown, Jr. was

one who managed to join. The grandson of Samuel Morse also applied, listing as a qualification that he had "inherited the family genius and will serve in whatever position I am appointed." Dr. V. T. McGillycuddy served as an "astronomic" or surveyor; he was later to become famous as an agent at Pine Ridge. Custer was directed to determine sites for military posts and routes, but he obviously was to survey for forest and mineral wealth as well, since a number of prospectors and scientists accompanied him. In all, over a thousand men outfitted in more than a hundred wagons entered the Black Hills under Custer's command.

Newspaper reporters with Custer sent back glowing reports of wealth, and some initial official dispatches suggested gold in paying quantity. Although the final official reports concluded gold mining would not pay, many unofficial prospectors were by then on their way. The army managed to turn back a few of these parties; it even escorted some out with punitive measures. Still, extensive exploration was under way. Near Lower Brule at the newly constructed military post, Fort Hale, the army investigated rumors of an expedition originating there, but Lieutenant William Dougherty found no supporting evidence. His commander believed the Lower Brule patrolled the White River trail to such an extent they would turn back any gold seekers.[34]

Elsewhere other Dakota did encounter small parties of whites attempting to penetrate their lands. On numerous occasions they attacked and sometimes killed such trespassers. In short, the attraction of the Black Hills for whites was causing considerable anxiety among the Dakota. They had expressed their feelings in council with the land commission, and they next turned to open violence. It is remarkable that their leaders were able to keep open warfare in check. Some leaders in the United States Army probably welcomed an open fight, and the Custer expedition appears much like a deliberate provocation.

Once official reports were in Washington, the Bureau of Indian Affairs assumed gold prospectors would be discouraged so their troubles among the Dakota would disappear. In making this assumption, the commissioner of Indian affairs failed to appreciate the extent of hostility already raised among the Indians. Even at Lower Brule, far removed from the Black Hills and with only an indirect attachment to them, reports of unrest circulated in the summer of 1874. Repeated trouble over trade led to an open confrontation, and general warfare was possibly quelled only by the chance presence of Bishop Hare. The military dispatch reported that a Brule-Ponca named Omaha had threatened the trader and agent, broken into the stores, and finally fled.

> At the request of the agent, I sent mounted men in pursuit, who captured his mule, but the Indian escaped . . . . A courier was sent to the Indian camp 7 miles below with instructions to the Chiefs to capture and bring in the offender. In the space of about four hours some 250 chiefs and warriors, mounted, appeared at the post with the Indian, but refused to surrender the prisoner unless the trader was given up to them. They assumed a menacing attitude—all were heavily armed, some with two pistols and repeating rifles. I at once placed my howitzers in position. The agent demanded the prisoner. After a long parley the chiefs advanced with him . . . .[35]

The talk continued the next day when Bishop Hare appeared to persuade the Lower Brule to keep the peace. Hare was so occupied with other troubles that he gave little attention to the incident. He had just returned from extensive negotiations with the northern Sioux. Afterwards he wrote his sister that he had become so involved with Indians and the government that he expected to be reviled, "sometimes by rogues and sometimes by sentimental philanthropists."[36]

While Bishop Hare anticipated further troubles over the Black Hills, Washington relied on the negative reports of mineral resources to discourage further exploration. Little did the Bureau of Indian Affairs realize the extent to which frontiersmen were committed. A Sioux City organization had strongly urged opening the country as early as 1872. Territorial influence was at work on the Bureau's superior, secretary of the interior Columbus Delano, as well as in Congress. Of course pressure from the military continued. More than twenty Sioux City residents had followed Custer and established "Harney City" in December of 1874.[37] They were turned out, however, by the military in the spring. Only isolated prospectors remained, scattered in the Black Hills, but during that summer they were joined by some 800 more. Gold fever was too much for the military.

Bishop Hare provides a pragmatic evaluation of events:

> *I was outspoken in my denunciation of this flagrant violation of the sacred obligations of a great to a weak people. I foresaw, however, that no power on earth could shut out our white people from that country if it really contained valuable deposits of gold. I went, therefore, to Washington and urged upon the President that a Commission of experts should be sent out to explore the country and steps should be taken to secure a surrender of the tract in question from the Indians on equitable terms.*
>
> *. . . The desire for the acquisition of this country was so ardent and influential, that the Government was practically driven to negotiate with Indians to secure a voluntary sale of the coveted territory.*[38]

A settlement for the Black Hills was foreseen as a matter of course by most whites on the frontier. One victim of a Dakota raid sought to be compensated from the Black Hills settlement, "whatever it was to be," months before a commission for negotiating was even appointed.[39]

The appointment of a commission was foreshadowed by an invitation to numerous Dakota chiefs for a visit to Washington. Red Cloud and others met with President Grant and the Dakota governor but refused to negotiate. They maintained they did not have the necessary authority, and negotiations would have to be conducted in the Dakota Nation by a commission. Eventually Senator W. B. Allison of Iowa chaired such a group consisting of Collins, Comingo, Hinman, and Palmer. Only Hinman had had any experience with the Dakota.[40]

The charge of the commission was in keeping with the government's policy toward Indians. On the one hand, it wanted to stand as a benevolent protector, while on the other, it demanded the land that Indians tenaciously held. In meeting with some 35,000 Dakota from six agencies, plus a few thousand "roaming Sioux," the commission was instructed:

In negotiating with these ignorant and almost helpless people you will keep in mind that you represent them and their interests not less than those of the government and are commissioned to secure the best interests of both parties as far as practical. [Taking the land] originates solely from a desire for peace between them and the whites since it has been impossible to prevent white persons from entering their country.[41]

Further bargaining points were included. The commissioner of Indian affairs noted that the annuities provided by the 1868 treaty had expired, and most of the Sioux Nation was now dependent on the annual charity of Congress. Its charitable intent would certainly change if the Dakota refused to negotiate. Finally, the Indians were to be invited to make an inspection trip of Oklahoma. Many Dakota were already familiar with Oklahoma Indian Territory, and they dreaded it. Perhaps the threat of removal originated from a sincere desire in Washington to improve life for the Indians, but it was used as a major weapon by westerners in the bargaining process.

The special Indian commission finally met with the Dakota in September 1875. The army persuaded most prospectors in the Black Hills to leave, hoping to provide a more favorable climate for negotiations. Instead the move probably fortified the Dakota in their resolve to hold on to the land. From the start they displayed such hostility to the commission that removal to the Indian Territory was hardly mentioned. Meanwhile the governors of Nebraska and Missouri, who wanted Oklahoma opened to white settlement, were violently protesting any Sioux settlement there. In negotiating a price, the commission found that the Dakota had a fair idea of what the Black Hills were worth—$30 to $40 million; and their initial offer of $6 million was met with scorn. When a final offer of $400,000 a year for a mining lease was rejected, the haggling ceased.[42]

About 300 Lower Brule had attended the general council with the commission. They had regularly visited their Brule cousins at Rosebud on any pretense so their presence could be expected. Although none of the Lower Brule were mentioned by name in the reports of the commission, the meeting must have provided an opportunity for Iron Nation and other headmen to see how white men could be opposed. One outcome of 1875 was that future commissions met separately with the various agency groups figuring that reduced numbers would lessen the opposition. However, Iron Nation and others had already learned some tactics of resistance which they frequently employed in the next few decades.

As the council of 1875 began to disperse with no prospect of accomplishing its aims, the commission resorted to some fine legal points to absolve the government from its obligation to keep whites out of territory belonging to the Sioux Nation. These rationalizations carried little weight in Washington where eastern humanitarians denounced them. Alfred H. Love, author and opponent of the Army, enlisted the aid of Quakers to denounce the Black Hills exploration.[43] Still the commission's tactics served to disrupt the Dakota as they made preparations for winter.

The winter of 1875–1876 was a particularly hard one with life further complicated by decisions made in Washington. President Grant gave orders that all Indians were to move into their agencies by February 1876. Those bands that refused were to be rounded up by the military. Many Dakota regularly spent the winter at the agencies, but following a customary pattern they left in the spring to join hostile groups in the Powder River drainage. In March of 1876 General George Crook, veteran

Indian fighter in the northwest and southwest, also left for the Powder River to ensure that the Indians complied with the presidential order. When he finally met the Indians his force was driven off after burning an Indian camp. Finding himself low on supplies, Crook had to return to Fort Laramie after having failed to round up any Indians. A victory over the military was attributed to Sitting Bull and Crazy Horse, and their numbers increased as the Indians, who only wintered at the agencies, joined the hostiles. Even a few of those who resided regularly at the agencies may have left for the hostile camps, but surely their numbers were small. At the time, however, the military and frontiersmen vehemently attacked the peace policy of providing subsistence for the agency Indians, who were now accused of joining the hostiles. The charge does not seem justified. According to local agents who were checking almost daily, almost all the regular agency Indians remained on the reservation.[44]

The force of warriors that was steadily building in Montana reached about 2000 men in the summer of 1876. It should be remembered that this group was encumbered by women and children and was not any better prepared for warfare than usual. Although they were on the alert after General Crook's early spring offensive, they had conducted their annual Sun Dance early in June and were earnestly pursuing the bison. Meanwhile three different army forces were marching on them, from the east, the west, and the south. In mid-June the first contact was made by Crook who engaged in intensive combat with a large, determined force of Dakota. The Indians fought with an intensity and persistence that should have warned the army that desperation and experience were making the Dakota a new type of fighting force. Crook, of course, did not have time to relay such a message to the other columns even if he had perceived the change. On June 25, 1876, in an attempt to exonerate himself, Lt. Colonel George A. Custer attacked the main force of some 2500 Indians and had his command of over 200 men completely annihilated. This battle of the Little Big Horn has probably been described in more detail than any other in all the Indian wars.[45] The Indian victory netted them nothing in the long run.

While these major events were occurring, life at Lower Brule proceeded much as usual. The agent and the officers at the nearby military post had no inkling of the fighting in Montana nor were they aware of any unusual build-up of Dakota forces because few Lower Brule or Crow Creek had left. Agent Livingstone was occupied trying to secure a safe place for his agency while agent Thomas A. Riley was being initiated into agency life at Lower Brule. The separation of Lower Brule and Crow Creek had been a gradual process with Livingstone still having some influence at Lower Brule even though officially only at Crow Creek. Little is known of Riley. He was appointed to head the White River Agency in July 1875 but seems to have arrived after several months' delay. His reports indicate a thorough clerical knowledge of the Bureau of Indian Affairs and a typical small-scale bureaucrat's approach to problems. During the spring and summer he concentrated on getting new buildings erected. He also wrote several letters pleading for a change of name for his agency since his mail was continually misdirected to a White River Agency in Colorado.

It is hard to imagine how Riley reacted initially to the news of Custer's defeat, but he was soon caught up in charges that he had allowed all the fighting men at Lower Brule to leave the reservation. A story in the *Sioux City Journal* on July 27th, 1876, alleged that all the Lower Brule had joined Sitting Bull. The next day Riley reported that "none of the Lower Brule are absent."[46] For the most part, the Missouri River agents seem to have made little attempt to convince local newspapers that the agency Indians had remained on the river. They did affirm their presence to Washington although some of the agents seem to have failed to realize the gravity of the situation. When Livingstone reported that he had just heard the news of Custer, he noted that conditions at Crow Creek were not affected in any way. In fact, half of his report details his lack of rations and an invasion of grasshoppers that "destroyed in a few hours what remained of the crops that had not been previously destroyed by drought and frost."[47]

The failure of the agents to clarify the situation resulted in inflammatory cries from the press about the agency Indians. The news of Custer did not reach Yankton until July 7th; it then came via Chicago and Salt Lake City. The local editor used the battle news to condemn the whole peace policy. He described the defeat as:

> . . . a cold blooded, barbarous massacre of men, anyone of whom is of more consequence in the estimation of the world and the eyes of the Lord than the entire forty thousand loafing Sioux to whom the government is furnishing sustenance, "aid and comfort," and arms and ammunition with which to carry on their wholesale hellishness. Will the controlling powers not now realize that Indians are not men. Or must we have a few more sanguinary examples of their brutish composition before the false philanthropists of the east will let go their hold of the delusion which has so long bound fast their prejudices to the idol of a morbid fancy?[48]

The writer was certain that at least two-thirds of the fighting force of "twenty to thirty thousand" [about ten times the actual number] were agency Indians who would soon be back at their respective agencies drawing rations. As evidence the paper offered numerous rumors. An unidentified Lieutenant Edmunds

> . . . reports that the Lower Brule—that is all the fighting men of the tribe—all left the agency some two weeks ago. Government rations have given them courage to kill white men and they have gone to join Sitting Bull. It is now some ten years or more since the Brules were placed under the civilizing process, and they have accumulated enough arms, ammunition, ponies and muscular courage to enable them to kill a good many white men.[49]

While Indian policy was under such attack, Riley and Livingstone appear to have taken little notice of the newspaper remarks. During the emergency, they continued to submit routine requests and trivial accounting of goods received. In August, Riley proudly announced completion of his building plans, and as if that were a peak in his career, resigned in September. Of course all the Dakota agents were under pressure, from the frontier and Washington alike, and a few resignations were necessary. Riley was a likely candidate because he had become embroiled in charges and counter-charges among his own employees, and it was obvious he was incapable of administering an agency. Lower Brule had grown to nearly a dozen employees in addition to the agent, and another nine or ten whites now resided there.

Riley's resignation was just one more event among many disruptive ones. The war with Custer had inflamed the frontier and demands for removal of the Dakota Indians ranged from genocide to forced migration to Oklahoma or what was then Indian Territory. The conflict opened the way for further pressure on the Black Hills and rights of way through Indian country. Still another commission from Washington appeared among the Dakota in the fall of 1876 urging the Indians to sell their land and reminding them of all the threats being bandied about on all sides. This time the commission visited the separate agencies and prevented any massing of Indians. The commission secured more signatures than usual for a sale of the Hills by promising to drop any idea of removal to Indian Territory which all the Indians strongly opposed. The Indians themselves appear to have been most confused. Custer may have been killed, but by fall hostile Indians were scattered widely as the might of the federal forces became apparent.

At Lower Brule in 1876 only a handful of whites were living among nearly two thousand Indians; yet they had not seemed to be in any grave danger at any time. The former band organization was apparently still intact. The fall agreement for sale of the Black Hills had been signed by nine chiefs: Iron Nation, Medicine Bull, White Buffalo Cow, Little Pheasant, Buffalo Head, Standing Cloud, Useful Heart, Long Bear Claws, and

Only Man. Some of these band leaders may have given a different name in signing the 1868 treaty since the Dakota sometimes acquired new names. Factional differences among the Indians were also present, but the major difficulty in these first years of reservation life was subsistence. The band leaders clearly were keeping the peace while the Indians were settling into a total dependence on rations and annuities, little realizing economic dependency would make them politically powerless.

Many whites, on the other hand, saw such lack of power as indicative of a low stage of civilization. As dependent savages, the Dakota should not be allowed to stand in the way of "progress," interpreted at this point as an expansion of Dakota Territory. If the Dakota did not make an adaptation to an agrarian way of life, they simply would have to become extinct. The next decade did little to change these great and tragic differences in outlook between the Dakota and whites.

chapter 4
The Desperate Years – 1877-1890

The Battle of the Little Big Horn was to have profound effects on all other Indians including the Dakota. After the initial shock of the army's losses and General Crook's ensuing success in rounding up most of the dissidents, the humanitarians split into two factions. Those who supported President Grant continued to advocate a peace policy. Some reformers, however, who generally opposed Grant now backed a frontier perspective that called for military domination of all hostile Indians. When the furor over Little Big Horn subsided, several reform organizations started. The Women's National Indian Association was founded in 1879 to mobilize public support for the Ponca; Philadelphia Quakers founded the influential Indian Rights Association in 1882; and New York Christian philanthropists organized the Lake Mohonk conference in 1883. Its annual meetings offered an important platform for reform during several decades. Almost all these reformers held that Indians were the racial equals of whites, but they saw little of value in Indian culture. As a result they pursued a goal of total assimilation.[1]

Meanwhile westerners continued to stereotype them all as Indian friends or "Friends of Mr. Lo." Before long the differences between westerners and easterners found expression in national politics. Under President Grant, the government had aimed to fulfill treaty obligations and ensure peace through a rationing system. The religious denominations were allowed a major voice in federal Indian policy, partly as an attempt to end the widespread graft and corruption brought about by rationing. Honest control of the annuities and rationing eventually prevailed. However, the policy was essentially one of segregating and keeping Indians on the reservation.

This treatment of the Indian as a different class of citizen now came under attack. The reformers who backed Grant urged that the peace policy take a direction that would absorb the Indian into the dominant society. Many of the reformers were in a mood to forgive the whites in the South and to reinstate them as full citizens. The enthusiasm carried over to Negroes, who were at least guaranteed equal protection under the Constitution even if not rushed toward full assimilation. When reconstruction efforts were frustrated by no quick solutions in the South, reformers turned their attention to the Indians through the 1880s.

The Indian organizations sought full assimilation of the Indian population and denounced the reservation system for isolating the Indian inhabitants. Ironically the reservation system had created powerful Indian leaders such as Red Cloud. The Indians who resisted the agents found favor with the eastern friends; moreover, since they generally kept order agents delegated more and more authority to them. This situation allowed the Indians to continue their customs, although these practices were resented by the reformers and missionaries who wanted to assimilate the Indians.

Most eastern sentiment was in favor of repressing aboriginal religion and politics on the one hand, while emphasizing education and agriculture on the other. More boarding schools modeled on Carlisle were built in the East; even more emphasis was given to farming on the reservation. Education, of course, has always been accepted by Americans as a magic key to change, but faith in its power was particularly strong in the late nineteenth century. The accompanying emphasis on agriculture arose directly out of the agrarian era. Indians were supposed to join with whites in converting North America into one vast farmland.

The individual most responsible for forging an Indian policy along these lines was himself a German immigrant. In his assimilation Carl Schurz became a close friend of Abraham Lincoln and later was appointed secretary of the interior under President Hayes. Schurz' career as a reformer began in Germany but reached maturity during the Reconstruction era in America. Later, in the cabinet, he turned his attention to Indians and generally overshadowed the once prestigious Board of Commissioners of Indian Affairs. No doubt his own success at assimilating into American life biased his outlook; certainly he ardently believed that American society was a noble achievement and full participation in it was best for everyone. In a published letter to one of the Indian friends in Boston he succinctly expressed his philosophy:

As to the ultimate end to be attained there can scarcely be any difference of opinion between us; it is the absorption of our Indian population in the great body of citizens under the laws of the land. You will also agree with me that this should be brought about in a manner least dangerous to the Indians themselves as well as to American society.[2]

Schurz, as secretary of the interior, stressed education as an essential step in the process, but time and again he had to face the immediate problem of loss of Indian land. Also, education might require a generation or two, and the reformers were not generally patient people. Helen Hunt Jackson, author of *A Century of Dishonor,* was leading a campaign to save the Ponca Reservation and prevent their removal to Indian Territory. She demanded that Schurz side with her cause. The secretary saw it as a lost cause but wanted to prevent similar tragedies. He answered Mrs. Jackson:

> The study I have given to the Indian question in its various aspects . . . has produced in my mind the firm conviction that the only certain way to secure the Indians in their possessions . . . is to transform their tribal title into individual title, inalienable for a certain period; in other words, to settle them in severality and give them by patent an individual fee—simple in their lands. Then they will hold theirs, and they will, as a matter of course, have the same standing in the courts, and the same legal protection of their property.[3]

Schurz foresaw that even with a generous assignment of land to Indians, there would still be surplus tracts at some reservations. He proposed that this land, not claimed by Indians, be sold and the proceeds used for Indian education.

The idea of assigning individual tracts of land to Indians was discussed as early as Andrew Jackson's time, and even Thomas Jefferson had proposed making Indians full citizens. What Schurz proposed, however, were concrete steps for fulfilling these goals. He was joined by many congressmen under pressure from Indian friends throughout the East. The prominent spokesman in Congress was Massachusetts Senator Henry Dawes, who finally wrote the legislative details that eventually became the Allotment Act of 1887.

In short, the national reaction to Custer's defeat was a move toward assimilation of the Indian population. At least strong pressure groups in the East and a sympathetic secretary of the interior urged that policy. By 1887 the legislation for it was in effect. Whether Schurz recognized it or not, the provision of opening excess lands to white settlement made the policy attractive to many westerners as well. Although most of them were certainly not ready to accept Indians into their communities or to treat Indians as equals, they were willing to go to almost any length to acquire Indian land.

On the reservations themselves the national movement had

no immediate consequences. At Lower Brule, William Dougherty had replaced Henry Livingstone as agent in 1878. Past scandals still tainted agency life, and Livingstone had been accused of graft. Livingstone's diary contains no hint of malfeasance and his relief from duty is privately recorded with great surprise. His March 21, 1878, entry comments simply, "Weather continues delightful." His next day's entry is: "Capt. D. [Dougherty] with a detachment of U.S. troops presented themselves this morning and took forcible possession of the agency. Can obtain no satisfaction in regard to this extraordinary measure." The bewilderment continued the next day. "Everything at a standstill, Capt. D. has taken possession of my personal property as well as the public property. I am not allowed the use of my private house. What is the meaning of this high-handed outrage is more than I can understand. L. [his wife] is very poorly but is keeping at better than I could expect."[4] Livingstone's case was slow to be prosecuted. More than a year later he was finally acquitted in Yankton with no concrete evidence of guilt, but he had acquired a ranch and was building a house in Yankton. He had made many sympathetic friends in Yankton who were generally unsympathetic toward the Bureau of Indian Affairs as well as to Indians. Dougherty believed there would be little chance to convict a Dakota agent of fraud regardless of evidence, and although Livingstone was found innocent, he was never reinstated.

Dougherty had served at several military posts before being assigned to one at Lower Brule. He was no stranger to agency life, but he attempted to fulfill some general policies that had little chance of success. His record book of 1879, for instance, is filled with many references to a goal of reducing the pony herds on the reservation. The Lower Brule herded more than 2000 horses and many frequently crossed reservation lines. The Indians constantly complained that neighboring whites were stealing their ponies while whites believed any horse they lost must have been stolen by Indians. Dougherty was expected to solve every one of the horse thefts. He felt his efforts should be directed at encouraging the Indians to farm or at least to substitute cattle for horses so he exhibited little patience for resolving the thievery.

Dougherty also had to contend with a continually shifting population. Kinship ties cut across reservation and even tribal lines so Dakota families were welcome almost anywhere. A family might tire of Yankton Agency; a spouse might die; a malcontent eased out; for whatever reason, many families came and went at Lower Brule. The agent, who was responsible for issuing an exact number of rations, had to keep accurate accounts as to which families were assigned to him for maintenance. A typical transfer letter to Dougherty reads:

Badger Head, family number 214, consisting of one man, one woman, one boy and two girls are dropped from the rolls of this agency. They claim to be Brule who wish to be transferred to Lower Brule agency.[5]

As if these details were not enough, Dougherty also had to complete special forms for the Bureau of the Census. In a fairly typical month he might have eight to ten family transfers. Most likely families came to Lower Brule from Yankton while they left for Rosebud, but the transfers involved all the Dakota reservations to some extent. Other Indians, on temporary visits, had to be issued passes, and records were kept of all these individuals on pass. Contractors of all kinds solicited the agent's aid in securing contracts, but a major task was simply keeping proper records of receipts, vouchers, and bills of lading.

Beef contractors posed special problems. They drove their herds to the reservation line, and then secured grazing for the cattle while they supplied appropriate amounts of meat. Often they could not secure adequate grass or water from neighboring whites and asked the agent for permission to graze on the reservation. The contractors waged continual hassles over payment for these grazing rights. Finally, when they moved the

With the end of the bison herds, the Plains Indians were forced into a dependency on cattle issued by agents. The beef ration was often critical for Lower Brule subsistence. Photo from the South Dakota State Historical Society.

cattle in for slaughter, Dougherty had to weigh each one and could only receipt for poundage, a regulation necessitated by the scrawny cattle first provided by contractors when purchase was made by the head. The Indians, who felt the cattle belonged to them, did not appreciate why a contractor needed to run the cattle over the scales and get a proper receipt before slaughter. In times of need, the Lower Brule felt no constraint in taking cattle from the contractor before they were turned over to the agent. Dougherty, of course, had to adjust these differences.

In the fall the problem was even greater. A beef contract stipulated that the government could demand 25 percent more or less cattle at delivery than specified in the contract. A contractor rounded up his cattle in Sioux City and started them up the Missouri Valley in September or October. He could secure very few head near Lower Brule, so he pressured Washington and the agent to decide exactly how much they needed. When he finally arrived, he and his men wanted to depart as soon as possible to avoid the winter and reduce costs. The agent needed the contractor to keep the herd intact and on hand. Once deep freezing weather set in, all the cattle could be butchered and stored until spring, but the meat could be lost if frozen too soon. Contractors, of course, wanted to turn over all the cattle at first frost; Dougherty needed to keep the cattle alive as long as possible.

Faced with problems of this magnitude, Dougherty must have been tormented by additional small problems such as: a centennial request for Indian artifacts, a rebuke from the Treasury Department for using the wrong form for a report, the request from a neighboring military post for a plow and wagon, and the necessity of recording and depositing the money paid to Indians for wood cut on the reservation.[6]

Even with the aid of a clerk, it is difficult to imagine Dougherty doing anything more than keeping up with the paperwork. Yet he planned buildings and managed to add and replace several structures. He also worked diligently at persuading the Indians to farm. For 1879 he reports two hundred acres under

cultivation. However, a white supervisor known as a boss farmer plowed and cared for fifty acres; the remaining one hundred
and fifty were in sixty-three tracts. Although the statistics meant
that families averaged less than three acres, they suggest an
honest report of what was happening. A significant number of
families were trying to farm, even if it was a minimal effort
probably done mostly by the women.

The government was involved minimally in education since
it had turned over major responsibility for schools to the
churches. Bishop William Hare directed his energy to a program of building and staffing schools for the many Dakota
reservations assigned to the Episcopal Church. He was further
concerned with a secondary level boarding school being constructed at Yankton. At Lower Brule several day schools for the
elementary level were planned; more importantly, the Bishop
had directed a young Santee Indian, Luke Walker, to settle at
Lower Brule. Walker was one of the first Dakota be become an
ordained Episcopal priest. He and his family came under the
influence of Bishop Whipple in Minnesota where he became a
deacon in 1871. After training he joined the Santee on their
Nebraska reservation and became a priest in 1876. In 1879
Walker arrived at Lower Brule where he served as missionary
until his death in 1933. Married to a white woman, he knew both
worlds well and must have been an important mediator for the
reservation. Unfortunately his life has been reported only
briefly.[7]

By chance national policy coincided fairly well with what
was actually occurring at the reservation level. Bishop Hare's
plans had always emphasized education and conversion of the
young. He now found the government more cooperative than
usual and was able to implement an extensive school plan. In
terms of missionary effort he had on hand a dedicated Indian
who could and did reach the Lower Brule. Dougherty was simply continuing the part of Grant's peace policy that had called
for farming; as a military man he was serious about carrying out
orders. If his Indians were to farm, then he made sure there

were farming efforts. It seems likely the Lower Brule did do more farming under him than under any previous agent.

Dougherty probably found other orders such as the formation of a police force more to his liking. Adherents of the peace policy were always advocating removal of U.S. troops stationed on or near reservations. They planned to replace soldiers with a loyal Indian force. The necessary legislation was passed in 1878. Most adherents of Indian assimilation backed the idea of building a force, believing it to be a step toward becoming a white community. At Lower Brule, the agent had established a small force late in 1878. Almost surely the force must have been composed of full-bloods because Dougherty reports only six mixed-blood families on the reservation. On most reservations these police forces were mixed-bloods or even marginal white men. George Hyde reports that the police were subordinate to Indian chiefs, not the agents, on most other Dakota reservations.[8]

Whatever the composition, this first force was unsatisfactory; Dougherty reports he dismissed the entire 1878 group and reorganized it in 1879.[9] These police probably came from the more "progressive" bands, ones that actively cooperated with whites. However, there is little mention of the usual progressive-conservative factionalism at Lower Brule at this time while it is common on other Dakota reservations. Dougherty only mentioned that three of the chiefs were somewhat progressive; he maintained that among all the Lower Brule, "tribal spirit and customs still prevail."[10] Certainly he realized that the police could not be entirely loyal. Justification of that suspicion arrived in the spring.

At the Rosebud agency in the spring of 1879, the Brule were preparing for a Sun Dance. The newly arrived agent there did not think to suppress the dance, and Chief Spotted Tail sent out invitations to the other reservations. White Thunder carried the news to the Lower Brule. When he discovered an Indian police force there, he goaded the Indians into revolt. More than one hundred warriors shot up the police barracks, raided the homes of the police, ran off their horses, and killed chickens, dogs, and pigs.[11] The police force resigned in a body. Most of the Lower Brule later deserted their farm patches and moved to Rosebud for the forthcoming important Sun Dance. Dougherty, probably wisely, did not attempt to use force to prevent the Indians from going. He held up the coffee and sugar rations for some of the chiefs which saved face for him while it did not seriously affect the Indians.[12]

This bit of violence against the Indian police force was the last act of armed resistance the Lower Brule would ever display as a group. After all, even the hostile Indians to the north had been effectively subdued by General Crook by 1877. Most Dakota were totally dependent upon government rations; and the number of agency employees continued to grow, supplemented by missionaries, traders, and neighboring ranchers. The Lower Brule were in their desperate years, torn by the intensive assimilative pressures while remembering how good aboriginal life was. Whenever they tried to live in the old ways, however, they ran counter to white expectations of what was best for them. For several years they would struggle to find some way of accommodating to the new way of life.

Yet the Dakota had little time to seek such a solution. The frontier newspapers, speaking for most of the territorial population, sought to expand settlement west of the Missouri River. The Yankton paper was particularly critical of the Rosebud Agency when it appeared to sponsor the 1879 Sun Dance, which it described as "Heathenish Hoodoo." The editor deplored the event because it would attract at least a thousand Indians from Lower Brule at a time when they should have been attending their crops.[13] This view, however, was nearly reversed a week later when the paper gave several columns to a description of the Indians' progress toward civilization. A special correspondent described a carpet factory at Yankton which employed Indian workers and declared the Crow Creek Indians were equally progressive.[14] Whenever the newspapers were ready to editorialize at length about opening the Sioux Nation, they commented favorably upon how advanced the Indians were, implying they no longer needed the protection of the reservation. By the end of 1879, the Yankton paper was advocating support for a bill in Congress that would allot the Dakota lands. It observed that 40,000 Sioux presently had rights to 40,000 square miles, obviously a needless waste. The land should be opened "to laboring people anxious to utilize its richness."[15]

This self-contradiction of the press was characteristic for the period. The fluctuation in attitude was typical of other papers as well. Initial reactions to any Indian act that seemed hostile were exaggerated or capitalized on for sensationalism. Yet within a week, an editor might reverse himself in the next edition, having nothing but praise for the progress Indians were making. The newspapermen obviously had a vested interest in an expanding population and did not want to frighten homesteaders with stories of hostile Indians. Yet they did overreact to any sign of hostilities. Sometimes they may simply have wanted to sell newspapers, but their motivations generally seem much more complex. While they deplored certain Indian practices on the one hand, they often praised what other Indians were doing. There is even a nostalgia occasionally for some aboriginal value or practice. It would seem the editors generally lacked feelings of racial prejudice toward Indians, but they were intolerant of cultural differences. On the few occasions that they sympathized with an Indian trait, it was because the practice or value coincided with their own or possibly because it was safely in the past.

Although the editors were ambivalent in their attitudes toward the Indians, they consistently urged appropriation of their land and westward expansion. Hopefully the Indians would take their place, with some equality among whites perhaps, but definitely within white dominion. Clearly the frontiersmen were not to be prevented from opening the lands between the Missouri River and the Black Hills. In retrospect, it is difficult to see how Dakota Territory could have moved toward statehood with a western and eastern population separated by an Indian Nation.

The urge toward expansion was a result not only of increasing population but also of the advancing railroad. By the late 1870s the Chicago and North Western Railway Company had plans to lay tracks between Tracy, Minnesota and Pierre, South Dakota. In a competitive move the Chicago, Milwaukee, and St. Paul projected a parallel extension of their line. By 1880 it ran between Canton on the Iowa border and Chamberlain, South Dakota. Pierre, the creation of the Chicago and North Western Railroad, began a long-standing competition with Chamberlain.[16] Although the railroads are relatively unimportant today, they have been replaced by parallel highways.

At Lower Brule, agent Dougherty looked forward to the arrival of a railroad with great anticipation. At one point he had hopes that the Milwaukee and St. Paul would cross the Missouri River at or near the Crow Creek Reservation.[17] A convenient railroad would certainly have simplified the reservations' logistics because the government was providing nearly total subsistence for 2000 Indians at Crow Creek and Lower Brule. Dougherty also foresaw a time when Indian farmers could ship their produce eastward by rail. Such a forecast was more dreamlike, rather than just optimistic, given conditions in 1880. The government was providing the Lower Brule with more than $60,000 worth of rations a year for subsistence alone.[18] The weekly issue was a major activity for the agent and other personnel. For the Indians it was a social event as well as a vital one for their subsistence. In 1880 the following sums were budgeted for rations: beef, $41,000; corn, $3500; coffee, $3000; flour, $3000; sugar, $3000; bacon, $2500; hard bread, $2000; pork, $1000. Also rationed were soap, tobacco, hominy, beans, and baking powder. Additionally there was the cost of the agency and the treaty annuities which kept the Indians clothed and further supplied.

In terms of farming, the Lower Brule showed no significant change; Dougherty reported 200 acres of corn sown in 1880 and thirty-five acres of wheat. His mention of a few acres in oats and vegetables indicates that he was clutching at straws. Although the agent never condemned the Bureau's insistence on farming, his enumerations of difficulties in the annual report for 1880 reveal the folly of the policy.

> *Notwithstanding the encouragement and substantial means afforded by the department to the people of this tribe, during the recent year, to enlarge their farming operations, they have not fully justified my expectations . . . . That more was not accomplished is due to circumstances beyond my influence, viz.:*
>
> *First, the breaking plows purchased and sent out by the department last winter were incomplete . . . .*
>
> *Second, the fence wire purchased by the department on the 4th of June, 1880, in Chicago did not reach here until the 13th of August—too late to be used this year.*
>
> *Seed wheat was distributed to those who offered to cultivate it and several small fields were very successfully grown. Several of the Indians on seeing the grain spring up like grass concluded that the rain had destroyed it, and plowed it under and planted corn.*[19]

Despite such problems Dougherty remained undaunted. In his support of farming he was willing to experiment, and on one occasion he obtained tobacco seed on his own to broaden the farm efforts.[20] While he encouraged this farming, he continued to disparage aboriginal practices. He reported some success in ending polygyny which he saw as female degradation. He also had ordered his police to stop some of the more "immoral" dances, and he asked for directives that would outlaw medicine men.[21]

It is little wonder that he placed great hope in the railroad as a civilizing force, and he reacted angrily when he discovered opposition to it on his own reservation. In late 1880 a petition to stop the railroad was sent to the secretary of the interior bearing nine "X" signatures of the Lower Brule chiefs. The logical extension of the Chicago, Milwaukee, and St. Paul Railroad west from Chamberlain would have entered the northern part of the Lower Brule Agency. It was planned to pass not far above agency headquarters at the mouth of White River. The Indians probably would have opposed the encroachment, but Dougherty may have convinced them that it would be in their interests. However, it appears that at least one of the traders, George Felt, did not want the railroad. Since Dougherty had closed down his store, it may have been that Felt was simply against anything Dougherty wanted. Whatever the details, Dougherty accused the Post Commissary Sergeant at Fort Hale of forging the document in conspiracy with Felt and his clerk David Rencontre. Thomas Wetherell, a military post trader, and a French trader were also implicated. Dougherty admits many of the Lower Brule had become highly agitated because of the traders' machinations and were close to raiding the railroad workers on the east bank. He credits his chief clerk with settling the dispute in his absence.

Dougherty was particularly busy as an agent because he handled the business of both Crow Creek and Lower Brule. Initially he also travelled to proposed sites along the Missouri River for the Spotted Tail and the Red Cloud Agencies. In the late fall of 1880 an agent arrived for Lower Brule to allow Dougherty to spend full time with the Crow Creek. Although Dougherty was so strong-willed that he frequently antagonized the chiefs, he made more enemies among those whites he suspected of graft. The Indians generally liked and respected him, and even after he left the reservation, they sought his help in emergencies.

Dougherty's replacement at Lower Brule in 1880 was Major W. H. Parkhurst. Parkhurst arrived without experience as did many an agent before him. Dougherty turned trader Felt's key over to him with a minimum of explanation for having closed the trader's business. Felt soon persuaded Parkhurst to reopen the store, and then conspired with the Indians to oppose the railroad. When Parkhurst learned the Indians had agreed to a Washington trip, the first for the Lower Brule, he believed that everything was calm, but he quickly found himself between Dougherty and the Indian traders.

However, such conflict was routine for an Indian agency, and Parkhurst was soon into the new year adjusting to the myriad reports sandwiched between charges and counter-charges. The greatest problem that faced him was how to advise the Indians in regard to land rights. Population growth in the Black Hills combined with that in the Missouri Valley forecast an opening of more Dakota lands. Many sincere men thought the safest guarantee for Indian possession of land was to assign them individual tracts. Yet if such assignment were made, much Indian land would be lost when opened to white settlement. Parkhurst and Dougherty seem to have adopted a wait-and-see approach, but they did encourage the Lower Brule to submit to the secretary of the interior a claim and description of the land they felt belonged to the Lower Brule, since the reservation was still in the anomalous position of being defined as a reservation within a reservation.

The petition probably did little to serve the intended end, but it documents the Indian interpretation as to the origin of the Lower Brule; how they separated from the Upper Brule or Rosebud Brule; and what they believed were their customary lands. The document is worth quoting at length because it apparently is the earliest Lower Brule interpretation of their history. It also suggests how complex early boundary disputes could be. Dougherty's military background and Western experience gave him the background for demarking the reservation, but the latter part of the letter must have been a more literal translation of the Indian explanation.

Sir: As the time has arrived when the subdivision of the Great Sioux Reservation is both imminent and necessary, the undersigned chiefs of the Lower Brule tribe of Sioux acting under instructions delivered in a council of the Tribe at Lower Brule Agency prior to their departure for Washington, respectfully submit the following description of meter [?] and bounds to be those that limit and bound the territory occupied and owned by the Lower Brule tribe for so long a time that the memory of man goeth not to the contrary, and that they believe, and are convinced that this long and undisputed tenure and occupation constitutes, and vests in this tribe, a right and title, prior to and more complete than the right and title of any other tribe or subdivision of the Sioux Nation that may have heretofore arisen . . . .

Beginning at the point on the Niobrara River where it is intersected by the Western boundary of the Ponca Reservation, thence up the Niobrara River to Antelope Creek, near the 102 meridian, thence up Antelope Creek to its source, or head, thence across the table land to the source or head of White Clay Creek, thence down White Clay Creek to its confluence with the White Earth River, thence down White Earth River to the mouth of Butte Cachee Creek, thence in a straight line through the Bad lands to the mouth of Sand Creek, at its confluence with the South Cheyenne River, thence down the South Cheyenne River to the mouth of Bull Creek, thence up Bull Creek to its head or source, thence in a straight line across the table land to the head or source of the main branch of the Bad River, thence down the Bad River to the mouth of White Clay Creek, thence in a straight line to the head of Antelope Creek, thence down Antelope Creek to the Missouri River, thence down the Missouri River to the point where it is intersected by the boundary of the Ponca Reservation to the place of the beginning . . . , and excepting from the area described, Cedar Island in the Missouri River and the Military Reservation at Fort Randall.

The undersigned chiefs do further say in support of this claim that in the year 1826, the whole Brule Tribe was encamped at the Lost Timber, near the head of the Niobrara River, that a division of the tribe there took place in consequence of a quarrel about a woman, and of a conflict with each other, in which many on both sides were slain, that the majority of the people went from there to the South Platte River, and that the part of the tribe now known as the Lower Brule Tribe retired to the head of the White Earth River, and that by mutual consent the line dividing the two parts of the tribe was declared to be at or near White Clay Creek and Antelope Creek, that for several years afterward the Lower Brule people lived permanently at C[illegible] Creek and planted there, and that subsequently some of them moved over to the Keya Paha River and made gardens at Turtle Hill [south of Winner], that during all this time the principal chief of *the Brule Tribe lived with the Lower Brules, and remained with them until he died, and that no tribe, or part of a tribe has up to this time ever claimed any part of the territory described. They further say that in 1855 General Harney took many of the Upper Brule people prisoners in a battle and took them to Fort Pierre on the Missouri River, and that when he released them they returned to their own territory on the South Platte and in 1866 the Lower Brule people came in from the head of the White River and encamped near the present agency. At the request of General Harney and General Sanborn, and that they have remained there in peace and friendship with the government up to this time.*

> *Signed Iron Nation, Medicine Bull, Handsome Elk, Dead Hand, Little Pheasant, Bull Head, Big Mane Headman Bear Bird*

By this agent,
  William Dougherty[22]

With the arrival of spring in 1881, Parkhurst assumed the full burden of agency life. He too had high hopes of stimulating farming, but the year proved discouraging. The acreage broken actually decreased, and no wheat was sown. In his annual report, Parkhurst was still in awe of the weather describing the winter in some detail. As for the summer it was "extraordinary" hot, and the "crop of corn this year, I fear, will be nearly a failure."[23]

To compensate for the lack of farming, the agent noted progress elsewhere. Thirteen bands, an increase of four, had moved closer to the agency generally or were more accessible as they settled in the valley of the White River. Most of the Indians were living in log cabins instead of tipis, and the Episcopal Indian missionary, Luke Walker, was praised for his efforts. Parkhurst had plans for a hospital and had organized a police force of eight privates, a sergeant, and a captain. The force, however, was too small to prevent liquor smuggling and illicit woodcutting. It had stopped a number of "immoral" dances, and Parkhurst predicted that the annual Sun Dance in 1881 would be the last one attended by the Lower Brule. Further, the Indians were looking forward to their visit to Washington, including even Medicine Bull, who had been wounded accidentally in the spring.

While the Indians sought some accommodation, not really ready to farm but recognizing they must move to protect their land, white pressures grew. Herbert Welsh, a nephew of that veteran activist in Indian Affairs, William Welsh, toured the Dakota reservations in 1882 and 1883 and left tourists' accounts of the agency. Although Welsh and his co-founders of the Indian Rights Association in 1880 were biased toward seeing progress whenever possible, they provide a different view from official agency reports.

I was the guest of the Reverend Luke Walker. It was Sunday and a day of beauty. I watched with great interest the Indians assemble for service. Many of them came in wagons—the gay scarlet and plaid shawls of the women fluttering picturesquely. Most of the men were on ponies, dashing and wheeling over the hills with a peculiarly Indian recklessness and grace. The men were dressed in civilized fashion—that is, in calico shirts and woolen trousers, roughly made, with the seams outside. Most of them had blankets, which they wrapped around them. They wore their long black hair in plaits.

It was not long before the church was filled. It was not a scene to be forgotten: two priests, a white man and a Sioux, kneeling together at the altar; the wonderful reverence and earnestness of these people of a despised race; the strangeness of hearing the Episcopal service in the soft, musical Dakota ....[24]

Here [at Lower Brule] we were the guests of the Reverend Luke Walker, a full-blooded Sioux Indian and a clergyman of the Protestant Episcopal Church .... The aspect of affairs at Lower Brule had, during the past few months, been unfavorable, and the conditions of the Indians unsettled. Their Agent [Parkhurst] has very recently been removed by the Department, and Mr. Gasmann, formerly at Yankton Agency, appointed in his place. The appointment I regard as most op-

portune . . . . The Indians have received him with open arms, and upon many occasions during our visit expressed great pleasure at his appointment.

On the afternoon of the May 25th, we drove five or six miles from the agency to "Little Pheasant's" camp, at the mouth of White River, where a small settlement of Indians has been planted, and Bishop Hare has stationed a mission chapel . . . . These people have been doing fairly well in their movement toward civilization. They occupy the arable bottom lands along the Missouri, and have 200 to 250 acres under cultivation. They, with the rest of the Lower Brule, have been much alarmed at the proposition brought to them by the Sioux Commission which would throw all the land they now occupy into the possession of the white man.[25]

This commission that had so alarmed the Lower Brule and alerted the Indian Rights Association had been sent to arrange further land cessions from the Dakota. Commission membership was oriented toward the westerners and headed by Newton Edmunds, former territorial governor. The Indian Rights Association favored the general policy, but it felt left out of actual proceedings and mistrusted members of the commission. Bishop Hare, equally concerned, also became involved along with the missionary at Crow Creek, the Reverend Heckaliah Burt.[26] When Burt described the situation to William Dougherty, who had been transferred to the Southwest, Dougherty offered to take leave to counsel with the Indians in confronting the commission. Parkhurst, of course, was obligated to aid the commission and charged Burt with improper meddling. He must also have resented the Indians' seeking Dougherty's aid rather than his own, but his actions certainly did not please the commission either. The commission accomplished so little that it sought scapegoats among most of the agents. After reporting that the Lower Brule refused even "additional privileges" offered as "inducement for them to sign," Edmunds observed:

The Lower Brule and Crow Creek Indians are in close confederation, and it was not considered best to go to Crow Creek until the

Brules had yielded in their opposition to the views of the department in regard to what is best for them.

The commission has been seriously embarrassed and delayed in its efforts by the active interference of Captain Dougherty of the U.S.A.— who has urged them by letter and telegram not to consent to the agreement and also by reason of want or lack of control of agent in their management.[27]

Edmunds moved on to Yankton leaving Judge Peter Shannon at Chamberlain to negotiate further. The third member of the commission, James Teller, had returned to Washington for help from his brother, Henry Teller, secretary of the interior. Meanwhile the Lower Brule prepared to leave for Washington, arranging their transportation through sale of beef hides. (Who owned the hides of the ration cattle was a perplexing question that raised numerous problems for at least a decade.) Judge Shannon asked for an order stopping the sales in order to keep the Lower Brule on the reservation. George Hyde well summarizes the incident: "In all our official dealings with the Sioux there is nothing remotely to be compared with this for despicable meanness."[28] Secretary Teller seems to have ignored Shannon's request, but he did empower his brother to inform the Lower Brule that two-thirds of the Dakota had already signed the agreement to cede land. Thus, the Lower Brule were to be moved unless they agreed to sign. Their agent was also employed in the threat; its vagueness can be seen in a letter Parkhurst sent to the Reverend Luke Walker, who was advising the Lower Brule.

Reverend Luke Walker: My Dear Sir—I have seen the commission this morning and have had some talk with them which I wish to state to you. Mr. Teller has just returned from Washington, and states that the feeling at the Secretary's office is this: First, that the plan of the Department in relation to this agreement will be carried out whether the Brule sign or not, as the number who have signed the agreement are more than necessary by the Treaty of 1868; Second,

The beef issue often caused problems over allocation. Dakota values generally insured a more or less fair distribution. Photo from the South Dakota State Historical Society.

*that the Lower Brule Agency may be, and probably will be, abolished
during the coming year, and probably the coming summer; should this
be the case the tribe will have to move somewhere, just where to be settled by order of the Department; and it does not matter whether they
wish to go or not, they will be, moved if needed, by the military;
Third, in the case they do not agree and do not sign and are moved,
they will get nothing for the improvements made, houses built, lands
broken or anything at all; but in case they do agree, they will be paid
for all these things at a fair price; Fourth, they will get no advantage
given them even if they are moved in a body, and they will, in fact,
cease to be a separate tribe, with no agency, no homes, no land, except
such as may be designated by order of the President, and which may be
taken from them at any hour by the same authority.*

Sincerely yours, W. H. Parkhurst.[29]

In addition to this threat, the commission renewed its
efforts at Crow Creek. There the status of the reservation was
in question. It appeared the Crow Creek Reservation could be
dissolved by presidential authority; under great pressure the
Crow Creek chiefs signed. Upon returning to Lower Brule, the
commission met as much opposition as ever, and none of the
Indians would sign. Edmunds and the other commissioners
submitted a final agreement to Washington with fewer than four
hundred signatures. They proposed that only three-quarters of
the chiefs and headmen needed to sign, not three-quarters of
the adult men although the 1868 Treaty specified clearly all
adult males. That logic had succeeded in 1876 when the Black
Hills were taken; but the Indian Rights Association and other
Easterners rose in defense this time. The agreement failed to
secure the Senate's approval; in fact that body specifically directed that the agreement be returned for signing by three-
quarters of the adult males.

For unknown reasons, Interior Secretary Teller reappoint-
ed the members of the old commission who did not even trouble to return to the reservations. Their interpreter, the
Reverend Samuel Hinman, was sent to collect signatures with

the aid of the agents. Hinman gathered many names, some of teen-age boys, at Pine Ridge before reaching Lower Brule and Crow Creek where John Gasmann had replaced Parkhurst as agent.[30] Gasmann did not back Hinman in his more obvious false threats, and the Lower Brule and Crow Creek Indians gave no consent to the agreement. In the meantime Bishop Hare, who was a long-time enemy of Hinman, had written to the chairman of the Senate Committee on Indian Affairs, Henry L. Dawes, appraising him of Hinman's tactics. Dawes formed his own committee to investigate matters at the Dakota agencies. The committee bypassed Edmunds and his commission, and the senator was soon in direct contact with the Indians.[31] Dawes soon learned what nefarious tactics were being used by land commissions, and as news reached the defenders of the Indians in the East, a solid opposition developed to any further land concessions obtained by commissions.

The oppression wrought by the land commissions appears to have produced some solidarity among the Dakota, and communication among Indians on the agencies increased during the 1880s. However, no overall leadership developed despite the impressive talents of men such as Red Cloud, Spotted Tail, and Sitting Bull. Indians at each of the agencies were still responsive almost solely to the chiefs at their agency; even this leadership was minimal as leaders continually appeared and disappeared. At Lower Brule, for instance, the number of band chiefs fluctuated between nine and thirteen. Although Iron Nation and Medicine Bull were prominent men, some Lower Brule had primary loyalties to other chiefs. The Reverend Luke Walker, some of the policemen, and whites who married into the tribe had also assumed leadership roles in new contexts. Moreover, the Dakota simply did not subscribe wholehearted loyalty to anyone. A man could and did move his family to another band or even agency when he disagreed with leaders. No one was in a position to assert great authority, and agents, of course, waivered between delegating and denying authority to the chiefs. The situation was one that made sources of power ambiguous and caused the Indians to employ devious forms of sanctions. Much the same situation prevails today, and a tactic to remove a reservation policeman in 1958 was used as early as 1882 to remove agent Parkhurst. Such tactics usually go unrecorded, but the 1882 episode is well-documented.

Parkhurst had been caught between Dougherty and the Edmunds commission and appeared to the Indians to side primarily with the commission. Since they had no direct control over him, they resorted to charging him with immoral behavior. In a letter thanking the Commissioner of Indian Affairs for their boarding school, the Lower Brule complained that Parkhurst "is always at that school with that lady teacher and stays there until the midnight and sometimes after midnight."

Even worse from the Indian viewpoint was that the teacher did not properly care for the children and one had died of neglect. In a confrontation with the parents, the teacher had sent for Parkhurst.

> *When he came to the school he was very mad and took his pistol from his pocket and go towards the woman point the pistol at her. When he came near the woman, then she took a large stick from the ground and struck on the right hand so the pistol drop from his hand and he clap her with his hand and fought with the squaw, at happen some of the Indians were there and so they stopped and separated them. Now Dear Friend the squaw is only a woman and the agent is a man he ought not fought with a woman or attempt to shoot.[32]*

Parkhurst responded by cutting off rations for a month; the Indians retaliated by withdrawing their children from school. Despite the conflict and Parkhurst's obvious inability to get along with the Lower Brule, his removal seems to have stemmed more from his failure to comply with the aims of the Edmund's Land Commission. All the Lower Brule chiefs[33] did not carry a fraction of the weight the secretary of the interior did in selecting an Indian agent.

Parkhurst's replacement, John Gasmann, had learned to

Big Mane, one of the Lower Brule band or *tiyospaye* leaders of the late 19th century. Photo from the South Dakota State Historical Society.

work with the Dakota as agent at Yankton. He fared much better with the Lower Brule although he assigned Henry Gregory, a clerk, to them while he located at Crow Creek. He was soon in trouble with the frontiersmen because the Lower Brule instituted a toll charge on cattle herds crossing their reservation. The incident is confused because of charges that members of the old "Indian ring" were really behind the toll and because of rivalry between Pierre and Chamberlain as a crossing point to the Black Hills.[34]

Novel sources of income, such as tolls, must have had a powerful attraction for the Indian agents. The Indians obviously were not going to become farmers as their romantic Eastern friends dreamed of and commissioners planned for. In 1885, only 650 acres of Lower Brule land were cultivated, and an observer notes that "farming thus far has been unimportant."[35] By this time Gasmann had been replaced by W. W. Anderson as agent. Anderson turned his full attention to Crow Creek while subordinates, over whom he exercised little control, administered Lower Brule.

To J. B. Harrison the sub-agency was "miserably inefficient, unprofitable and unwholesome."[36] Harrison was a typical Indian benefactor, and his report is revealing of their attitudes. He observed that the Lower Brule land was poorly suited for farming and that the Indians ". . . will ultimately have to depend very largely upon stock-raising." Yet he immediately rationalized that an allotment of land, designed to encourage farming, would benefit the Indians because ". . . a definite subdivision of the land which is in any degree adapted to agriculture will be useful by providing for each family an anchorage to a particular spot."[37]

Meanwhile the Indians managed to save some of their ration cattle and started two small herds. These cattle were sometimes grazed along Medicine Creek and in the Little Bend area. A few Lower Brule began settling in this region north of their agency, foreshadowing a later shifting of the whole reservation northward. This enterprise in cattle received no help or recognition from the government beyond the encouragement of the agent. Although most agents at some time or another recognized the advantages of raising cattle, they persistently pursued a farming policy. At times an agent obviously reported simply what his superiors wanted to hear, but generally the agents expressed sincere conviction that farming was desirable. Anderson's 1886 correspondence is illustrative. His early letters have a missionary's zeal about farming while his later letters deal with a multitude of minor crises and ignore agriculture. His initial confidence is expressed in a statement of his objectives:

> To get these Indians out of the old ruts and fit them for citizenship will prove best for them and the country. There must be something radically wrong when ablebodied men are seen begging their bread. Such a state of affairs is degrading to freemen and disgraceful to the Government.
> There are three things I have been trying to impress on these Indians viz: 1) to become self supporting; 2) to send their children to school; 3) to take up land in severalty. I have dealt fairly and plainly with them, appealed to their manliness, told them what a glorious privilege is that of being independent, and tried to stimulate them to better efforts.[38]

Two months later Anderson engaged in more mundane matters such as establishing jurisdiction over an Indian who had murdered another Indian. Territorial officials ignored the problem because of the cost involved. Soon thereafter one of the white employees who supervised farming was engaged in a brawl with Chief Useful Heart. The chief broke a sack of corn over the farmer's head when he felt he had been cheated on the amount of corn issued to him. Useful Heart was one of the remote White River Brule who were more conservative than those at the agency. When the agent sat to hear both sides, the chief confronted him with a drawn gun, and Anderson's police were unable to arrest Useful Heart. In a moment of panic Anderson asked Washington for authority to request troops. It disgraced an agent in the late nineteenth century to ask for military help, and Anderson must have realized his career was endangered. Finally a U.S. Marshal pacified Useful Heart with the aid of Yellow Hawk, the chief of police.[39]

Anderson was soon back to his paternalistic self. He consistently spoke of his "firm but gentle" treatment of Indians and of government's responsibility for "civilizing" them. The irony of an "uncivilized" frontier in contact with the Indian was of course lost on Anderson but preserved in his correspondence. For instance, in one of his longest letters to establish the guilt of an employee, Anderson concludes: "It was a disgraceful affair and Altman and Mullins stood for several minutes like two school boys bandying the words, 'you did' and 'I didn't.' I do not think they are proper persons to *civilize* the Indians and think that both of them should be dismissed."[40]

Anderson was particularly interested in dismissing Altman who apparently had close relations with the Indians. At one point some of them petitioned the commissioner to make Altman their agent, and on one occasion Anderson accused Altman of encouraging "barbarous dances and other uncivilized practices." To some extent at least the Indians' customs of bride price, simple divorce, polygamy, self-torture, and the give-away at death persisted. Anderson attempted to suppress all of them. The major means of forcing this change was through education, and Anderson planned several schools. He was encouraged by the prospects of compact settlement at Lower Brule, where no one farmed, in contrast to the more scattered farming families at Crow Creek. Anderson must have seen the paradox that increasing farming would hinder school attendance as families settled on their scattered allotments, but he made no attempt at a resolution.

Indeed a national policy of forcing Indians into farming was officially formulated in the Allotment Act of 1887, also known as the Dawes Act. The history of allotment is well enough known that it needs only brief summary here. Perhaps its best justification is that events forced such a step. The chief author of the policy, Senator Henry L. Dawes, eventually took such a view. "It was born of sheer necessity. Inasmuch as the Indians refused to fade out ... and the reservation itself was slipping away from him, there was but one alternative; either he must be endured as a lawless savage ..., or he must be fitted to become a part of that life and absorbed into it. To permit him to be a roving savage was unendurable, and therefore, the task of fitting him for civilized life was undertaken."[41] With the advantage of historical perspective, George Hyde presents a contrasting view about both the necessity and motivation for allotment.

> *The idealists imagined they knew what was best for the Indians, and they were determined the Sioux should do their bidding. This bill was intended to please all parties concerned. It gave the Dakota whites the Sioux land they desired, it protected the rights of the Christian missions ..., and it gave the Indian Friend groups full scope for meddling .... The bill had the hearty support of everyone—except the Sioux Indians, the Democratic administration, and the public.[42]*

The background for allotment lies in a complexity of factors that are still not fully known. The effects, for instance, of agrarianism, racial stereotypes about Indians, the philosophy of social Darwinism, and free enterprise, as well as the political maneuverings between Republicans and Democrats, all contributed to the drafting of allotment policy and its implementation. Whatever might have been substituted for it can never be known; it is evident that events in the West demanded some major change from the earlier peace policy.

Dakota Territory was experiencing boom times during the 1880s. The grasshopper plagues had been brought under control, and although droughts occurred along the Missouri, eastern South Dakota enjoyed adequate rainfall. More importantly, the settlers were introducing controls over their environment. A variety of spring wheat resistant to drought was grown widely;

new plowing and reaping techniques allowed further expansion. Markets for the grain expanded widely because of the new railroads. By this time several lines entered Sioux Falls; its population jumped from 2000 in 1880 to more than 10,000 in 1890. As statehood approached, a number of towns vied for designation as capital. Although Huron and Pierre were consistent leaders, even a town like Chamberlain had hopes. Its paper claimed that the opening of western South Dakota would mean Chamberlain

> ... *will be the gate city to millions of choice areas* ... *It means pre-eminence of Chamberlain as a jobbing and manufacturing center. It means that two years hence Chamberlain, the most beautifully located city in the Northwest, will be the metropolis of South Dakota.*[43]

As frontier times in the Black Hills drew to a close, a stable, expanding population formed the western border of Dakota Territory. The large-scale gold mining operations that contributed to this growth were supplemented by large-scale cattle ranching as it became more profitable to raise cattle on the northern Plains than to drive them there all the way from Texas.

The great Sioux Nation, lying between these two developments, was an obvious obstacle to inevitable expansion. If the land commissions had opened the reservations to settlement solely through purchase, the government would have had no obligations, beyond those of treaties and the peace policy, for the "reservations" to be created within the Sioux Nation. It seems quite possible that pressure on the Indians, under these conditions, could have led to a complete loss of lands. Obviously the outcome can only be speculative. What did happen, under the Dawes Act, was that full responsibility for Indians was placed upon the federal government. With allotment, Indian land became a trust responsibility of the secretary of the interior, which gave the Bureau of Indian Affairs almost complete control over Indian lives. It is ironic that a bill intended to incorporate Indians into the larger society instead converted them to dependency and bound them in increasingly complex ways to a federal bureaucracy.[44] The government misled frontiersmen as well as itself into believing the new policy would soon lead to assimilation. A frontier editor, for example, wrote:

> *The government is finally beginning to adopt the belief that the best and quickest way to civilize the Indians is to break up their tribal relations and bring them into closer relations with the whites. This is contrary to the view held by the crank philanthropists of the east . . . . The present relations of the Indian tribes begets communism and a certain clanishness that can never be reformed, except it be broken up.[45]*

Steps toward allotment proceeded quickly at Lower Brule. Surveyors arrived at the reservation in the fall of 1887. Little Pheasant and other White River Brule threw the surveyors off the reservation, but Anderson arrested the chief and four other leaders. The surveying began again, but allotment was delayed for various reasons. Before the policy was implemented, the government decided it was necessary to open the Great Sioux Nation by major land purchases. Another land commission, this time chaired by Richard H. Pratt of the Carlisle Indian School, visited the Dakota reservations in the summer of 1888. He met with little success except at Lower Brule, where he may have employed illegal tactics to secure compliance. At any rate the mission failed. In 1889 Washington pressed even more strongly for cession of 9 million acres, leading the way for legal allotment among the Dakota. Major General George Crook, veteran Indian fighter among the Sioux, was appointed head of a commission. His work, described by Hyde as a "shakedown," induced the necessary three-quarters of the adult males to sign an agreement to give up the land.[46] Crook made many pledges that he may have recommended to an unresponsive government knowing they would not be fulfilled. Few Indians were likely to have understood that Crook's qualified promises were not binding on the government. The help of local agents must also have been important. At Lower Brule, a Doctor Goodrich from Chamberlain had urged the Indians to refuse signing as had Easterners of the Indian Rights Association. The agent immediately wrote Washington complaining about the "unprofessional, underhanded, and ungentlemanly" doctor and requested permission to bar him from the reservation.[47]

The problems of land and subsistence caused increasing tension among the Lower Brule and other Dakota. The Missouri River reservations were totally dependent upon rations and annuities, and these sources frequently were manipulated arbitrarily by the agent. Many other whites were entering the reservation and were becoming a significant part of reservation life. Three white men and their families, who were farming at Lower Brule in 1889, raised more than 3000 bushels of wheat and employed a few Indians part time. Two white traders were engaged in business, and three or four teachers lived among the Indians more or less permanently. Although the Episcopal missionary was an Indian, he lived much like a white man, and his wife, Sophie, was also white. A few white missionaries occasionally lived on the reservation and often visited. The agent employed an increasing number of whites; unfortunately not much is known about the background of these contacts for the Indians.[48] But in effect all the whites who lived on the reservation dominated Indians in one capacity or another. Although most of them saw themselves as serving the Indians, it must have been clear to the Indians that they were becoming more subservient to an increasing number of whites. They must also have begun to imagine that they were inferior beings because of their dependency.

The diversity of occupations for whites followed the introduction of much of the dominant culture: government, trade, farming, formal education, dress, craft occupations with wage work, a money economy, and religion. The response of the Dakota to these innovations varied among individuals. Some individuals accepted and tried to learn new ways. A leading chief, Iron Nation, eventually led large numbers in this adaptation. Others, like Little Pheasant, resisted the change, and dissension among the Lower Brule marked the end of the nineteenth century.

In 1890 a new agent, A. P. Dixon, started his administration with an awareness that the Indians were troubled, but he attributed it solely to a pending transfer of agency headquarters and a relocation of reservation boundaries. General Crook's agreements to open the Great Sioux Nation were implemented for the Lower Brule by legislation in 1888 (25 Stat. 94) and 1889 (25 Stat. 888). These measures created six Dakota reservations, and opened the remaining land to public domain after providing allotments to individual Indians. The Lower Brule Reservation was shifted northward to its present location, noted by the accompanying map. Because the agency headquarters near Oacoma would then be outside the reservation, Dixon recommended a relocation to approximately the present site. The new agency was nearer the center of the reservation, on level bottom land, and more conveniently located in relation to the Crow Creek Agency.

Some Indians had already settled in the new area, but a faction led by Iron Nation wanted to remain south of White River. An agreement in 1889, however, converted this area to public domain. The agent was faced with the problem of persuading this group to move north. In an act of compromise, the Indians south of White River were offered land at Rosebud providing the Upper Brules would accept them, but several technicalities prevented this alternative. The disorder must have made it even more clear to the Indians how capricious and unpredictable was the power to which they were so completely subjugated.

In retrospect it was an obvious time for trouble, but agent Dixon was wholly unaware of the ferment. Only a week before he would have to jail twenty Lower Brule, he sent a four-page report to Washington detailing building and relocation plans. He argued the merits of new lumber at length ignoring Indians until the last sentence of the letter, and this addition is only a brief extra argument for removal.[49]

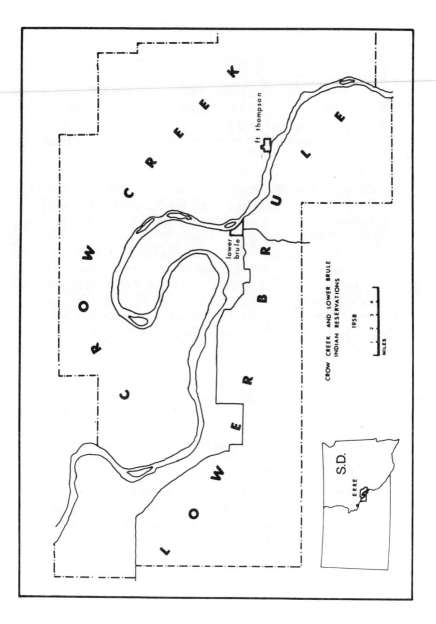

CROW CREEK AND LOWER BRULE
INDIAN RESERVATIONS

1958

1 2 3 4
MILES

ft thompson

lower brule

S.D.

PIERRE

In short, the Lower Brule were desperate for solutions to their numerous problems. War, or the use of other violence, was clearly hopeless. It is no wonder that a religion promising a Messiah, revival of the past, and an end to domination should have appeal to the Lower Brule and other Dakota. The religion took the form of the Ghost Dance, a ritual originated by a peaceful Paiute. On the Plains the ideology became more militant and spread widely. Soon it was among the Lower Brule. Even some of the much more acculturated Yankton Sioux began Ghost Dancing. For the smaller reservations, the movement is not so well-documented, probably because it did not present as much of a threat to whites as on the large reservations. James Mooney's documentation simply notes that no military aid was called for at Lower Brule or Crow Creek, and it could be assumed that the Ghost Dance did not reach them.[50] However, the Chamberlain newspaper reported on a large party of Yankton Indians visiting at Lower Brule who carried the message of the Messiah. The paper asserted that the Yanktons believed "His coming" would result in much good to all; the tone of the article actually condones the visit.[51]

Only two weeks later the editor recognized the movement as disruptive. The paper reported, "The jail at Lower Brule Agency is filled to overflowing with Messiah crazed redskins. A dose of confinement is likely to cool their ardor."[52] In another column the paper expressed sympathy for Iron Nation, who had suffered an accident feared to be fatal. The Chamberlain paper maintained its sympathy toward the neighboring Lower Brule. For example,

Seventeen Lower Brule Indians were taken to Fort Snelling, where they will be confined. It did not hurt President Harrison's feelings to permit these comparatively harmless Indians to be arrested, but for the Lord's sake keep hands off such pleasant and agreeable gentlemen as Sitting Bull, Hump and Red Cloud.[53]

But in mid-December the paper indicated a complete loss

of sympathy and outright ignorance of what the Ghost Dance meant. A full-page advertisement is headlined "Ghost Dance Prices!, of a few of our goods during our Messiah Craze."[54] It is no wonder that the paper failed to carry any significant news of the final outbreak at the end of December. The frontiersmen had failed to understand it from the first. The final fight must have been embarrassing, and of course there was always the fear of frightening potential settlers. In early January the Chamberlain paper reported on a children's party at the Episcopal mission at Lower Brule; late that month a weekly column from a correspondent at Lower Brule began. The column contained such items as how many Indians had their hair cut; when Miss Hyde, the school teacher, visited Chamberlain; and the possibility of a separate school for the white children.[55] When the agency employees petitioned for their school, Anderson missed the irony of their request for a separate school at a time when national policy called for rapid assimilation.

The reporting of the Pierre daily paper was more detailed than the Chamberlain *Democrat,* but no more enlightened about Indians. It too failed completely to understand the Ghost Dance and treated it as a joke as late as December 16, 1890. Some examples best illustrate the attitude of the press:

> *Maybe the Sioux Indian Messiah who is hourly expected to arrive and turn the entire earth over to his people will find opposition from an unexpected quarter. The democrats will be at hand.*[56]
>
> *The reports of Indian uprisings generally circulated in the East do not give people who live in close proximity to the red-skins any uneasiness. They know a pound of raw beef-steak will appease the wrath of the most ferocious buck on the reservation.*[57]
>
> *There is a disgusting amount of chaff over the Indian outbreak. Indian outbreaks are over with. The good old red warrior is of the past. [A few] make a bluff of going to war in order to work the government for more grub and "fixings." There will be no more Indian wars.*[58]
>
> *The Indian Messiah, it is safe to say, beats a presidential election*

*or a Johnstown horror in furnishing matter for the news columns of
the eastern daily press. It will have a nine days run and then collapse.*[59]

Bishop W. H. Hare provided a few firsthand observations
and reported the Indian belief that a wave of earth was to descend on all whites and those Indians behaving like whites. The
Bishop saw a quick end to the dance once the Messiah failed to
materialize.[60] Like the editors, he saw no serious trouble ahead.

By the end of November the Pierre paper was scoffing at
the movement in one column: "With the first real snow storm
of the winter the Messiah craze will come pretty near being
snowed under." Yet another column on the same page saw a
necessity for the army to show a firm hand and return the
hard-core Ghost Dancers to the reservation.[61] Clearly the paper
did not want to alarm citizens nor frighten prospective settlers,
but at least a few men in Pierre were beginning to realize the
Indians were in earnest about the new religion. On December
15th the paper printed a short, first-hand description of Ghost-
dancing at Cherry Creek, Cheyenne Reservation with a comment that the dance ". . . put me in mind of a Methodist revival
more than them of anything else."[62] Less than two weeks before
the Wounded Knee massacre, the Pierre paper continued in this
vein. On December 16th a column joked about the Ghost Dance
being started by an Eastern correspondent, and on the same
page Sitting Bull's death was announced. "A Report Comes
That the Old Dusty Has Cashed in his Chips; His Son with Six
Other Indians and Four Police Join Him on the Trip." The
editor commented that he should have been hanged anyway
fourteen years ago so there can hardly be any sympathy. Fortunately the death would "put an end to the disturbing elements."[63]

It is hard to imagine that newspapermen could have been
so unaware of events among neighboring Indians, but communication across the Missouri River was still slow. Although
railroad and telegraph connected Pierre to the East, no regular

ties ran to the Indian reservations. The first news of Wounded Knee, two days after the event, appeared on the back page under the head, "Pierre Potpourri."[64] Through the first two weeks of January only brief, noncommittal reports on the fight appeared. What can be assumed to have been a paucity of news at first seems likely to have been followed in the West by a suppression of news later. The *New York Times* in one issue devoted about as much space to Wounded Knee as the Pierre paper did for all of January.[65]

Although the New York paper assembled details from various military posts, its editorial revealed little understanding of the situation. It believed a simple administrative change could solve an exceedingly complex problem.

> *If the Indian Bureau were transferred to the War Department, it would be swept and garnished. The Indians would be safe, in the hands of officers of the Army, from the plunder to which they are exposed at the hands of the broken down political hacks who man the Indian agencies.*[66]

The papers on the frontier likewise resorted to simple solutions in such a time of stress. In Pierre an editor deplored the effects of the uprising upon future settlement and the present bad image of the state. He concluded that the only solution was to send all Sioux to Indian Territory.[67] Other "villains" were attacked with sarcasm. For instance,

> *Senator Dawes wants the battle of Wounded Knee investigated . . . . Senator Dawes belongs to the most effete caste of society in the effete east, and his desire is no doubt prompted through his sympathy for the noble red man that exists in his imagination.*[68]

The fight had prompted the expression of many fears and prejudices. Captain W. E. Dougherty, a former Lower Brule agent, had returned from duty in the Southwest to participate in the military engagement at Wounded Knee. He reported:

"General Miles tells me that the Messiah craze is the outcome of a great conspiracy among several tribes of Indians, extending as far west as Nevada, and that the Mormons are at the bottom of the whole thing...."[69] Dougherty does not directly contradict his superior, but this experienced observer's own view was: "It was apparent enough to anyone who had ever lived with these Indians that from the first there was no intention whatever to go into open and defiant revolt."[70]

In historical retrospect it is clear that the Indians intended no violence. The many accounts of Wounded Knee differ only on small detail. A good general account is provided by Robert Burnette, a Rosebud Sioux:

Panicked at the news of Sitting Bull's murder, a band of about three hundred Sioux under Chief Big Foot fled their reservation. Some of these Indians were believers in the so-called Ghost Dance religion, a fusion of Christianity and Indian spiritism that preached the return of the buffalo and the spirits of dead Indians and a sort of earthly paradise where the white man would have no place. The Ghost Dance cult was peaceful, but nervous frontier whites interpreted the strange trance dances as a resurgence of Indian militarism. When the Ghost Dance started at his reservation, D. F. Royer, the cowardly young agent at Pine Ridge, began to send hysterical telegrams to Washington asking for help. When Big Foot's band bolted, the Seventh Cavalry was sent to bring them in.

The cavalry, some six hundred men with four Hotchkiss quick-firing cannons, apprehended the fleeing Sioux and marched them to a place called Wounded Knee. The soldiers gave the Indians food and rendered medical aid to Big Foot who was dying of pneumonia. But they also searched the captured Sioux for weapons.

The morning after the Indians' capture, 29 December 1890, another search for weapons began. According to the army version, two young Indians refused to give up their new Winchesters. According to most Indians, the army began to fire rifles and cannons without provocation.

The "battle" that followed the first wild shots was one-sided and brief. A handful of Indian warriors pulled concealed weapons or wrested arms from soldiers and put up a courageous fight while the women and children fled screaming across the frozen prairie. Most of the men were dead within minutes. Troopers pursued the women and children for two and three miles firing point-blank at their backs.[71]

This account is especially useful because Burnette provides another one of events at Wounded Knee in 1973. Burnette, a Marine veteran and also a long-term veteran of Indian politics, reports on the basis of first-hand observation.

I was in Saint John's Hospital in Rapid City recovering from surgery when the Wounded Knee clash began. On 11 March I joined hundreds of other people in driving to Wounded Knee to meet those who took part and see the village for myself.

I was appalled at the change that had taken place since my last trip there. The trading post, the church, and the log houses had all been riddled with federal bullets, and it was a miracle that only two of the defenders had been hit. The quality of the entrenchments was not very good. Some of the barricades and obstacles were made of cinder block. I winced to think what would have happened to anyone crouched behind these cinder blocks if they were struck by large-caliber slugs. Their shattered chunks would have been almost as lethal as bullets. Inside the perimeter was the AIM "tank," a U-Haul van the activists had plastered with mud as camouflage and used for patrol work. Anyone sitting over the front-mounted engine of the "tank" would have been roasted alive if a single tracer hit it.[72]

The misperceptions in 1973 recapitulate those that occurred in 1890.

Dougherty was one of the few who had grasped the nature of the Ghost Dance and the events at Wounded Knee in 1890. In the spring of 1891, the commissioner asked the Dakota agents, "What were the real causes of the outbreak?" At Lower Brule, Dixon saw only superficial ones:

It is without doubt, that there existed previous to the outbreak among the Indians, a feeling of dissatisfaction growing out of a failure to receive a regular and full rations, and the delay in shipment of Annuity clothing, owing to the dilatory manner in which the Indian Appropriation Bill was handled by Congress, all of which was explained to the Indians but imperfectly understood by them. This state of mind rendered them susceptible to outside influence which was extended from their near neighbors, the Rose Bud and Pine Ridge Indians to participate in the so-called "Ghost Dance," and they were fast becoming impregnated with the pernicious belief and evil consequences attending. The attempt to suppress this practice and the refusal of the Indians to discontinue these dances, was the immediate cause of the hostility at this Agency, and the consequent arrest of 22 Indians, the incarceration of 17 of them at Fort Snelling Barracks, Minnesota, for a period of 8 weeks.[73]

It seems likely this agent never did see the significance of the Ghost Dance as a reaction of a proud but beaten people who found themselves in an extremely frustrating situation. Their agents changed every two years or less; the rations and annuities they saw as their right were frequently treated as a privilege by whites; chiefs were esteemed in one context, then ignored in another; treaties and regulations were imperfectly understood; most of all, the Indians saw their lands continually eroded by white ownership. In 1850 with the demise of tribes like the Mandan the Dakota were sovereign over almost all of what is now North and South Dakota plus sizeable parts of Nebraska, Wyoming, and Montana. Only forty years later they were confined to a dozen reservations, each averaging the size of a single county.

Ironically the last major opening of Dakota land, under the treaty negotiated by General Crook, came at the end of boom times. Drought set in at the end of the 1880s, and fewer people were willing to homestead. The demand for land decreased even in eastern South Dakota. The land speculators, who had been among the most vociferous demanding opening of the Sioux Reserve, were not willing to invest in it after the land became available. The expected flood of settlers was more like a trickle.

Approaching statehood further diverted the attention of politicians from the Indians and their land. People in Yankton realized that its location was unfavorable for a state capital, but they meant to retain the state offices as long as possible. Meanwhile numerous other towns advanced their claims. For a while Bismarck served as the Territorial capital, but in 1889 South Dakota voters approved a constitution. At the same time they elected their first state governor, divided the territory into two states, were admitted to statehood along with North Dakota, and accepted prohibition. People in South Dakota had experienced so much "progress" in 1889 that one can understand why they saw little future for the Indian or had little patience for anyone who might hold up further "advancement."

The year of the Ghost Dance, 1890, saw a continued rapid political pace. Drought and the high-handed, monopolistic practices of the railroads had slowed the economic boom, but a farmers' alliance launched an independent party that later served as a base for the Populist party. The Democrats were recovering from the stigma of Civil War days while questionable Republican tactics further weakened their former control. The question of a capital site, after much agitation and questionable maneuvering, was finally settled in favor of Pierre. In short, political ferment was at a peak among the white population in 1890; they had no time for Indians nor any patience with a minority that stood in the way of expansion. It is no wonder so few people at the time comprehended the meaning of the Ghost Dance or sympathized with the survivors of the uncalled for and brutal suppression at Wounded Knee.

Many histories of the Sioux end at 1890. The date marks the close of a colorful, exotic life as well as the last pitched battle between the Dakota and whites. Henceforth the Dakota realized their destinies depended on accommodation with the dominant society. Although some Indians continued in a state of despair, many others turned to new solutions. Complete answers have not yet been found; staggering problems still exist; but desperation is no longer such an overriding part of Dakota life.

chapter 5
Years of Accommodation – 1891-1924

After the suppression of the Ghost Dance, Indians of the Plains rapidly moved toward ignominy and anonymity. The frontiersmen were caught up in politics with the emergence of the Populist third-party movement that created complex shifting alliances among them. For once the Indian friends and foes left Indians alone to seek their own solutions. The reformers in the East had won their way in instituting allotments and were turning to new interests. Their concern with the national economy and particularly the worldwide and severe depression of the mid-1890s diverted their attention from Indian affairs. No doubt the lack of progress in allotment and the tragedy of Wounded Knee further induced them to turn elsewhere.

At Lower Brule, the 1890 decade began with the relocation of the agency and a redefinition of reservation boundaries. The United States government decided that the original reservation blocked a convenient westward route from Chamberlain. The White River Valley provided one of the best accesses to the Black Hills, and the Lower Brule occupied most of it. If the Lower Brule Reservation were moved north, it would also place the new agency closer to Crow Creek. The two agencies were again consolidated for a few years. Any conscientious agent must have been troubled about the distance between the two. A new pontoon bridge at Chamberlain had at least reduced the hazards of crossing the Missouri River, but the two reservations were still a day's journey apart.

In anticipation of the relocation, no expenditures were made on agency buildings, and agents postponed decisions whenever possible. Agent A. P. Dixon throughout the early 1890s argued once more for stock-raising but reported he would maintain an emphasis on farming while that remained federal policy. He did urge further employment of Indians and his reports indicate that wage labor was becoming one form of accommodation. Two Lower Brule men were employed by the agency in carpentry, two in blacksmithing, three as laborers, and one as interpreter. Sixteen Indian police and three part-time judges also drew salaries. Other men received pay as temporary workers for hauling supplies. Likely a few may have worked for white farmers or in town. It is difficult to determine what this income meant for the average Lower Brule family. Dixon does provide one of the earliest accounts of cash income for his consolidated agency:

> During the year 2,200 beef hides . . . netted them $1.50 per hide, or $3,300. They have received for labor and services $12,529, and for transportation of government supplies $1,216. . . . They have been paid by the government $655 for wood . . . and $7,197 for wheat, oats, corn and use of hay lands.[1]

It is likely the Crow Creek Indians received most of the money for the farm produce; if it were divided equally among the Indian families at both agencies, it would have yielded an annual per capita income of $12. However, if the cash income went mostly to a relatively small number of families, as is probable, these persons would have shown others possible means for coping with new conditions. Dixon's correspondence suggests a variety of such accommodations. He noted that the older

Indians simply brood over their "subdued condition and loss of territory and freedom." He deplored their lack of interest and noted they "are seldom willing to favor or accommodate a white man without being paid." Many other Indians remained south of the White River. This faction refused even to make plans to move to the new reservation. They constituted a majority of the Lower Brule population and an embarrassment to Dixon because they sought to relocate among the Upper Brule at Rosebud Reservation.

However, approximately a third of the Lower Brule were seeking a new livelihood, and they gave the agent considerable cooperation. About 130 families had chosen to live on the new reservation. This group had constructed log houses on land they planned to take in severalty. Dixon described them as among the "most intelligent and progressive" members of the tribe. He issued to them all of the stock cattle and the seed grain. With the aid of the white agency farmer the progressives had broken 1200 acres, put up 1200 tons of hay, and cut one hundred cords of wood. Even if Dixon exaggerated these figures, a few families must have been nearly self-supporting. Yet Dixon admits that all the Indians still relied on subsistence rations, and the progressive group suffered a hardship from having to travel so far to his agency at the old site. This situation would continue for several years. The physical separation of the two factions, as shown on the accompanying map, meant that the progressives could have followed their accommodations to white ways with less resistance than usual from the conservatives. It should be noted, however, that the distance did not produce complete segregation. The Lower Brule continued to visit readily throughout the reservation and frequently traveled to other reservations. Social gatherings must have been numerous because Dixon devotes much of his report to Indian dances. His writing reflects upon his attitude and accommodation as well as that of the Indians:

Social gatherings are permitted among them twice a week at

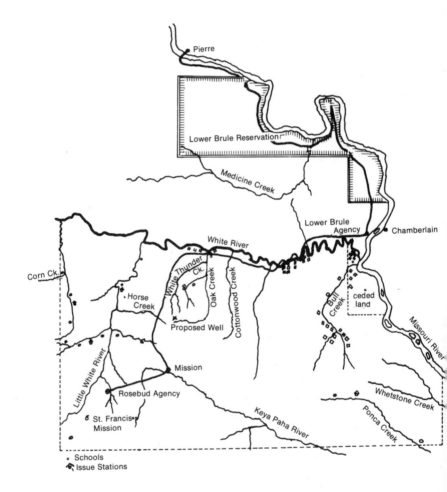

Pierre

Lower Brule Reservation

Medicine Creek

Lower Brule Agency

Chamberlain

White River

Corn Ck.

White Thunder Ck.

Oak Creek

Cottonwood Creek

Horse Creek

Bull Creek

ceded land

Missouri River

Proposed Well

Little White River

Mission

Rosebud Agency

St. Francis Mission

Keya Paha River

Whetstone Creek

Ponca Creek

• Schools

⚑ Issue Stations

*which dancing is participated in to a moderate degree, but no objec-
tionable features are introduced. At these gatherings may be found Indians, church communicants who do not uphold dancing in any form,
but are drawn there out of a social spirit to discuss, in council, their
tribal affairs, the various stipulations of treaties, subjects of agriculture, stock raising, etc. . . .*[2]

While the dance was taking on new functions and probably
also new forms, other parts of the social order were likewise
changing. For instance, only nine cases of polygamy, "of long
standing," were noted for Lower Brule, and marriages were
now performed by ministers or priests. Dixon assumed the
Lower Brule family was changing to the white form but large,
extended families continued to reside in the log cabins. To be
sure, family and other kin relations were changing; yet they
would not necessarily become identical to that of whites.

New adjustments can only be glimpsed at this time even
with the aid of historical perspective. The increase in acreage
plowed and bushels harvested was encouraging compared with
earlier years, but the Lower Brule-Crow Creek Agency was far
from self-sufficient. Rations still poured in and must have accounted for more than three-quarters subsistence. During 1892
the agency supplied 3.25 million pounds of beef on the hoof.
Every week, for every 100 persons were also issued: ten pounds
of bacon, three pounds of beans, four pounds of coffee, seven
pounds of sugar, and fifty pounds of flour. Baking powder, salt,
soap, and annuities of hardware and clothing were also furnished. Obviously the Lower Brule were still subject to the
beneficence of the federal government.

On the reservation itself the major concern among the
Indians was with reservation rights. The Lower Brule Reservation had originally been in the ambiguous position of being
designated, in effect, a reservation within the Sioux Nation.
When that nation was reduced to reservations, the Lower Brule
boundaries were redrawn and the reservation moved northward. For a while agency headquarters were outside of the

Agents discouraged social gatherings organized by Indians, but they did not hesitate to assemble Indians for their own purposes, as when a photographer visited in 1914. Photo from the National Archives, Record Group 75.

southern boundary of the reservation. More significantly, the Indians south of the agency desired to settle to the west at Rosebud Reservation rather than move north. The motivations of this latter group are largely unrecorded; local agents and special agents offer conflicting or superficial opinions. Whatever the reason, they held out so forcefully that legislation in March, 1891 (26 Stats. 1009) allowed them to transfer to Rosebud providing all the Indians would agree. That is, the White River faction could move to Rosebud to take land in severalty if they transferred their rights from Lower Brule to the Rosebud Indians. The measure had to be approved by three-quarters of the adult males both at Lower Brule and Rosebud. In 1892, when a special agent held the first election, he was unable to secure the consent of three-quarters of the Lower Brule. Later it was the Rosebud Indians who refused the necessary consent.

In the summer of 1893, Frederick Treon became agent after previous service of half a dozen years as physician at Crow Creek and Lower Brule. Treon was feuding with agent Wright at Rosebud, and he believed Wright's contacts in Washington were encouraging the White River faction to favor Rosebud. Treon insisted all the faction would move to Lower Brule if it were not for outside interference. In the fall the bickering finally led to action, and a hundred of the White River Brule left their homes and moved to Fort Randall where they occupied the abandoned barracks. Treon was furious when he received the news. He ordered fifteen Lower Brule police, plus five from Crow Creek, to proceed to Fort Randall under the direction of his two agency farmers, J. B. Smith and O. H. David. Treon does not explain why white farmers led the force rather than the Indian police chief.[3] At Fort Randall the police disarmed the dissidents after a brief struggle and pursued several individuals across the river onto the Yankton Reservation. The police and their captives then made the hundred-mile trip up river to the agency where Treon jailed the leaders and made the others encamp. Among the jailed, and probably the main leaders, were Medicine Bull, Long Crow, Black Dog, Fool Hawk, Hawk Wing,

Lone Pine, Ashes, Surrounded, and Left Hand Thunder. Treon now saw his chance to force this group upon the new reservation. Soon he had them at forced work building houses for themselves and preparing the new agency grounds. He also put more pressure on the White River residents who had not left for Fort Randall. After collecting some of these families, agent Treon suddenly faced a logistic problem. Winter was fast approaching, and his new agency was short on rations. He wrote several desperate letters to complete the necessary transfers.

It is remarkable that Treon did not encounter even more trouble. Despite his comparatively long residence with the Indians, he shows little sympathy with them or insight into their ways. In his 1893 report all he found to say about their customs was:

> *The Sioux Indian is rather indolent and still clings to some of his old-time customs, but it is only fair to say that these people are slowly advancing. They have a mania for dancing, and it has been the practice with many of them to meet for that purpose as frequently as once a week. In view of the fact that they hold their dances in overcrowded rooms, the participants nearly or quite nude, the excitement very great, the people stimulated by relating stories of bravery, often giving away horses, pipes, etc., some of them traveling long distances, losing several days from work, I shall order them held at longer intervals. I am aware that some innocent amusement should be given them in place of the dance.[4]*

Treon remained agent for several more years. Probably the peak of his career at Lower Brule was the transfer of agency headquarters in 1894. The new location was on a river terrace high above the Missouri River. It resembled a military compound in some ways. A grass square, like a parade ground, was surrounded by a concrete sidewalk with commodious frame houses along the boundary. These houses were for the interpreter, several clerks, an engineer, a blacksmith, farmer, carpenter, and physician. A spacious, imposing house for the agent dominated the compound. Behind one side of the square was a police barracks; buggy and storage sheds were built on the other side. A school complex was separated from this scene by several hundred yards. It consisted of dormitories for boys and girls, a laundry, a dining hall, commissary, and principal's cottage. An Episcopal church stood at one end, and a Catholic church would soon be added at the other end. Luke Walker continued as the Episcopal minister. Another full-blooded Indian, Joseph Rogers, had served as Presbyterian missionary to the White River faction; the Presbyterians continued to hold occasional services at the new agency.

As a result of the move, a day school forty-five miles west of the old agency at Driving Hawk's Camp, and a school at the mouth of White River were abandoned. An industrial boarding school at the agency was allowed to deteriorate and was replaced by a new complex of eight buildings at a cost of $32,400. This large, expensive enterprise served only 128 pupils.

All the building made Lower Brule one of the most imposing towns between the Missouri River and the Black Hills in 1895. Treon was an ambitious man with a large staff. In addition to the frame buildings for whites, he had convinced some Indians to build log cabins near the agency while arguing with others to build homes on their allotments. By 1895 he had persuaded all but twenty-five families to accept an allotment. He also pursued introduction of an up-to-date water works, and artesian wells were drilled for the agency center. The agent hoped to conquer some day the periodic South Dakota droughts with artesian waters. His ambition is reflected in a petition of the Lower Brule which suggests that councils of Indians spoke for the Lower Brule long before they were legally recognized by the Indian Reorganization Act in 1935. Thus the petition is worth examining in full:

We the undersigned civilized claimants of the Lower Brule Reservation do want help and favor of you.

Buildings for whites on the Lower Brule Agency in 1914. The agency resembled other South Dakota towns with houses for white employees placed around an open square. Photo from the National Archives, Record Group 75.

The Great Father wants all Indians to be self supporters. This we have tried to fulfill, and also is what we want, but some of our friends, the whites are not friendly to us. They have even urged some of the Allotted Indians to leave their homes.

If we could see anything that would be benefit to them, we would be the first ones to leave here and go there but as we cannot see anything of said kind we have made up our minds to stay.

Those that are here we want to raise stock, but lacking two important things which are these. Artesian wells, and a fence around our reservation, if this is granted to us we would have no trouble from our friends the whites.[5]

The petition was signed by Eagle Star as "President of the Civilized Counsel," George Estes as secretary, and Big Mane, Black Elk, Lone Horn, Long Claws, Black Foot, Thundering Bull, Big Star, Bad Horse, and Alex Rencountre.

Petitioning was only one form of political accommodation the Lower Brule were learning at the close of the century. Allotment policy projected that Indians would be citizens at the end of a trust period, twenty-five years from allotment or earlier if they proved themselves competent. Many of the Crow Creek Indians in particular were expected to be citizens before 1900, and local politicians were already considering their strength. One of the earliest typewritten documents in the Lower Brule-Crow Creek record is a letter to President McKinley's commissioner of Indian Affairs that complains of agent J. H. Stephens at Crow Creek. He was accused by J. M. Greene, a Chamberlain attorney, of mistreating one of the agency farmers, Van Patter. A handwritten postscript is of more interest than the letter itself:

Should it be recommended that one of the farmers at that agency be transferred it is I think with the purpose of striking at VanPatter. Of the three farmers there Sutton and VanPatter are Republicans and as these Indians will be entitled to vote at the next election we want them under the proper influence, and as farmer Jones is a Democrat and a hot one *if any transferring [is] to be done let him go where he can do no harm.*[6]

Indian land, as well as votes, was being carefully watched by whites as the century drew to a close. Across the nation land titles were transferred to whites almost as soon as patents in fee simple could be acquired from the Indians. The Bureau of Indian Affairs became alert to the problem and asked for special statistics on land holdings. These figures show that all Lower Brule allotments were completed in 1898 while none of them had been converted to fee simple. The agent, B. C. Ash, also maintained that all Indians were living on their allotments, which seems doubtful, but he must have convinced many individuals to settle on tracts scattered over the reservation. He further reported that allotment "has a very beneficial effect upon the Indian, as it stimulated individual rights and gives them something they can call their own, and induces them to stay home,"[7] while at the same time he noted that no Lower Brule land was adequate to provide a living by farming. Ash's exaggeration of the importance of "staying home" derived from his misunderstanding of Indian economics. His condemnation of the Indian custom of give-away provides some of the best first-hand information on the practice at his agency:

> *The entertainment of numerous visitors is nearly as demoralizing as the making of frequent visits, and always creates what are regarded as reciprocal rights and obligations. Crops are abandoned, horses and cattle are neglected, smaller stock and poultry cannot be kept at all, and a great deal of property is always recklessly distributed in making presents. The latter is of course practically a matter of exchange or barter, but no particular transaction is closed until the visit which inaugurated it is repaid, and business principles are entirely disregarded.*[8]

What Ash failed to understand was that the give-away was never intended as an exchange of goods. Rather the emphasis was upon social relations and the giving and receiving of material goods were simply symbolic of new or reinforced relationships. Since the different groups of Dakota all produced essentially the same goods, trade or barter made little sense in terms of profit. As a means of establishing social relations, however, exchange of goods was vital to a people scattered widely but needing to continue as a social entity.

For the Lower Brule the social ties they maintained by the give-away, intermarriage, visiting, and other means were largely between Yankton and Rosebud. The Lower Brule ties to the two reservations had always been strong, and in 1899 the Indians living south of White River who still desired to live at Rosebud were finally allowed to do so. The annual census of the Lower Brule agent reports a drop from 858 in 1898 to 390 a year later. The final move required another treaty written in March, 1898 and soon ratified. That summer the Indians finally achieved their desire to relocate among the Brule at Rosebud. Their ties to the Lower Brule Reservation have remained strong, however, and sixty years later visits between Rosebud and Lower Brule were still popular and frequent. In 1956, of forty-two inter-reservation marriages half the spouses were either from Yankton or Rosebud.[9] The loss of population to Rosebud meant that Lower Brule land would appear "underutilized," at least to white frontiersmen, and pressure for ceding a part of the reservation began in 1900.

The preceding ten years had seen comparatively little pressure on land. When the Great Sioux Nation was opened in 1890, townsite boomers made Fort Pierre and Oacoma appear prosperous. Oacoma grew up around the former Lower Brule Agency, but its demise coincided with the decline of western growth. Drought and depression forestalled settlement; yet as the stagecoach route opened to Rapid City, towns such as Hayes, Kennebec, Midland, and Presho got their start. The large open-range ranchers soon expected railroads to follow the coaches, and the ranchers thrived as the railroads drew closer. However, the railroads also brought homesteaders and an eventual end to the open range.[10] For the Lower Brule the settlement meant a white expansion along their northern and southern boundaries, complete enclosure by 1900, and pressure to cede the western part of their reservation.

Reformers of the period, generally known as Progressives, were still too busy to come to their aid. Although Theodore Roosevelt was well-acquainted with the Dakota, his major interest in the West was conservation. While he added thousands of acres to national parks and forests, more and more Indian land was being lost. Other reformers, led by the Muckrakers, were involved with trust-busting, poor working conditions, big city bosses, toxic patent medicines, and slum tenements. Exploitation of children and Negroes outrated Indian land exploitation. The year the Lower Brule lost a major segment of their reservation, 1906, the reformers' attention was focused on meat-packing.[11]

This new pressure for their lands had begun at the close of the century. Several severe winters, such as those in 1896 and 1897, had cost the Indians nearly all of their range cattle. By 1900 a special agent was reporting that the Lower Brule were asking to cede 50,000 acres in order to purchase cattle and fence their reservation. This agent argued that the Lower Brule were the most progressive Dakota west of the Missouri and that their lands were far more suitable for grazing than farming. However, the agent provides no factual evidence about the land; rather he concentrates on the progress of the Lower Brule. His report enumerates the number of shingled roofs, the number of shingles on order, and notes that china cupboards are being issued as quickly as the agency carpenter shop manufactures them.[12] It is clear he was building a case to prove the Lower Brule competent or sufficiently civilized so that they could sell their land. The local agent, B. C. Ash, obviously concurred in the decision, possibly he even originated it. At least his reports fully corroborate special agent McLaughlin's previous one. For some unexplained reason the Lower Brule population increased markedly at this time from the 390 reported in 1899 to

475 the next year. Some Lower Brule might have returned from Rosebud had they anticipated per-capita payments from a land sale.

Although R. H. Somers replaced Ash as agent in 1902, he too recommended acceptance of the McLaughlin Treaty, actually a congressional act, to acquire part of Lower Brule. Overall Somers made as few decisions as possible so he did not strongly urge the ceding. He concentrated instead on suppressing Indian dancing and other social gatherings. Once he even managed to prevent Reverend Walker's Sunday night Bible services. The Indians had agreed to limit their celebrations to the Fourth of July as Somers insisted, but they petitioned to be allowed to rehearse two or three times a month.[13]

Somers' appointment as agent derived from hostilities in 1901 that probably had forced Ash's resignation. The event was the last one to involve some continuing violence and open gunplay; it serves well to mark the end of frontier days at Lower Brule. The hostility had its roots back in about 1885 when Handsome Elk had wounded some Lower Brule police. He was sentenced to one year in the state penitentiary, probably the agency's first felon. In the fall of 1900 he again clashed with the police when they arrived to chastise Handsome Elk for beating his wife. One of the policemen, Spotted Horse, had a personal grudge against him and upon Handsome Elk's escape, the police set a trap. Some evidence suggests that Handsome Elk was killed from ambush by the police although Ash's version speaks only of resisting arrest. Still there was enough talk about the incident that Ash resigned, and Somers was appointed to replace him. He too met with similar difficulties. In the fall the daughter of Little Crow became ill. Although the agency doctor insisted she be kept at the hospital, Little Crow removed her, forcing the agent to send police for his arrest. A dozen or more Lower Brule, in protest, showed up at the jail to take Little Crow's place. In the ensuing scuffle Little Crow fled, and a policeman was wounded. Agent Somers ended up sentencing two others to the jail at agency headquarters, and held the rations of the others. Somers' actions were later justified upon formal investigations by a special agent, but it is obvious the Indians never held him in high regard.

Although in 1903 an agent had much less control over withholding rations than formerly, he still held near dictatorial powers. The Bureau of Indian Affairs had inaugurated a make-shift "labor policy" encouraging the employment of Indians at agency work instead of simply issuing rations. Since Congress never authorized the program, sufficient funds were never available, and many Indians were unable to secure the wage work. Consequently a local agent held considerable power because he controlled the jobs. For example, Somers had Indians at work fencing the reservation, building roads, and doing odd jobs. About twenty-five families had some cattle, but altogether less than 1400 head were grazing on the reservation. At this time a special agent, J. F. House, reported that he thought the Lower Brule were "the poorest of the Sioux I ever visited," and were "far from being self-supporting."[14] Although his observation was just the opposite from the one made by Special Agent McLaughlin only four years earlier, Agent House arrived at the same conclusion made by McLaughlin. Proceeds from the sale of reservation land should be used to purchase cattle "as soon as possible."[15]

Approval for sale of the land was finally completed in April, 1906 (34 Stat. L., 124). After purchasing the land, the federal government opened it to homesteaders. The Lower Brule received $115,000 for more than 55,000 acres. Although 21,000 of these acres were judged first-class land, the Indians were paid only $2.50 an acre for them. Land judged fourth-class sold at $1.25. Proceeds from the sale were set aside for the Lower Brule to purchase stock for themselves. It was a slow process. Somers writes that in 1907 he had purchased 474 heifers and 24 bulls for the Lower Brule who had built sheds and put up hay. However, Somers also reports that he had placed nearly 5000 head of stock upon the reservation under the permit system. This form of lease netted the Indians $16 per capita for the year.

It is likely that Somers preferred the ease of leasing land to whites, who would then be responsible for the herding, rather than overseeing Indian herders. Such an arrangement, of course, scarcely benefited the Indian.

There is no evidence that Somers was personally benefiting from the permit system or that fraud was involved in the delay in building a herd. The local agent received no encouragement from the hierarchy above, and it would have taken great courage to abandon the official policy on farming when the Commissioner of Indian Affairs was making such incredulous statements as:

> For myself, I hold very radical views on this whole subject [allotment]. I do not believe that these Indians [the Sioux] as a rule will ever make a success of farming, no matter what particular branch they pursue, or no matter how much they are assisted at the outset. I consider the policy of trying to make every Indian into a farmer whether he will or no, which has come down to me through so many years of failure, all wrong in conception and therefore impracticable in execution. But so many good persons still cling to the old notion, that I am stretching every resource at my command to give it the most favorable experiment possible.[16]

By 1909 the Indians owned 825 cattle and more than 1000 horses. This herd was augmented with an issue of 2050 cows and 68 bulls. The agent planned to issue most of the cows on a per-capita basis, four head to each Lower Brule Indian. No allowance was made for family size or whether a family had access to water, land, hay, or other essential items for ranching. James McLaughlin, now an inspector in the Indian Service, approved the distribution but did make some reasonable recommendations about winter care, use of bulls, and building a horse herd. In short, the Lower Brule were in the cattle business for better or worse. In retrospect they appear to have started well, but the odds against them far outweighed whatever luck they possessed.

The Lower Brule were not the only Dakota ceding land in the early 1900s. Much of the eastern part of Rosebud was being opened for homesteading as well as parts of the Cheyenne River and Standing Rock Reservations. The latter-day homesteaders in these areas arrived to break the prairie, build tarpaper shacks, and discover in a few years they could no more support themselves by farming than the Indians. What they thought had been good luck in winning by lottery the right to purchase a homestead turned out generally to be bad luck. The pioneers soon departed except a few who leased or purchased additional acres to convert to ranching.

Some details of this process are preserved for The Strip, as the western part of Lower Brule was known, in a highly readable account by one of the participants:

> *Every homesteader who had a tug that would fasten over a double tree, a wagon that could still squeak, or a flivver that had a bolt in it, went into the transportation business—hauling the seekers from Pierre or McClure to look at the land.*
>
> *A generation before people had migrated in little groups in covered wagons to find new land. Now they came by automobile and railroads ... but the spirit that drove them was still the pioneer spirit, and the conditions to be faced were essentially the same—the stubborn earth, and painful labor, drought and famine and cold, and the revolving cycle of the seasons.*[17]

For two decades these last pioneers flooded into western South Dakota. Far more people came than could ever make a living, but they had to discover the mistake through trial and error.[18] Settlers around the Lower Brule in 1890 were few and scattered along river or creek bottoms. Only 233 whites lived in Lyman County which then stretched from Oacoma to Murdo.[19] By 1900 ten times that number had settled, and between 1900 and 1910 there was a three-fold expansion to 10,848. In anticipation of further growth, county boundaries were redrawn. Half of Lyman County was added to the new Jones County, but the settlers were discovering the area would not support them. By 1920 the combined population of both Jones and Lyman counties was only 9595. This reversal began a continued downward trend in population. The 1920 population of Lyman County alone was 6591. It dropped to 6335 in 1930; to 5045 in 1940 and 4572 in 1950. This decline in the county surrounding Lower Brule simply reflected a process that was occurring throughout South Dakota west of the Missouri River. For this area the population jumped from 44,000 in 1900 to 138,000 in 1910. The bulk of these settlers were homesteaders who brought an end to the open range and a striking reduction of the large herders. Droughts, especially in 1910 and 1911, soon reduced the homesteaders in turn. A special state census in 1915 revealed only 120,000 in the area. The west river country had lost more than 17,000 persons in five years.

In a few places farmers persisted, but they had to have unusual access to water and somehow to have increased their acreage. Elsewhere some ranchers made adjustments to the newly developing cattle technology. If they were able to acquire land and capital, they became successful providing a market for the unsuccessful homesteaders. These ecological adjustments produced a sparse population throughout western South Dakota; only a few towns grew up along the access routes between eastern prairie and the Black Hills.

A similar process was occurring at Lower Brule. Once their reservation had been allotted, the Indians came under intense pressure to settle down and farm. By 1895 they had been so bullied or bribed that most were scattered over the landscape. Soon, however, they too were drifting into the favorable areas such as the river and stream bottoms provided. Although these settlements were new, the practice of banding together along a protected area was a well-entrenched practice. Both the aboriginal summer and winter encampments had offered a rich social life for the Dakota. Furthermore, from the fur trade to the rationing period, strong feelings for community life persisted. A dispersed settlement pattern was antithetical to Dakota ideals

White homesteaders in a South Dakota sod house. Photo from the Friends of the Middle Border Museum, Mitchell, South Dakota.

of sharing, visiting, and exchanging children as well as the more obvious social forms such as the dance. The white innovations such as churches and schools further encouraged more compact settlement. Early in the twentieth century almost all the Lower Brule were living in six locales. About one hundred each were at the town of Lower Brule, along Medicine Creek, and in the Fort George bottoms. Fort Hale and Cedar Creek had sixty each; another thirty persons were in the Little Bend.

The folly of the allotment system was clear at Lower Brule and many other reservations by 1910. Federal policy, however, was slow to change. The 1912 report of the Commissioner of Indian Affairs shows a determination to keep Indians on their allotments. Some tribal development was to be allowed in exploitation of natural resources such as oil and timber, but overall the Bureau still pursued Dawes' dream:

> *Present policies . . . center upon individual Indians and individual Indian families, seeking to give each Indian the knowledge of health which will enable him to compete with his fellow Americans, to place each Indian upon a piece of land of his own where he can by his own efforts support himself and his family. . . .*[20]

At Lower Brule very few families were yet able to support themselves. Rationing still continued at a cost of nearly $6000 a year for approximately 500 people. The bulk of the rations continued to be beef, flour, bacon, beans, and coffee. The practice of hiring Indians added another $3500 to the economy, but it employed only sixteen individuals. A further supplement consisted of a cattle issue of 1000 head. In spite of former complaints about an abundance of horses, nearly a thousand of them were also issued. Even after this issue, the largest Indian herder had only 125 head of cattle. In contrast, white ranchers were grazing 5000 head on the reservation under the permit system that allowed them to do so.

Although the Indian economy remained undeveloped, the bureaucracy at Lower Brule was flourishing. Interestingly, a special agent had recommended earlier that the administration could be made more efficient by letting the agent serve also as school superintendent. This economy measure was followed by the hiring of additional farmers and other school employees so the agency grew even larger. In 1910 it must have been quite an outpost. A stagecoach ran daily between Reliance and Lower Brule even though a government telephone connected the agency to the Reliance telegraph. During the decade, concrete sidewalks replaced wooden ones; more and more buildings sprang up. By 1915 garages were being added. It was all right to store buggies in a stable, but apparently automobiles needed their own structures. Consistently a series of agents or school superintendents deplored the inadequacy of the sewer system, and they maintained sanitary conditions were the major problem of the agency.

Meanwhile Indian lands eroded both literally and figuratively. One agent noted that "The results of issuing patents in fee on this reservation does not produce the desired results but rather leads to extravagance and shiftlessness."[21] Future agents, like this one, would maintain that they discouraged patenting to prevent sales, yet the very next year the agent quoted above requested a new clerk because of "heavy land sales." Meanwhile as white ranchers did well on leased Indian land, the Indians were being urged to farm on poorer land. In 1913 an eager agent had directed his additional farmers to concentrate on a "demonstration" plot using the most up-to-date seed, techniques, and equipment. As early as June 28, it was clear that wind erosion and high temperatures had demolished the farm. Surely the effort must have vividly demonstrated to the Indians the futility of farming, if they needed such a lesson; but one wonders why the white men were so slow to reach the only logical conclusion. After such dramatic evidence, the agent only haltingly advised against the practice: ". . . it would seem that the efforts which we make to force the Indians, year after year, to continue agricultural pursuits are ill-advised."[22]

Only gradually were Indian farm efforts supplemented by

encouragement in stock-raising, possibly because local agents exaggerated their farming reports to please their superiors. Still they consistently mentioned issue of heifers and bulls to individuals or to form a tribal herd. Unfortunately the history of the ranching effort is neither known nor well-reported. Almost all the local agents indicated at one time or another that ranching was feasible, if not ideal, and that the Indians were interested. However, in 1914 a blunt, forthright agent for the Lower Brule reported: "Probably 10,000 head of heifers have been issued to these Indians in the past twelve or fifteen years with the result that there is little over a tenth of that number on hand at the present."[23] In this agent's opinion, it was too easy to get permits to butcher or sell; he also documented the frustration of keeping accurate records: "It [the livestock] slips away here and there." Despite his awareness that the cattle industry was unsuccessful, he proceeded with the distribution of 500 head of heifers he assumed would be the basis of a tribal herd.

The reasons the Indians failed to become cattle ranchers are far from clear. Gordon Macgregor briefly touches on the problem for the Dakota at Pine Ridge, but he concentrates only on the economic conditions of World War I and its aftermath.[24] Malan and Schusky provide a contemporary study of Pine Ridge ranchers but offer no historical background.[25] One of the most penetrating economic analyses is available in "Rosebud Reservation Economy," but again concentration is upon modern conditions.[26] To some extent white competition denied the Indians full use of the range. The BIA was under continual pressure from Indian owners and white ranchers to use immediately reservation grassland. Furthermore, most agents understood very little about ranching although they occasionally employed competent stockmen. A few Indians, almost always the most acculturated, did accommodate to ranching but Dakota reservations were never well-utilized for that purpose.

The answer to this problem of why Indians were unsuccessful in ranching must lie mostly in cultural factors. An economist might explain that people on a poverty level cannot afford or manage capital accumulation. Any goods they acquire go immediately into consumption rather than investment. The same explanation, but in much more understandable and humane language, is also given by the novelist, Dan Cushman. In *Stay Away, Joe,* he pictured a Plains Indian family that sincerely believed it would be able to build a herd from a starter crop given it by a benevolent government.[27] In less than a year the herd just slipped away here and there as the family met the social demands of friends and relatives. Outsiders fail to appreciate how people on a subsistence level can seldom manage long-range goals when faced with present-day hunger.

Solutions to the complexities of the problem certainly eluded the local agents at Lower Brule. While the reservation economy stagnated, a series of agents concerned themselves in large part with Indian morality and attributed much of the immorality to frequent dancing. Annual reports consistently included new regulations imposed by the agent to reduce the number of dances and to ban inter-reservation visiting for the purpose of dancing. Efforts were still being made to restrict dancing to the daylight hours and only on national holidays such as the Fourth of July and New Year's.[28] This emphasis on "morality" stemmed in large part from Washington where the commissioner was taking time to write individual Indians on the subject:

John Small Waisted Bear,
My Friend:
I have been reading the Brule Rustler. In it I notice that you have a race horse which you wished to take to Kadoka but when you were told that I did not think the race horse business was good for Indians you said: "Alright, I won't go. I guess that's the best way."

I want to say to you that I am glad that you see racing horses is not a good business. I think, however, that an Indian who is interested in horse racing . . . should be able, with the help of his Superinten-

A Lower Brule 4th of July celebration about 1914. Old costumes were incorporated into national holidays. Photo from the National Archives, Record Group 75.

dent, to improve his Indian ponies into horses which will bring good money. Why don't you do this?[29]

The Bureau's interest in the direction of Indian attitudes even went to the extent of advising on celebrations. In response to a poster for one Fourth of July celebration, the acting commissioner objected to a four-day observance, recommending two days for the next year. He also urged that in the future "The sunrise charge and sham battle be discouraged."[30]

As European nations moved toward world war in 1915, BIA concern with "morality" declined. Indian affairs received a lower priority than usual, but the war did raise the question of where Indians stood as United States citizens. Although most Indians, especially those on the Plains, were patriots of the first order, here and there across the country some Indians refused to be drafted because they were not yet considered American citizens. Iroquois patriots, refusing to claim citizenship, still joined in the war effort; and one group of Iroquois dutifully declared war on Germany.[31] Many Indians, of course, joined the armed services and the reservations were called upon to help on the home front. For instance, Commissioner Sells wired Lower Brule:

War situation makes it imperative that every tillable acre on land on Indian reservations be intensively cultivated this season to supply food demand particularly wheat, beans, potatoes, corn and meat. Call farmers and leading Indians together immediately for organized united effort under your control and supervision. This is of the highest importance and requires aggressive action. There must be delay [sic, apparently "no" delay] in anything necessary to insure results. You are authorized to take older boys out of school for farm work. Wire what may be expected and report progress by letter.[32]

In addition to taking older boys out of school, federal policy also moved toward taking more land out of Indian owner-

FOURTH OF JULY
CELEBRATION

at
LOWER BRULE AGENCY

JULY 1st: Parade 8 a. m.
12 m. Basket dinner
1 p.m. half mile race and repeat
2 p.m. potato race
? p.m. foot race, 100 yard dash

JULY 2nd: 6 a.m. Daybreak charge
9 a.m. 1 mile relay race
10 a.m. sack race
11 a.m. broncho riding
12 m. basket dinner
2 p.m. quarter mile pony race
3 p.m. base ball game
5 p.m. dance

JULY 3rd: 6 a.m. Sunrise Charge
and Sham Battle
9 a.m. race 1 mile and repeat
10 a.m. wheelbarrow race
11 a.m. orange eating contest
12 m. basket dinner
1 p.m. shinney game, 10 men on
each side

JULY 4th: Sunday, an old fashioned
camp meeting with basket dinner. The entire day given over to religious meetings

COMMITTEE

High Elk, President
Spotted Horse, Vice President
William Iron Elk, Secretary
Ashley Sawalla
Amos Boy Elk
Samuel White
Dan Grass Rope

James Dismounts Thrice
Whirling Iron
Yellow Wolf
Thomas Bow
John Fire Cloud
Bear Heart

It is against the federal laws for ANY ONE to introduce intoxicating liquors on an Indian Reservation.

It is better to be safe than sorry.

Both white and Indian speakers will address the crowds during the day on appropriate subjects.

ship. A former tribal chairman of the Rosebud Reservation asserts:

Many of the Indian servicemen in the First World War returned to find their lands confiscated by the state. In the Indians' absence, the government, in order to buttress its "assimilation" policy, had issued "forced patent-in-fee" titles to Indian land. This made the land on which these titles were issued taxable by state and county authorities, and removed the land from the trusteeship, as provided by treaty, of the federal government. When the taxes, of which the Indian soldiers were ignorant, went unpaid, the local authorities "assimilated" Indian land.[33]

Probably the war had added pressure for this step, but more importantly, allotment was recognized as a complete failure as the means of assimilation. Instead of giving up the policy of assimilation, however, the government had turned to other means. In addition to allowing increased land sales, it placed great faith in education. To the Indians the policy simply meant further land reduction. A part of the 1918 policy statement issued by the Interior Department is explicit on this point:

We have begun the speedy release from guardianship of all Indians found to be competent to transact their own affairs, giving to all such a full control of their property of whatever description and recognizing their status to be the same in every respect as the white man's.[34]

The claim that this step plus new directions in education would provide full assimilation was couched in patriotic terms appropriate for a time of war, especially one that was fought to make the world "safe" for democracy.

It is not too much to say that [the policy] has developed notably the Indian's confidence in the Government, made him feel that its flag is his flag, its weal his weal, its warfare his warfare, its destiny his destiny. It has revived the dauntless spirit of his ancestry and trans-

formed it into the valorous stuff of American patriotism. . . . This poli-
cy I believe can not fail to dissolve tribal bonds, remove interracial
barriers, rescue the Indian from his retarding isolation, and absorb
him into the general population with the full rights and immunities of
our American life. . . .[35]

While grand goals and words flourished in Washington, affairs at Lower Brule proceeded much as usual. The omnipresent Bureau of Indian Affairs maintained a close supervision of every activity. When superintendent Garber reported the annual election of a Lower Brule Business Committee to advise the superintendent, the Washington Office immediately inquired as to whether the officers were "industrious, sober and progressive Indians, their degree of Indian blood, their education."[36] Upon reflection, Garber concluded the committee was not representative and arbitrarily called for another election. In the second election, most of the original committee was returned except for some Indians who had achieved citizenship, known as "patent-in-fee" Indians. Some new officers were also included. The elected chairman, Henry Useful Heart, was vetoed by Garber because of "lax morals" and use of liquor. Without consulting any Indian, he named Daniel Grass Rope as chairman. Garber probably failed to realize the extent of his dictatorial methods, and certainly he missed the irony of his action's occurring just at the time when the world had ostensibly been made safe for "democracy". He seems fully sincere, after vetoing and appointing officers, to claim in the very same letter that the business committee "takes up with the [Indian] Office, through the Superintendent, *all matters* in connection with the tribal affairs of the Indians of this reservation [author's italics]."[37]

Garber presided over the demise of the tribal herd as well as shepherding the business committee. The herd had struggled along with little formal accounting until 1917 when a special investigator made a thorough report on its history. He traced records for several years showing that in 1913, fifty-five

Mr. Grass Rope, a well-known Lower Brule. Photo from the South
Dakota State Historical Society.

head of two-year heifers were purchased; the next year 500 head more were added plus fifty-five bulls, and seventy-five more bulls were added in 1917. Total costs were more than $40,000. In 1917 the herd totaled 359 cows, 83 heifers, 118 bulls, and 311 yearlings and calves. The herd should have totaled twice as much; moreover the excess number of bulls indicated poor management. In addition, heifers often were bred at the wrong time of year; feed was inadequate; the manager was inexperienced; shelters were poorly constructed; cows were not culled; and Indians probably stole calves for their individual herds. Investigator C. M. Knight further reported that the Indians strongly favored a division of the herd.[38] A slightly later report confirmed the figures provided by Knight. Bureau figures showed $64,221 spent for cattle at Lower Brule, more than half from tribal funds, between 1914 and 1918, but in 1918 only 387 animals were reported for the tribal herd.[39]

However, the idea that a tribal herd might be inappropriate for the Indian economy was slow to penetrate officialdom. Local officials still believed Indians were incapable of managing large herds, and arguments were advanced that the tribal herd should be maintained at least as the basis for building individual owners. Under such policy the tribal herd was meant to furnish "starter head" to Indians who could gradually pay back this loan through future calf crops. On paper the idea appears to be sound and it has actually worked in a few places. Such cooperative ventures, however, seldom have proved effective among Plains Indians. As Indians today remember the system, full-bloods frequently accused the mixed-bloods of taking more calves than they deserved while mixed-bloods blamed full-bloods for never doing their share of work. No doubt internal bickering was almost as important a reason for the failure as the technical reasons enumerated by Inspector Knight. Unfortunately the record remains cloudy.

High beef prices in 1917 and 1918 motivated unusually high cattle sales. These market conditions coincided with the arrival of new superintendents at Lower Brule. The one for

1918, E. M. Garber, had some praise for the tribal herd idea and claimed to have doubled its size through judicious purchases, but he concluded his report on cattle with a recommendation to sell the tribal herd. The 1919 successor, F. Campbell, barely mentioned cattle except to note that the citizen Indians were selling out because of good prices, and the Indians who were non-citizens would sell whenever permitted. However, a few Indians continued to build large herds and invested all they could. These operators wanted the remnants of the tribal herd issued in order to acquire them. Apparently the contemporary pattern of individual ownership with bureau supervision was beginning to take shape at this time.

If these factors had not been sufficient to reduce the tribal herd, the arrival of BIA superintendent C. H. Gensler guaranteed it. Gensler considered himself a long-experienced "practical" farmer and expert on Indians because of previous service on the Havasupai Reservation in Arizona. He firmly believed in the demonstration farm method and began extensive plans for one upon his arrival in the winter of 1920. From Gensler's initial enthusiasm, one wonders if he might not have contemplated a cotton crop as well as the alfalfa, oats, corn, beans, potatoes, and wheat he talked about. Cattle had little place in his plans for the Lower Brule future, and he was quick to point out the heavy loss of cattle in the 1919–1920 winter. The scabies as well as the weather that struck the herds convinced Gensler that: "The outlook here for the future is the general farm rather than the cattle range. The days of the large herd has passed."[40] At the end of the 1920 summer, Gensler was forced to report that the season, but apparently not his idea of farming, was "almost a total failure." Grasshoppers and the typical "unusual summer conditions" had worked their havoc. Once more a demonstration plot failed to demonstrate to a superintendent the impracticality of farming; nevertheless it did dampen his enthusiasm. The next year he continued to talk of "general farms," but no longer was he so positive that farming could solve all the problems of the Lower Brule.

Gensler's other recommendations are of a much more serious nature and must be examined in depth—those that involved land sales. Most Indians today see the federal government's relation to the tribes as nothing more than one large real estate transaction. Anyone the least bit familiar with Indian problems recognizes that land records and land transactions were a major part of bureau activity. The charge that United States and Indian relations were practically nothing but a series of land transfers is made most effectively by Vine Deloria in his book entitled, *Custer Died for Your Sins*.[41] The question of interpretation is far from settled; most writers have seen the relationship as one full of complex factors. Probably the truth lies somewhere in between; certainly Deloria's charge has been sufficiently documented to deserve serious attention.

At Lower Brule, superintendent Gensler's recommendations on land could be interpreted as collaboration in a land grab. Taken at face value, the recommendations could also be interpreted as the serious and well-meaning thoughts of a sincere but mediocre and naive bureaucrat. Gensler's "logic" is perhaps the poorest of the Lower Brule superintendents in the early twentieth century, but all of them presented similar recommendations on land. Of course the Washington office did not necessarily respond to all these low-level recommendations, but doubtless much sympathy for such a viewpoint existed within the Bureau of Indian Affairs.

It should be recalled that Gensler had served on a southwestern reservation before arriving at Lower Brule. His 1920 recommendation, therefore, is not exactly that of an initiate; he was familiar with the problems of patent-in-fee, the difficulties beginning to arise from the division of allotments into heirship land, and the growing complexities of other land problems. His yearly report, in reply to a guideline with questions, assessed the Lower Brule situation in these terms:

The net results of the issuance of patents in fee is rather difficult to define. To examine it only from the use made of the proceeds of the sale of this land, a large part of which is sold, the issuance of a patent in fee is a failure. But it is an unfortunate fact that those who squander their money will do it whether they get it now or later and for those of that caliber the quicker the money is used up the better as they will then go to work. I believe they should be issued quite liberally.[42]

It does not require much cynicism to interpret Gensler's reasons as another simple-minded rationalization for selling Indian land. His recommendations the next year do nothing to dispel such interpretation. Again, after complaining that the able-bodied were not using their land, he urged that only the old and disabled be permitted to lease: "This would produce lots of idle land but would at least cut off the easy money due from rents and would do away with the excuse that their lands are leased as a reason for not working."[43] He continued in this vein a year later: "These Indians are very lazy and the matter of their ever utilizing their land is doubtful and the fact that they can lease their land only encourages shiftlessness."[44] Fortunately for the Lower Brule, the Plains economy slipped into a depression, and no one had the capital to buy Indian land. In 1923 Gensler offered ninety tracts of Lower Brule land but could sell only eight. In the next year's bidding, one hundred tracts were available but again only eight sold. Still the land sales and particularly the land leases had increased to such a large scale that Gensler admitted in 1924 that his bureaucracy had been swamped by the complexities. Papers that should have been signed by both parties, cancelled checks that should have been filed and countless other miles of red tape had made it impossible to maintain all the files required. While the economy had slowed the land sales, red tape had reduced the issuance of patents-in-fee. Only two were issued in both 1923 and 1924. The bureau had prevented itself, because of myriad regulations, from carrying out recommendations such as Gensler's.

One must sympathize with the view that Gensler was simply out to transfer Indian land to white title as quickly as possible. In retrospect his reasoning resembles a simple facade for quick land sales. However, another interpretation is possible. Gensler, like other Indian agents or superintendents, was given complete charge of an Indian reservation. He expressed a clear-cut duty to help the Indians, meaning by "help" that he would help them become more assimilated. He faced a hopeless situation although he could not recognize it at the time. No Indian communities had ever been assimilated into white society to the extent envisioned by whites. The process took much longer than was anticipated in the nineteenth century; moreover it was not and is not the only alternative for Indians. Many Indian communities were and are changing but not solely in the direction of becoming more like white ones. Thus Gensler existed in a situation where, with the best of intentions plus major authority and responsibility, he could satisfy neither himself nor his superiors. Unable to understand the complexities, he could hardly blame social or economic conditions; obviously the Indians must have been to blame instead. Therefore he soon saw them as "lazy," "hostile," or "ignorant," and his recommendations grew out of these ill-formed and unintelligent stereotypes.

National policy reflected in many ways what seemed to have been going on in Gensler's mind. Interior secretary Hubert Work and BIA commissioner Charles Burke were concerned with shaping Indians into U.S. citizens. On June 2, 1924, Congress granted citizenship to all Indians regardless of property status, although the act explicitly stated that citizenship would not affect any other rights Indians held.[45]

In many ways the 1924 legislation was one of the most important steps in the history of the government's relations with Indians; yet it received comparatively little attention then or now. Often the Citizenship Act has been passed off as the only event worthy of note between the Dawes Act and the Indian Reorganization Act of 1934. For the Bureau of Indian Affairs the granting of citizenship was seen in part simply as an expedient solution to some sticky problems.

For instance, at Lower Brule the boarding school had closed, and only public schools were available for the Indian children. Gensler reported the local school boards were using numerous devices to exclude Indian children even though he had "... been careful not to send Indian children to these schools about whom the Whites could make a legitimate complaint." Gensler's rationale for proceeding slowly was: "After all, the tax returns here show practically none paid by Indians and every Indian parent, whose child attended public school, with but three exceptions are full citizens. This is a treacherous subject to discuss with these taxpayers and it is one of the current and everlasting topics of discussion."[46] Even though citizenship for a majority of the Lower Brule had not made it easier for them to attend public school, the BIA did not alter its view that citizenship would relieve the bureaucracy of responsibility for Indian education. In fact, BIA commissioner Burke saw citizenship as solving nearly all his problems. On the eve of citizenship an influential book, *The Red Man in the United States,* was published whose author, G. E. Lindquist, predicted that "The Indian appears not as an interesting relic of the past, but as a future citizen, at present in a difficult stage of transition, but destined ultimately to be merged, like other racial groups, into the general population."[47] Commissioner Burke went even further in endorsing the view and the book:

> *Practically all our work for the civilization of the Indian has become educational: teaching the language he must of necessity adopt, the academic knowledge essential to ordinary business transactions, the common arts and crafts of the home and field, how to provide a settled dwelling and elevate its domestic quality, how to get well when he is sick and how to stay well, how to make the best use of his land and the water accessible to it, how to raise the right kind of live-stock, how to work for a living, save money and start a bank account, how to want something he can call his own, a material possession with the happiness and comforts of family life and a pride in the prosperity of his children; teaching him to see the future as a new era and one inevitably different from his past, in which individual ambition,*

unaided by the show and trappings of ancient custom, must contend with the complexities and competition of a modern world.[48]

An equally pressing problem was growing in the courts where Indians could expect little justice. Gensler warned of trouble in this area in 1923, noting that "criminal cases in Circuit Court handled by the state are a farce except we hire Council [*sic*] to assist the state."[49] Apparently he was convinced that at least one Lower Brule Indian had good cause to seek recovery from a popular white rancher, but Gensler reports that no white man would ever be convicted on the basis of an Indian's testimony.

Again Gensler felt citizenship for the Indian would end such problems because it would place Indians on an "equal footing" with others. Ironically the bureau itself was not proceeding consistently on that assumption. During and after citizenship legislation, the government moved to suppress the religious rights of Indians. Clearly the bureau understood citizenship to mean only that Indians were to become like whites, not necessarily to enjoy the same rights. In 1923 Gensler reported at greater length on the undesirability of Indian dancing than on the injustice received in the state courts. He detailed how the Lower Brule had met to adopt rules and regulations in regard to dancing. For instance, no "educated" Indian was allowed to dance, the Indians were to furnish lists of participants at dances, and they were limited in any gift-giving to the Fair Association meeting (resembling a county fair) or the Fourth of July celebration. Gensler concluded for Commissioner Burke that: "It is my humble opinion that they have responded wonderfully to the suggestions you offered them."[50]

Opinions about dancing came to dominate Indian affairs in 1923 and 1924 overshadowing news of citizenship. The *New York Times* took the position that if emigrants could become citizens in five years certainly Indians deserved citizenship after one hundred years. It failed to go much beyond this argument, however, becoming more engrossed in the debate over Indian dancing and ritual between novelist D. H. Lawrence[51] and Herbert Welsh and the Indian Rights Association, plus the Baptist Convention and numerous missionaries who had pressured the bureau to suppress all "objectionable and immoral" features of dancing. Although the Southwest Indians were the major target, there was also concern about "excessive" gift-giving in the Plains. Burke, if not secretary Work, was receptive to the pressure and had directed agents to limit dance and ritual wherever feasible. Neither Burke nor the missionaries ever detailed what was immoral about Indian dancing or the give-away custom. Ironically this close supervision of Indian morality by the Department of the Interior was occurring just as the Teapot Dome scandals were brewing. Apparently Burke had relied heavily upon a body of testimony collected by missionaries from dubious sources in justifying his suppression of dancing. The Indian Defense Association, led by John Collier, who later became one of the most notable Indian commissioners, charged Welsh and the Indian Rights Association with disseminating propaganda that swayed the bureau "to compel Indians to surrender their aboriginal beliefs." Collier warned civil libertarians:

> It is important that the public shall not lose sight of the existing fact, that the Indian Bureau in theory and in practice denies liberty of conscience to the Indians. It should not be inferred from Herbert Welsh's letter . . . that Secretary Hubert Work and Commissioner Burke have brought the religious persecution to an end, have abrogated the amazing code of religious crimes or promulgated any religious bill of rights for the Indian.[52]

Collier, speaking for the faction of Indian friends who valued cultural pluralism, held the position that citizenship for Indians meant equal protection under the law and that the law was a means for preserving their differences.

Thus on the one hand Burke and Welsh, who had left the Indian Rights Association, saw citizenship for Indians simply as a step in the assimilation process. Collier and the Indian Rights Association, on the other hand, saw the act as a step toward cultural pluralism. In 1924 Collier's view was not widely shared although the *New York Times* showed some sympathy for it. However, within ten years Collier would be Commissioner of Indian Affairs and initiate a major reorganization of policy based on a philosophy of cultural pluralism or the encouragement and preservation of Indian cultures.

Nevertheless, under the Burke administration, the Citizenship Act produced little change for Indians. At Lower Brule, agent Gensler failed even to refer to the legislation in his 1924 report. Far from seeing any protection of Indian diversity, Gensler noted in poetic style how far the Lower Brule had advanced toward civilization. In concluding, he rationalized that the consolidation of Lower Brule with Crow Creek was indicative that the Indians of his agency would soon be absorbed.

Among the Lower Brule there was fear and resentment that the loss of their own agency would reduce necessary services. They realized citizenship alone could do little to alleviate the discrimination found in the schools and courts. Indeed citizenship was interpreted as an end to any special federal services and recognition of their special rights as created by treaty or acts of Congress. Even though the legislators who had written the Citizenship Act clearly intended to preserve such rights, it was logical for white South Dakotans to demand immediately why Indians deserved any special privilege once they were citizens "like everyone else."

Given these conditions the Lower Brule managed remarkably well. A few of them had started cattle herds and employed other Indians; many had built frame homes; most had drifted off their scattered allotments to form more viable communities around schools, churches, and post offices. Economically the Indians were not doing well; however, the end of World War I had brought depression everywhere on the Great Plains, particularly among ranchers. Problems abounded, but many of the Lower Brule were seeking more rational solutions. They no longer thought of violent resistance nor a return to former times through a messianic movement. Instead they were experimenting with new forms of governing bodies and finding ways to accommodate to the benevolent, dictatorial powers of the superintendent and bureau. Indians were petitioning the commissioner, and they were beginning to discover the direct link they had with Congressmen. Their accommodations with local whites are undocumented except for increasing intermarriage. Some Indians were beginning the migration from the reservation, and a few joint efforts between Indians and whites to improve social conditions were occurring in the churches. Indians still had a "long way to go" toward satisfying their own goals, but in the three decades following the Ghost Dance, they had at least laid a foundation.

chapter 6
Twentieth-Century Indians

The consolidation of Lower Brule and Crow Creek agencies brought a transfer of Bureau of Indian Affairs personnel and their services to Fort Thompson in 1925. Older Indians at Lower Brule today recall this final consolidation with some bitterness. They claim the move was the beginning of termination of federal services to them, and the town of Lower Brule has never been the same. However, the end of close, personal supervision by a resident agent possibly gave potential Indian leadership more opportunity. Certainly W. E. Duncan, superintendent of the consolidated agency at Crow Creek, found little time for the Lower Brule. He complained of much overwork for his staff after the August, 1925, consolidation and reported that the "efficient work of this unit has been practically at a standstill."[1]

Duncan's initial reports for the Lower Brule have a candor typical of new agents not responsible for past administrations. From these reports one is struck by the paradox between the way Indians were being treated and the fact that they had recently been declared citizens. Duncan describes much of this treatment as a matter of course, seldom seeing any of the paradox. The lack of insight and sensitivity displayed by most Americans

181

as well as official personnel has long been the major part of the Indian tragedy.

For example, due process guaranteed citizens under the Constitution was completely foreign to the administration of law and order at Lower Brule. Physical fighting among the Lower Brule was largely ignored although police often did investigate cases of wife-beating. Horse thefts were common, and car thefts were beginning. The latter would replace the former within twenty years. When crimes of this nature were "prosecuted," it was almost solely at the discretion of the agent. When Duncan disagreed with the way Indian justice was being administered by Indians, he simply took over. For instance, he reported in 1925: "The Indian court on the Lower Brule reservation was abolished during the year, and all cases of a trial nature are handled by the farmer in charge in conjunction with the Indian police."[2] The agent added that more serious cases were brought to him for adjudication. In a few cases he reported further to federal or South Dakota state authorities "when warranted." In his 1926 report, Duncan indicates he had modified the system so that Lower Brule justice was now administered by two Indian police and "some other qualified Indians to judge misdemeanors." Duncan does not indicate how these Indians were selected, but he must have appointed the two police and likely the others.

The law violations that primarily concerned Duncan were the illicit liquor traffic and the use of drugs. He believed peyote was being taken at Lower Brule in 1925, although in later years he explicitly notes they never used it.[3] However, there was an extensive liquor traffic, and Duncan attempted numerous methods to suppress it. When he could get federal officers to arrest a white offender, he believed there was a chance of conviction in federal courts, but he judged that a state arrest and conviction of a white man for victimizing Indians were virtually hopeless. White juries and probably the court officers of the state were not ready to consider Indians the equal of other citizens.

Nor was the Bureau ready to allow Indians the kind of

community self-government that other American communities enjoyed. Even today Indian communities are deprived of self-government although the deprivation today arises from a complex legal structure to be discussed later. In the 1920s the lack of self-government was simply the result of a firm conviction in the Bureau of Indian Affairs that Indians were incapable of managing their own affairs. Thus a white farmer was often deemed to be a more capable judge than any Indian. Duncan's observations on the business committee at Lower Brule are a clear documentation of the bureau attitude. He failed to mention the committee in his 1925 report while holding out hope that "younger and more progressive Indians" were about to "take over" the Fair Association, one of the few organizations that allowed even an expression of Indian opinion. In 1926 he dismissed the organization with one line: "There is one business committee at Lower Brule sub-agency but this committee does not often agree amongst its members."[4] The next year he further demonstrated his contempt for the members: "I appointed the president of the committee to the position of Police Private." He had even less use for the "so-called business committee" at Crow Creek which was "more of a hindrance than help."[5] This view of a supposedly self-governing body continued under the next agent, E. J. Peacore, who saw the two business committees in much the same light:

> A year ago there was a business committee at the Lower Brule subagency that was suppose to represent the Lower Brule Indians. Since I have been here I have heard very little from this committee, and believe it of very minor importance.[6]

Somehow these governing bodies struggled on although they were not allowed to make any significant decisions or supply more than a minimum of consultation to the agent. When E. B. Wright succeeded Peacore, he described the groups as "self-elected," implying he did not have to pay them much attention. In his opinion they remained "more of a detriment to the Indian than a help."[7] Despite such discouragement, the business associations may have provided the basis for the tribal councils several years later when the Indians were encouraged to be self-governing.

Since there was no self-government of any kind before 1930, the Lower Brule lacked any control over the education of their children. Their rights as citizens to participate in the school system were completely ignored. Once the bureau-sponsored boarding school was closed in 1921, Indian children were integrated into nine public day-schools that had been established by whites at several points on the reservation. Enrollment, however, was at the discretion of the agents, who sometimes barred children they found "objectionable." During the boarding school era, the Indian police had acted as truant officers frequently dragging children to school by force. Then when Indian families were more receptive to education, they found that public schools would not readily accept their children. Because the government paid the tuition for the Indian children, local school boards could not complain about the Indian as a non-taxpayer, but board members and county officials saw no reason to include Indians on their boards. This exclusion of Indians from control over education went unrecognized for years. Lewis Meriam and his associates recommended wide-ranging changes in Indian education, including adult education, but even this report in 1928 failed to recommend Indian participation in the control of the system.[8]

The token control the Indians were given during the 1920s in any kind of management consisted of forming a fair board. The board was responsible only for organizing an annual fair where agricultural produce was displayed, yet even here the agent frequently directed or revised Indian decisions. Agent Duncan took special interest in the annual fairs and noted that he had backed younger and more progressive Indians in controlling and managing the event. He predicted this change he directed would help "do away with the old time fair where Indian dances predominated."[9] In conjunction with fair activities, the agents encouraged 4-H Clubs among the youth and even a Federated Women's Club among the mothers. These imitations at being white generally had little effect. If anything the efforts provoked some biting sarcasm from the Indians' white neighbors that likely encouraged retention of Indian culture in the long run. For instance, the Chamberlain paper commented in September, 1924:

> The Lower Brule Indians held their annual 3 day fair and grand oratorical conclave at Lower Brule agency this week. Many came from surrounding tribes to help devour the roast ox, dance to the ravishing strains of the tom-tom and do their part toward making the show a howling success.
>
> The exhibits in quantity and quality surpassed those of previous years, demonstrating conclusively that "Lo the poor Indian" if given half a chance will become as sangfroid and sophisticated allee samee white man.[10]

The extent to which this white prejudice effected the preservation of Indian ways cannot be determined fully, but the Lower Brule did persist with their dancing in face of stern opposition from a series of agents. The view that citizenship should allow the Lower Brule religious freedom certainly had not penetrated to the agency level. Throughout the 1920s agents carefully watched the dances and tried to limit participation to Indians over fifty years old. They were concerned especially with young people returning from boarding school who showed any interest in dancing. Regulations continued that required a listing of participants, a termination before nightfall, and a limitation to dancing on "rationday." A major prohibition blocked the give-away, a practice at the heart of Dakota social life. Ironically, while the government was making these attempts to regulate Indian morality, it experienced the major political scandals of the Harding administration.

In the next administration the Indians experienced some relief from government supervision of their morals. Probably

Calvin Coolidge's relationship with Indians is best known from a famous photograph of him wearing a Sioux war bonnet. The newspapers of the day enjoyed suggesting Indian names for him, such as "Runs Deep." However, the event is of importance because it reflects at least some potential political power for Indians. South Dakota Senator Peter Norbeck, who was responsible for the war-bonnet presentation, made the following assessment:

The Indians of South Dakota are an important factor politically. There are 20,000 Indians of whom 7,000 vote. They hold the balance of power between the political parties.[11]

Norbeck, whose adopted name was "Charging Hawk," saw a potential that was never much utilized, but it was enough to make Congressmen pay a little attention to Indians. Gradually Indians learned that an unresponsive bureaucrat in the BIA responded quickly enough to a senator or representative. Clumsy as this political tie was, it was more than Indians possessed as business council or fair board members. Another political avenue the Dakota discovered was through the courts. The government's claim to the Black Hills is based on vague and ambiguous treaties and acts of Congress. As early as the 1920s the Dakota sued for $800 million to begin a suit which is still pending.[12] Today young Indian militants encamp on Mount Rushmore to remind a nation that this lawsuit never has been settled satisfactorily.

Although the Lower Brule were participating only marginally in these developments, they were gradually learning the art of politics. Denied any form of local self-control, they were beginning to acquire indirect controls over the bureaucracy above them. They also were discovering a political channel that generally respected their rights and gave them some legal recourse to the government that took their land. In short, they were learning to maneuver politically in the larger society even if they had little room. Given a more sympathetic chance in the next decade, they were able to prove they had benefited from their lessons.

However, the political experience of the 1920s was far outweighed by economic trends. In this decade the Dakota found themselves in even greater poverty than during the early years of reservation life. The cattle market had not yet recovered from the immediate post-war depression. Hot, dry summers occurred regularly with notable drought in 1925 and 1926. Wheat and oats often had to be cut and used as hay. When grazing deteriorated, the Indian ponies competed with cattle. None of the agents following Gensler ever had his enthusiasm for agriculture; their estimates for both farming and ranching at Lower Brule are consistently pessimistic. Even H. E. Wright's enthusiasm as a new agent was guarded:

The outlook for the Indian in future stock raising would be very good if he would become interested and take care of his stock. Many of the Indians will not take care of their stock. This class of Indians' sole ambition appears to be to kill their cattle for feasts and for present living, leaving the future to take care of itself.[13]

A year later the agent was openly discouraged about the prospects for agriculture. His attempt at humor is the only unusual aspect of his evaluation of farming in the early twentieth century:

During the year the grasshoppers were very numerous and did considerable damage. Potato bugs ate up the potato vines. Poisoned bran was used to kill the hoppers and all kinds of poisons were used to eradicate the insects on the potato vines. The potato bugs ate the poisons and appeared to relish on it.[14]

Generally the agents sought wage work for the Indians rather than encourage self-employment in agriculture. Even in this situation the Lower Brule frequently frustrated the bureaucrats. W. E. Duncan claimed employment opportunities were

A Lower Brule farm before and after heat and grasshoppers, about 1930. Photos from the Federal Records Center, Kansas City.

available near the reservation, but "The Indians on the reservation do not need any assistance in finding work. As a rule they do not want any regular employment."[15] Other agents were more optimistic about economic improvement through outside labor, but they noted that odd jobs or occasional work such as haying or fencing seemed preferred to steady employment.

Given the lack of any available earned income, agents had to view the sale of capital as necessary. Most of this capital was land, of course, but some other property was also sold. Again the various agents were remarkably consistent in their evaluation of land sales. They noted that the land sales were necessary because of poverty, but they reported such sales were regularly followed by the purchase of automobiles. Duncan wrote that "Probably ninety percent of the land patented is sold and probably half the proceeds squandered."[16] Wright confirmed this pattern several years later: "Of all the patents in fee issued to Indians of this jurisdiction prior to June 30, 1930, only five retained the land covered by patents so issued."[17]

By 1931 the Lower Brule approached rock bottom; even the market for land had come to a standstill because of hard times throughout the Plains. Thirty-six state banks closed in South Dakota in 1923 alone. Rural credit was hit especially hard because of a scandal in the state organization established to aid farmers.[18] With whites in such straits, Indians had even less chance. A Lower Brule holding of 160 acres was estimated to be worth less than $800. Monies reserved for per-capita payments to be used in time of need amounted to only twenty dollars apiece. A few cattle, milk cows, and pieces of farm equipment would have added virtually nothing to these meager assets.

Obviously the times were ripe for a major change in government policy toward Indians. The total Indian population had reached its lowest decline in 1920, and its growth in 1930 was hardly noticeable. The initial impetus for change arose out of a nationwide survey of Indian affairs by the Institute for Government Research. Lewis Meriam headed the staff which compiled a thorough study of Indians and the Bureau of Indian Affairs. The final report relied on an objective, well-documented approach that avoided rhetoric and emotion.[19] It showed without doubt Indians were the most deprived people in the country, and their plight desperately needed attention. Meriam strongly recommended new methods in education and foresaw economic improvement largely through improved schools. The emphasis upon education had been a major part of bureau policy after citizenship; Meriam called for improvements in the basic approach. The report was of more consequence, however, in its detail of Indian economics. For instance, Lower Brule was not surveyed by the Meriam staff, but the neighboring reservations of Pine Ridge, Yankton, and Rosebud were. The respective per capita annual incomes for these Indians were $86, $151, and $197. On the more than sixty reservations surveyed, 84 percent of Indians were shown to have less than a $200 annual income.[20] Figures on earned income, which excluded land sales, showed a per capita annual income of $22 for Pine Ridge, $77 for Yankton, and $44 for Rosebud. The dry statistical tables that presented these data became the ammunition for a major reform in Indian administration.[21]

Under President Herbert Hoover, the BIA attempted to instill a spirit of cooperation among the Indians. A new emphasis on day-schools began although Lower Brule was to remain without them. The Crow Creek superintendency generally changed only a modicum; agents no longer condemned Indian dances, and the general economy was blamed for Indian poverty almost as much as Indian lack of initiative. Finally, a marked change in Indian policy appeared in 1934 with the passage of the Indian Reorganization Act.

The Indian Reorganization Act had such far-ranging consequences for Indian policy in general as well as the Lower Brule that its philosophy and provisions are worthy of detailed examination. At a general level, the policy was a change from assimilation to cultural pluralism. The architect of this policy was John Collier, who had at one time headed the Indian Defense Association. Collier was beyond doubt the most colorful and controversial figure ever to head the BIA. His critics called him everything from visionary to communist; he was accused on the one hand of going too fast and on the other of attempting to preserve the Indian cultures as museum pieces. His liveliness and devotion to Indians cannot be denied, but certainly there is also a case to be made that the times helped to make the man:

> Hopelessly tangled in obsolete laws, nearly landless, poverty stricken, uneducated, prey to white interests everywhere, unable to defend themselves, and finally saddled with an administrative policy which regarded them as a dying people, more in need of race euthanasia than anything else, the Indians could hardly have been worse off. As far back as 1862 Abraham Lincoln said, "If we get through this war, and I live, this Indian system shall be reformed." But it is only now [under Collier] that this is really taking place.[22]

A unique feature of the new policy was that its provisions would apply to a tribe only after the tribe voted favorably to accept them. Doubtless local agents pressured their Indians to accept, but many tribes did not. The Lower Brule were among the first to vote its approval. The Chamberlain paper reported they were the second tribe in the nation to go under the provisions of the Indian Reorganization Act and had done so by a vote of two to one.[23] Other than these details the local newspapers showed little interest. The story was taken from a Washington source and received no additional local coverage.

The major thrust of the policy intended to give Indians the same rights to self-government that other American communities possessed. The powers of the local agent were ended; popularly elected tribal councils were to be the governing bodies. At Lower Brule the reservation was divided into half a dozen districts, and representatives were elected from each one. The initial councils must have been enthusiastic because a tribal constitution was accepted by the people and approved by the secretary of the interior as early as 1935. A Charter of Incorporation was added in July, 1936. The constitution served to define the means for self-government; the charter allowed the tribe to function as a business group.

A second major part of the new policy was directed at land and resource preservation. Allotment was ended. An individual Indian could sell his land only to the tribe or to another Indian. Ceded land that was still retained by the government was returned to the tribe. Further, a $10 million revolving loan fund was established that allowed the tribes to purchase land from whites. Marginal or badly eroded lands within the reservation were purchased as a conservation measure by the government and became, in effect, part of the tribal domain. For the first time in United States history, the trend of Indian land loss was halted; indeed it was even briefly reversed. On the Plains especially, a number of whites were eager to sell, and no other buyer was available. At Lower Brule 27,000 acres were added to tribal use between 1934 and 1937.[24] The land that became tribal estate went into trust status similar to that of initially allotted land. This status exempted the land from state taxation and protected it from loss through tax sales.

Final judgment of the Indian Reorganization Act is yet to be made. The number of tribes opting for organization under the act grew steadily, but Indian affairs stagnated during World War II. The post-war years brought another fundamental change in policy. It was obvious that the reorganization legislation was deficient in empowering Indians with self-government. Well-meaning constitutions were negated in effect by a simple clause that any decision with regard to trust property was "subject to approval by the Secretary of the Interior." Since almost all income for a tribe was derived from trust land or the resources from that land, decisions that involved this money were subject to the bureau acting for the Interior Department. For example, if a tribe purchased cattle, this property was in a trust status. It was marked with an I.D. or Indian Department brand, and was exempt from taxation. Most likely it would be grazed on some tribal land. Collier meant for the Indians to manage fully such a herd; initially tribal councils did make significant decisions. But if they mismanaged the herd, the responsibility for such mismanagement lay with the secretary of the interior. Given such circumstances, bureau officials could hardly do otherwise than circumvent Indian decisions with which they disagreed. Today Indian tribal councils continue to make many decisions, but they do so knowing their decisions will be acted upon only when they are in accord with the BIA. Thus tribal councils are generally ineffective bodies regarded with apathy by the Indians. In a few cases the governing bodies became even worse. A prominent Rosebud Sioux has described the policy in these terms:

> *The plan looked splendid on paper, and had the best of intentions behind it. But, in practice it was doomed from the beginning. The Indians were given a charade to play. No act of the tribal government, except the taxing of its own people, could be performed without the express approval of the BIA. Far worse than offering the Indian people a system of self-government that was composed merely of shadows, it offered them a system in which the Indians who became leaders, because they lacked real political power, found importance and profit by playing upon the greed, ambition, and desire for influence that existed within and without the reservation. Instead of a tribal government, many tribes discovered to their dismay that they had a tribal gang as their representative.*[25]

However, in the mid-1930s these political problems were of less importance than economic ones. Droughts, severe dust storms, and the Depression had struck the state. Throughout South Dakota, real estate values dropped 50 percent between 1920 and 1930. In the next five years they dropped another 50 percent. While production of crops and cattle remained almost stable, net farm income fell from $1000 in 1929 to $300 in 1932. The drastic drop in prices led to 34,000 farm foreclosures by 1932. As drought years followed, the population on relief rolls swelled to 40 percent; in one county near Lower Brule more than 80 percent of the white farmers were on relief.[26]

At Lower Brule the first agent acting under the provisions of the Indian Reorganization Act dwelt almost solely on economics in his initial annual report. He felt that "desolation seemed everywhere," and economic problems alone were nearly overwhelming:

To write of industrial development during the year 1934 one must be possessed of an imagination, both flexible and inaccurate, for such development did not exist.[27]

The one bright spot in the Indian economy was the establishment of the Indian Emergency Conservation Work as one phase of New Deal legislation. It afforded employment in a variety of jobs from building dams to planting trees, and the chance to conserve at least part of the water supply. Agent Hyde also had available "road funds" that allowed further employment while the Works Projects Administration hired still more Indians on the reservation. Hyde claimed that many Lower Brule worked "who had never worked before"; in his opinion this opportunity for wage work improved reservation morale greatly. Further, the income from wage work was supplemented with an issue of 1200 cattle for immediate consumption acquired under the crop reduction program of the Federal Emergency Relief Administration.

The work relief program at least held off immediate disaster while Hyde became familiar with local conditions. In his second year he came to realize the effects of land sales since allotment. On maps indicating white and Indian ownership, the Indians appeared to retain more than half the reservation, but Hyde learned that whites had purchased only the better land. In his opinion, four-fifths of the value of the reservation lands was actually in white hands.

One result of this pattern was that Indians generally had left their original allotments except in those few cases where timber and water were available. In the process of resettlement some Indians moved into the town of Iron Nation, but most of the Lower Brule settled at the agency in a large tent camp. This trend spelled the end of allotment as a means toward breaking the tribal spirit and replacing it with rugged individualism. Growing dissension might become a feature of community life, but beyond doubt the Lower Brule remained a community rather than a collection of individuals.

Planners within the bureau were now interested in stimulating community spirit; indeed they fretted over the Indians who sought the individualistic life of neighboring white farmers and ranchers. In a survey of potential communities for development at Lower Brule, the planners provide one of the earliest accurate descriptions of population distribution. Their motivations for the study were clearly stated:

> *On matters of common tribal interest, where a clearcut public opinion must develop, in order to make satisfactory decisions, the problem becomes most acute. It is much less a problem, however, where community groupings of the population which follow kinship or identity of culture can be organized into economic units for their separate advancement.*[28]

The population of the seven groupings was:

Area	No. of Families	No. of Individuals
Fort George	15	85
Cedar Creek	1	4
Medicine Creek	7	28
Iron Nation	9	41
Little Bend	4	25
Lower Brule, sub-agency	55	227
Fort Hale	5	33
Total	96	443

Fort George was farthest from the sub-agency both in distance and social attachment. It had good open range with wood and water. The population strongly resisted movement to the agency, and its members were more oriented toward Pierre. According to the planners, the community was divided into mixed-blood and full-blood factions who likely would not work together, but the factions were judged to be highly cooperative among themselves and interested in a cattle program. Cedar Creek was another natural range unit with water available. Although twelve families considered it their home, they had moved to the agency temporarily. These Indians were described as a highly cooperative full-blood community. Medicine Creek was a third natural range unit. Half the usual number of families there had moved to the sub-agency. Whether they would return was doubtful because Medicine Creek was badly checkered with white ranchers, and development would be difficult. Iron Nation was just north of Medicine Creek in the Missouri Valley. Indians had dry-farmed the area; irrigation here was feasible. Nine closely related families, headed by mixed-blood Susie Johnson, formed the basis for community life. Only four families lived in Little Bend in scattered settlement. No community existed yet, but the white-owned land in the area was readily being purchased since no whites remained. The bureau considered the area ideal for irrigation, grazing, and general economic rehabilitation. The survey staff agreed. Good grazing range and bottom farm lands also were found at Fort Hale. Seventeen families there had been reduced to five; they were reported as mixed-blood and accustomed to cooperation. A 2600-acre ranch that had recently been purchased from a white man was recommended for use as headquarters of the Brule Cooperative Livestock Association. A tribal herd was slow to develop; in 1935 Indian cattle were reduced to 250, and in the next spring the tribal herd was further reduced to eighty because of range conditions.

These six communities formed an arc around the old agency headquarters which had come to be known as the town of Lower Brule. The town rested on a flat plain only eight miles from Crow Creek Agency when ice on the river was solid or a ferry was running. Otherwise the commuting distance was sixty miles via Chamberlain. All agency activities were funneled through Lower Brule, so it became the central point of reservation activity. Besides the sub-agency office there were the government day-school, Catholic and Episcopal churches, two traders, a community center, jail, machine shop, and power plant. A row of two-story, clapboard homes called rehabilitation houses was built north of the square in 1936 and 1937. Planners estimated that only a dozen families had resided at the sub-agency before 1934, but since then the new homes and a tent colony had attracted more than forty families. Intensive land purchase for Indian use was made around the agency; an irrigated tract of fourteen acres was producing garden vegetables; a projected cannery was to provide employment through use of the truck garden. However, as early as 1938 the planners were skeptical that irrigated farming would do much to change the Lower Brule economy.

In fact, the planners were generally pessimistic although they did not hesitate to offer their scheme for economic development. Their analysis clearly indicates the dire straits of the Lower Brule; average family income in 1937 was just over $650, half of it from relief sources. Another critical aspect of income was that two-thirds of it was derived from government sources.

This latter factor particularly upset the economists. The severe part of the depression for the Lower Brule was in the 1920s. The emergency relief programs of the Roosevelt administration in the 1930s had not only raised their income markedly, but with the addition of aid from the BIA under Collier and special Indian benefits, Lower Brule average income was actually above that for neighboring whites. It was the first and last time that such a difference occurred. Although it did not last long, many Indians became strong supporters of Roosevelt and the Indian Reorganization Act. Indeed, since much of the IRA was identified with the New Deal, its supporters became known as New Dealers. Mixed-bloods consistently took advantage of relief work and IRA provisions while some full-bloods opposed a few of the innovations, such as representative government through an elected tribal council. Occasionally the full-bloods became identified as Old Dealers because of their opposition. It is likely that on some issues at least, the full-blood opposition was directed at the mixed-bloods rather than the merits of the issue. Unfortunately the evidence for this factionalism is scant. At any rate, World War II brought an end to almost all innovations and changed the economy far more than the Indian bureau technicians ever dreamed.

Estimated household income and its sources for fiscal year 1936-37.[29]

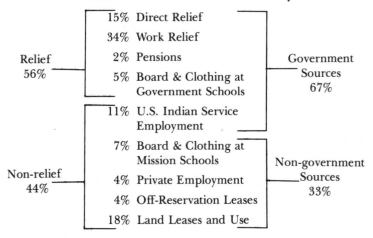

Relief 56%	15% Direct Relief	Government Sources 67%
	34% Work Relief	
	2% Pensions	
	5% Board & Clothing at Government Schools	
	11% U.S. Indian Service Employment	
Non-relief 44%	7% Board & Clothing at Mission Schools	Non-government Sources 33%
	4% Private Employment	
	4% Off-Reservation Leases	
	18% Land Leases and Use	

Large-scale migration to war plants and military service in the armed forces dramatically changed Lower Brule after 1940 although significant patterns of migration had already developed in the preceding decade. As the Indians had grown to depend upon relief work, they were drawn to the agency center. For a while the town of Lower Brule was in danger of losing its community character as the former agency headquarters became simply a collection of groups. One tent camp on church land lacked sanitation and protection from the weather. None of the encampments offered more than rudimentary conditions. Influenza struck hard in the 1937 winter. Only a few dances provided any social life, and morale suffered. The then agent Hyde had insisted that half of all summer wages be set aside for winter so some cash was usually available throughout the year. His direction in this respect was much like that of former agents and was hardly conducive to the tribal council's managing its own affairs. Still the decision carried families through the year.

However, more and more Lower Brule were leaving the reservation. A few went to other reservations, but a large number were moving to white towns and cities. Even though the actual migration was fairly substantial, the total population remained more or less constant. The constancy of the total population figures was a result of Indians from other reservations moving to Lower Brule; even more significant, it was maintained by a high birth rate combined with a declining death rate. This same pattern continues today.[30] The absence of a large number of enrolled Lower Brule complicated land ownership. The bureau planned to consolidate Indian-owned land as an accommodation for the proposed cattle ranges. Because it could not establish title with an absent Indian, securing heirship land was particularly difficult because all heirs had to consent even when selling to the tribe. Residents on the reservation, who were enrolled elsewhere needed land if they were to support themselves. Actually they held no legal rights at Lower Brule Reservation, but social and kinship ties obligated the Lower Brule Indians to provide for them. Of the 446 persons on the reservation in 1937, 66 were Indians from other reservations and four were whites married to Indians. Of the 609 Indians enrolled in the Lower Brule Tribe only 376 resided on the reservation.

The bureau also believed that the proportion of "Indian blood" is "always a most important factor in considering any plans for an Indian population."[31] The planners were not so naive as to believe that "blood" or genetics might actually determine behavior; instead they recognized that factional splits over the retention of Indian ways or the acceptance of white customs follow full-blood and mixed-blood lines and are a major basis of social organization. Evidence suggests that the individual's outlook is markedly influenced by his parents; unless one of them is white, basic aspects of the dominant culture seldom are inculcated.[32] Thus "degree of Indian blood" is a useful index of attitudes toward accepting or rejecting innovations from the dominant culture. The index is often unreliable, but its use is justified when other data are unavailable; unfortunately such is the case much of the time.

At Lower Brule in 1937 the population was classified as 40 percent full-blood and 60 percent mixed-blood, but only 20 percent of the population was less than one-half Indian. The bureau recognized that this distribution was especially difficult to interpret.[33] The mixed-blood population might be seen as outnumbering the full-bloods 60 percent to 40 percent. On the other hand, the "conservatives" might be expected to be comprised of those individuals with half or more Indian blood in which case 80 percent of the population would resist innovation.

The bureau was too optimistic, however, to dwell long on resistance to its programs. It believed that the large-scale conservation programs it had initiated would soon have the range land in optimum condition for Indian ranching. Its planners called for replacement of white-owned with Indian-owned cattle. Land consolidation might never restore the entire reservation to the Indians, but it could make available some large range lands. An economy built around cattle, with some dry farming and a little irrigation, was the proposed future for the Lower Brule in 1938.

The record does not show what the Indians thought of the plans. Certainly their economic life improved very much under the Indian Reorganization Act, and they encountered an entirely new attitude from bureau officials. No doubt many minor bureaucrats continued a paternalistic outlook while local whites retained their prejudices, but at least visiting dignitaries treated

Indians more or less as equals and believed their participation in decision-making was a necessity. Some improvement in Indian morale is apparent in one of the few Indian documents available from the time:

> For the past 18 or 20 years the Lower Brule Tribe has been ditched but now for the last three years our government try to get us out of the ditch. The Lower Brule Tribe were neglected for about 18 years, but about two years ago Mr. Collier came to us and see the condition we was in and sympathy with us and he promise us that he is going to get us out this ditch we are in. Now I say he got us out this ditch.
>
> We have in operation a good school. The children are getting noon dinners . . . . They are teaching manual training. They are adding a washroom and toilet on the schoolhouse. And we expect to have a better school than any on the reservation . . . . And we have a good community hall with a place to can, electric lights and hot air heater. And we have 17 new houses with basements and toilets.
>
> Now some of our young people are getting out on farms which is bought with Reorganization funds to stock up by live-stock. We got enough surplus land now that we can run 5,000 head of cattle . . . .
>
> And Superintendent Mr. Hyde and his assistants [Scott, Mountjoy and Reifel] all cooperate with us. And the stock association is going full swing. We got a herd of over 600 head. We have Indian directors for our association. Mr. Jim Byrnes, Mr. Alex Rencountre and Mr. Moses DeSmit . . . . We get a lot of function from this New Deal and we appreciate very much.
>
> The history of Lower Brule Tribe is a clean one. Our great chief, Iron Nation, was popular because he wasn't a warrior or a great medicine man or a Ghost Dancer. He was a chief and a peace maker. He got his people engage in peace and in farming and stock raising. The Iron Nation Tribe of Lower Brule was going to get 50 head of mares from the government and also 100 blankets but he gave this to other tribes to quiet their warriors so Iron Nation is a great peace maker . . . .[34]

The Lower Brule still maintain that Iron Nation was their outstanding leader and have named a tribal corporation for establishing industry after him. They also still believe the government owes them for the horses, but jokes about their "pony claims" carry a bitter overtone which suggests they never expect settlement.

Generally the American Indians favored IRA. Eventually more than three-quarters of the tribes accepted it, and not one ever voted to revoke the provisions. The policy found less success with whites. Congress was always reluctant to fund the revolving loan fund; western representatives were usually quick to point out any shortcomings doubtless out of concern for land reverting to Indian title. The *New York Times* showed some sympathy with Collier's hopes for Indians but only in a limited way. Early in the program the editorial page took note of a finding by anthropologist Clark Wissler that Indians now had one of the country's highest birth rates.[35] The editorial comment was:

> *The erstwhile vanishing Indian now has a birth rate that is probably the highest in the world [3 times the urban White rate]. The aboriginal inhabitants of the country seem to have found life on the reservations more healthful than when they ranged this broad continent.*[36]

The *Times* interpretation is worthy of note because it preceded the views of anthropologists, who at the time were developing the concept of acculturation and applying it to Indians. Still, it is unlikely the *Times* recognized that Indian cultures might continue indefinitely. Three years later Collier noted the high birthrate and added that many Indians were developing "surprising capacities as business men."[37] The next day the *Times* commented that Collier was late with his news of a high birthrate; they had reported Wissler's findings before. More importantly, they raised the question of how Indian cultures were to persist if the Indians were adopting white ways:

One might argue that the Indian is, after all, vanishing when Collier stresses his "surprising capacities" as a business man. A cooperative Indian dairy farmer is not quite the Indian of tradition.[38]

The experiment in cultural pluralism moved toward its end with the outbreak of war. Thus the Lower Brule, the second tribe in the nation to accept IRA, operated less than five years under the policy so far as it was actively backed by the government. After 1942 the Bureau of Indian Affairs held so low a priority that its offices were vacated in Washington for war-time organizations. It took up residence in Chicago for the duration; many of its personnel were transferred elsewhere. For instance, a number of the staff for the War Relocation Authority who administered the Japanese relocation camps were former Bureau of Indian Affairs hands; even anthropologists studying Indian education were involved in the transfer.

At Lower Brule in 1942 the Indians once more were urged to grow all the food possible, and a tribal herd that started at Fort Hale in the 1930s prospered in the 1940s. This herd provided jobs and experience as well as cattle for market. High beef prices encouraged individuals to develop their own herds. Many other Lower Brule joined the armed services; still other families left the reservation for wartime employment, working in munitions plants in Nebraska. The war gave the Indian ranchers an opportunity to engage in the white economy more extensively than ever before. Indians found themselves received more favorably by industry off the reservation as well, but it was the men in the armed services who encountered the unique situation of being accepted as the equals of whites. They learned new skills in the army and traveled worldwide; more significantly, they formed close associations with whites and learned intimately much of the dominant culture. Intermarriages increased greatly during and immediately after the war. In short, the war provided an occasion for large-scale acculturation under conditions more favorable than any government planners had ever conceived. Yet at the end of the war, large numbers of Lower Brule veterans and workers returned to the reservation. The ranching economy dropped off sharply, and the tribal cattle enterprise ended in 1953. Half a dozen small operators continued on their own and managed at a slightly better than subsistence level. However, they provided only a minimum of part-time jobs for a few other Indians.

Another major development during the war years that was to affect the reservation involved the Army Corps of Engineers and the Bureau of Reclamation. Serious floods in 1942 and 1943 sparked plans to control the Missouri River with a number of dams. The Corps of Engineers recommended massive earth dams on the Missouri while the Bureau of Reclamation favored reservoirs in the tributaries. Compromise between the two agencies resulted in the Pick-Sloan Plan which was authorized in 1944. The first dam, at Fort Randall, required purchase of a large part of the Yankton Reservation; the resulting reservoir was to flood 8000 acres of the Lower Brule Reservation. At Crow Creek even more land was inundated. Up river, the Oahe Dam reservoir flooded much of the Cheyenne River Reservation and parts of Standing Rock. An earlier dam in North Dakota at Fort Garrison had cost the Mandan and Hidatsa a part of their reservation; Sioux and Assiniboine at Fort Peck in Montana had given up land as well. Control of the Missouri River under the Pick-Sloan plan was possible only through condemnation of valuable reservation land. The money the Indians received as compensation was always planned as investment capital, but the economic schemes that followed never improved life very much.

The Lower Brule hoped to change this pattern. They faced construction of the final dam, Big Bend, just a few miles below the agency. The resulting reservoir, Lake Sharpe, would extend eighty miles to Pierre. The lake would completely cover the old agency grounds and almost all the town of Lower Brule. The low-lying river terraces that had been so good for hay and dry farming would be lost as well as the timber areas which sheltered cattle in the winter. Prior to construction of Big Bend

The Big Bend Dam, which flooded the former town of Lower Brule. (1970)

Dam, tribal council members hoped to have the Lower Brule economy stable enough to take advantage of the changes brought by building and the potential for tourism. They had reasonable hopes of securing a settlement of nearly $800,000 for the 8000 acres lost to the Fort Randall reservoir. With these funds they planned to initiate a number of individually-owned cattle herds. One major problem the council faced was that many tribal members demanded the settlement simply be divided among all members as a per capita payment. However, per capita settlements among other tribes had often resulted in little or no economic change so Congress, which had to appropriate funds for settlement, opposed such payments. Furthermore, since half of the Lower Brule enrolled members were off the reservation, per capita payments would divert half the money outside the reservation. Plans which called for investment in the reservation economy could keep all the money at Lower Brule. Obviously such a situation was full of political potential. The final Act of Indemnity involved intricate compromise.[39]

In the meantime, an even more explosive issue was crystallizing on the national level in the postwar years. Like everyone else, the Indians had welcomed the end of the war. The Pine Ridge Dakota made news by declaring themselves at peace with Japan:

> *In recognition of the end of hostilities, the Western Sioux sent a peace pipe to President Truman as a "tribute to the greatness of our President as a leader in war and peace." The pipe was once used by Chief Crazy Horse.*
> *The Sioux have been celebrating the end of the war with dancing and feasting since Wednesday [the 12th].[40]*

President Truman reciprocated by appointing Dillon Myer as Commissioner of Indian Affairs in 1950. Myer had had the unique experience of heading the only United States government bureau ever to have gone out of existence, the War Relocation Authority. Therefore, he was thought qualified to accomplish the termination of the Bureau of Indian Affairs. Under the Democrats, this policy of BIA termination remained only a vague idea; it got its real impetus from Republicans, when President Eisenhower appointed Glenn Emmons to head the bureau. Support from Congress for such policy was derived from House Concurrent Resolution 108 and Public Law 280. The former declared that official policy was to make Indians "subject to the same laws and entitled to the same privileges and responsibilities as are applicable to other citizens." The resolution further abolished a few local offices of the BIA. Public Law 280 authorized the states, at their discretion, to assume jurisdiction over Indian tribes; at any time they could substitute their laws for tribal law codes and their enforcement machinery for that of the Indian police.

The new town of Lower Brule, relocated during the construction of the Big Bend Dam. (1970)

A house moved from the former town. A number of full bloods refused to reside in the new town and had their homes moved to the bluffs overlooking Lower Brule. (1970)

The general policy, never fully systematized as the Indian Reorganization Act was, came to be known as termination. Its sponsors talked about it as if it would terminate the Bureau of Indian Affairs, but their actions suggested the first goal was to terminate Indians. In terms of economic programs, for instance, Emmons promised industrial developments for the reservation coupled with a relocation program designed to spur out-migration.[41] Most Indians soon experienced government pressure to relocate while they saw little or no industrial development. Emmons, from New Mexico, was accused of favoring the Southwestern Indians, especially the Navajo, with reservation development. At a national level of Indian organization, the customary factionalism between Southwestern and Plains Indians was increased, but even so the opposition to termination produced an unusual unanimity among Indians. The National Congress of American Indians, with all Indian officers and financed largely by the tribes, became an important lobbying group to halt further termination legislation. It had the cooperation of the Association on American Indian Affairs, the heir of the various eastern friends groups.[42] The policy was so controversial that a wide number of individuals became engaged in debate over it. Ralph Nader, just beginning as a crusader, reviewed the federal law that governed land transactions,[43] while one especially vitriolic article exposed greatly increased land sales under Emmons.[44] At no time since allotment had Indians felt so threatened by a governmental policy.

In an initial stage, termination called for ending government relations with five tribes, three of them small, little known, and powerless such as the Coushatta in Texas. But the two others, Klamath and Menominee, had valuable timber resources and some political know-how. They and their allies were soon able to picture termination as just another land grab by whites. When the market for lumber coincidentally became depressed, they were temporarily joined by unexpected allies in the lumber industry. Even so the tribes were eventually terminated. As predicted, tribal land and timber ownership erod-ed to whites, and nationwide Indian opposition to the policy mounted.

Therefore it was a major surprise when the Lower Brule requested to be terminated. They were the first, and the only, tribe ever to initiate a program calling for termination.[45] As a result, the Institute of Indian Studies at the State University of South Dakota sponsored a research program to investigate this unique request of the Lower Brule.

The Iron Nation Corporation has attracted various small indus-tries. The tribe invests in attracting businesses that will create jobs on the reservation. (1970)

It is at this point that I entered the history of Lower Brule, because I was sent there to learn why they should make such a choice in the face of united opposition from other tribes. I had just finished course work for my Ph.D. in anthropology at the University of Chicago and was ready to begin field work. Like many anthropologists before me, I had plans to work at Pine

Ridge or Rosebud. I was not enthusiastic about the initial inquiry to work at Lower Brule because I assumed the Dakota there were nearly acculturated. Since little had been written on any of the Missouri River reservations, I assumed there was little to find. But a brief visit to the reservation in January 1958 suggested these Dakota were still very much Indian; they had simply been forgotten because of their more colorful cousins to the west. In March I returned and settled for six months at the old agency headquarters. There I concentrated on the present conditions and the future outlook for the Lower Brule which is the subject of the next chapter. It was almost ten years later that I began research into the historical background which has been the subject of the previous chapters. The historical perspective, and perhaps some maturing in more than a decade, have changed my evaluations as to why the Lower Brule will persist as a distinct entity, but then as now I was firmly convinced that the Lower Brule community would last through the foreseeable future as an Indian community.

chapter 7
Dakota –Today and Tomorrow

My initial visit to Lower Brule was sponsored by Wesley Hurt of the University of South Dakota. On that first day we called at the home of Joseph Thompson, then tribal chairman, discovered that he was at Pierre and headed there. On our way he passed us. We turned around, again went to his home, and eventually received tribal approval for me to return in a few months for a survey of the reservation. That night on our return to Vermillion we were caught in a snowstorm, and I began to have doubts about how I was to survive even the final part of a Dakota winter. I also wondered how I would adapt to a life where chance meetings might be more important than the fixed, planned scheduling I was familiar with at Chicago.

When I returned in March and rented a trailer at Chamberlain, the Bureau of Indian Affairs provided a handyman who helped me locate next to the home of the tribal policeman. From his house I was soon attached to water and electricity although I kept trying to convince the bureau employee I should be located somewhere else, farther away from the old bureau compound and especially the police. Later I found this unplanned location had the unforeseen advantage of people com-

211

ing to me instead of the police, and their complaints against others soon had me deeply involved in community life. Chance appeared to serve me better than well-laid plans would have.

Furthermore, I found the Dakota remarkably friendly. Once it was established that I was not there in some position of authority, they were exceedingly open. Gradually it dawned upon me that few whites were ever on the reservation who could act as equals to Indians. The schoolteachers were not subject to the community because they were bureau employees; indeed they exerted considerable authority in hiring the bus driver and cooks as well as in directing much of the children's lives. The white storekeeper and his wife, who was postmistress, were both domineering figures. Most Indians were in debt to him continually, and he reminded them of the debt in numerous subtle ways. His wife was thought to hold back checks mailed to Indians when they failed to pay; she also interpreted the meaning of government regulations pertaining to welfare, agriculture, and other government programs. The Catholic and Episcopal priests were both missionaries and thus responsible to mission boards rather than to their congregations. Although these two priests were not particularly authoritarian, priests traditionally had been, and certainly Indians regarded them as figures of authority. The few white neighbors of the Lower Brule generally had little contact with them; when they did interact with Indians, it was often to employ them. All these dozen or so whites seemed well-meaning toward Indians, and probably they had the best of intentions in their relationships. Nevertheless they consistently urged the adoption of white culture either implicitly or explicitly, inevitably suggesting that Indian ways must therefore be inferior. More important, they were all in positions of authority, cutting themselves off from the social life of the Indian community.[1]

The Lower Brule responded to this authority in a variety of ways. For instance, the storekeeper and his wife frequently urged Indians to adopt "white-man's time." At meetings of the Sioux Valley Improvement Association, a group modeled on white civic associations, they regularly exhorted Indians to arrive promptly for the next meeting. Indians responded by passing motions to begin on time and imploring that their fellow Indians show up promptly. To me these resolutions always seemed sincere, but I soon learned that next week's meeting would begin as late as the previous one had. I also learned that Indians simply reversed the white pattern of meeting and visiting. Instead of visiting informally after a meeting, they visited before; then they left promptly when the meeting adjourned. In other instances, resistance to white authority was more marked. An elderly member of the Episcopal Church ended a long defiance of the young priest and his viewpoint by donating land to a fundamentalist church which later splintered the Episcopal congregation. In other cases Indians simply turned away from whites and ignored them as much as possible. The white school principal, for instance, felt the Lower Brule were markedly "uncooperative," and he sympathized with me because I was totally dependent upon their cooperation. In turn he spent no time in the community beyond what his duties demanded. He and his wife seldom spent a weekend on the reservation and looked forward to their visits with white friends. Joking and ridicule were other forms of resistance to whites, and the Dakota sense of humor could be used in many different contexts. Of course, it could not be used against ignorant whites, but it was most effective against Dakota in the Bureau of Indian Affairs or other authoritarian positions. Once I had learned something of the community and was judged not so ignorant, I found it used against me when I went too far in trying to organize, i.e. exert authority, in some teen-age activity.

In retrospect this variety of response to authority strikes me as only one part of a significant pattern. In most areas of life, the Lower Brule, and probably the Dakota as a whole, have maintained an unusual flexibility. Indeed it is tempting to think that the ecological flexibility achieved earlier on the Plains in response to summer and winter extremes has carried over to present reservation conditions. The adaptable winter *tiyospaye* and summer camp have been transformed into a nuclear family that in most cases has fundamental ties to a widely extended kin network. Virtually anyone can be incorporated in a family because of the looseness of the network, and the developmental cycle of the family allows still further variation to accommodate a range of life styles. To whites this form of family is frequently interpreted as disorganized, and a high number of Dakota families fail to meet white measures of stability or desirability.

However, these measures of family life do not take into account several factors peculiar to the reservation. One, the Lower Brule experience a very high rate of out-migration. More than half of the legally enrolled population resides off the reservation. In this process of migration, the handicapped are much more likely to be left behind. A number of single-person families are a result, with the individuals eligible for welfare such as Aid to the Blind or the Aged. Two, Indian teen-agers have a high dropout rate especially from boarding school. The Lower Brule had only an elementary school, and most of their high school students had to attend boarding schools, such as the one at Flandreau, South Dakota. The unpopularity of boarding school combined with other reasons leads teen-agers to return to the community with little to do.[2] Young women often become pregnant and children are born out of wedlock. Many Lower Brule express sincere concern about such births, but among the young there is little stigma against them. Most important, no one defines the babies as unwanted. Although some of the infants do end up in orphanages or with adoption agencies, most children find a home with grandparents or in some other family. Even after a girl marries, her children may remain well attached to the other family for some time.

Such behavior is part of a developmental cycle for the Dakota family which contrasts sharply with the ideal of the white middle class. For many of the whites who attempt to direct Indian life, marriage should be a giant step toward responsibility which is then fully cemented by the birth of children. The twenty-one and twenty-two-year-old white parent is expected to

Lower Brule homes in Pierre, South Dakota. (1970)

be fully independent to prove his or her responsibility. In marked contrast, the birth of children may precede marriage for many Lower Brule, but even then responsibility as interpreted by whites is postponed.

Marriage itself is generally a settling down of a couple who have long gone together. It is marked primarily by their occupying the same residence, often with the parents of one or the other. Generally one of the priests then persuades the couple to undergo a marriage ceremony at the church, but weddings are one of the least important church rituals. The Lower Brule are well aware that marriage immediately involves them in the white man's law, and their lives will only be further entangled with a foreign bureaucracy. The informal marriages can be ended with much less difficulty while a registered marriage can end in expensive divorce or cause endless complications over land ownership. Legal marriages offer no particular advantages to the Indians.

The early period of informal marriage allows considerable freedom for both partners. Between the ages of twenty and thirty, men come and go considerably. They can work off the reservation for months at a time or visit other reservations where they may live temporarily with a woman. Young women also work off the reservation or live with men visiting their reservations. Experience with contraceptives seems to be reducing birthrates, but any children born during this time generally find homes somewhere near the parents.

Sometime after age thirty, both men and women appear to whites to become much more responsible. Drinking and fighting bouts are infrequent, and the man may find fairly regular employment. Furthermore, he begins to assume some leadership role in the church, tribal council, or some other organization. Frequently he berates younger brothers who are behaving as he did a few years before. Generally he begins to take an interest in the community for the first time.

During this period children born earlier are brought back into the household. The older ones, especially girls, begin caring for younger ones, and the couple between ages thirty and forty may take in children other than their own. Some unusually large households of ten to fifteen persons are headed by husbands and wives at this stage. As the oldest children of such families begin to leave the household, grandchildren begin to arrive. Between ages fifty and sixty, a man's earning power begins to drop because he can no longer pursue strenuous agricultural work or find temporary off-reservation employment. However, as grandchildren are absorbed into the household, the husband and wife may qualify for Aid to Dependent Children. Somehow or other the couple manage to support themselves and continue to offer aid to children or grandchildren in times of stress.

Older couples generally maintain a separate household, but it is located close to kin and visiting among households is frequent. An elderly female usually finds a place with one of her children where she continues to help out with child care and household chores. An older man often maintains a separate house. Although his ties with kin are not so active as a woman's, kin are close by and aid him in distress. Aid to the Aged, pensions, Social Security, or lease income from a tract of land usually allow the elderly a degree of economic independence, but their social life is still well integrated with the rest of the community.

Formerly the elderly maintained an advisory role, especially in advocating peace, but this role has now noticeably declined. The elders generally have enough extra cash to buy a grandchild a special gift, but since they can seldom interfere with their children's lives, they command considerably more affection and respect than their counterparts in white society, who are so often defined as problems.

Of course, not all families cycle precisely in the way described above. Some couples settle down and raise all their own children after marriage; others never become respectable in white eyes, and one middle-aged couple who seriously neglected their children were held in great contempt by other Lower Brule. But this range of behavior is simply one more aspect of flexibility built into Dakota social life. Whereas the older kinship system allowed shifting between winter and summer organizations, the new one allows adaptation to a radically different environment caused by the presence of whites.

The first major change from the former system must have occurred with the appearance of the white man and the development of the fur trade. As the Lower Brule broke off from the other Brule to settle more or less permanently along the Missouri River, a compromise between the winter camp and the summer gathering had to occur. The bands that began to form in various locales around the agency seem to have been larger than the older *tiyospaye* but not nearly so large as the summer encampment. The establishment of schools and missions at first followed these camp lines, and even the early agents recognized various camp leaders as spokesmen for their respective groups. Later, however, whites figured it was more expedient to deal with only one or a few leaders, and the establishment of a single ration-issue station brought pressure on the scattered camps to come into closer contact. The pressure to maintain only a few schools and missions further encouraged consolidation of the bands. During this period, Iron Nation came to be recognized as chief of the Lower Brule, but he was more likely simply the first among equal band chiefs.

While at the local level white pressure worked to establish a chief spokesman for the tribe, national policy was being formalized to destroy all Indian political organization in order to assimilate individuals as rapidly as possible. The Allotment Act of the late nineteenth century was intended to scatter individuals over the reservation on their respective allotments. White neighbors were to have more influence over Indians than the former chiefs. Several agents after 1890 struggled valiantly to break up the community that had grown up around the agency. Agents argued with Indians to build a cabin on their allotment and to farm their individual land. At the same time a central school was being built which children were expected or even forced to attend, and most parents did not want to leave their children behind to board at the new school.

Furthermore the agency offered a number of jobs, providing the only regular employment on the reservation. Driving the issue wagons was particularly popular among the Dakota, but numerous semi-skilled jobs were also available from the government. Finally, of course, the social life of the agency was far more appealing to a people like the Dakota than the solitary existence of an isolated farmer on the Plains. Indeed, most of the Brule probably saw confinement to an allotment as a form of exile rather than a way of life. Whether their social organization could have helped in adapting them to such a way of life is doubtful; it did allow them the option of settling in the vicinity of the agency. The kin network ensured that whatever income or rations entered the community were distributed in fairly equal proportions. As a result everyone remained poor, but all managed to survive.

Part of a subsistence size herd of a Lower Brule rancher on summer pasture. (1970)

A new subsistence factor, cattle ranching, began to emerge in the twentieth century; it separated some nuclear families more than any other event. Several individuals built herds prior to World War I; the tribe experimented with a tribal herd between the wars; and since 1950 a few individuals have again acquired small herds. Ranching has meant a better than subsistence-level life for a few Lower Brule, but most profits from ranching have to be reinvested. No individual has become wealthy as a result of his herd. The few people who have succeeded at ranching have cut or reduced their kin network. Several ranchers have married white women, for instance, so that in-laws no longer make demands on them. More significantly the ranchers have been defined as mixed-bloods and have become marginal to the social life of the community even though they exercise some economic and political power.

Dakota—Today and Tomorrow • *219*

For other families welfare, poorly paid employment, or partial employment provides an income which is still fairly evenly spread through the community. Middle-aged men who are entering the respectable stage are also the most likely to have some wage income, which gets distributed among their household members and extended kin. Younger men who experience some windfall, such as rodeo prizes, are generous in sharing—usually to provide a drinking bout or vacation trip. Even older men will share when they can, giving to the church or sponsoring a feast to celebrate some feat of a younger relative. Thus church basket dinners are strikingly similar to the old give-away, once discredited and discouraged by the churches. Feasts given to honor a high school graduate are likewise reminiscent of the celebrations for the young man who successfully returned from a war party. In either case, the demands of kinship ensured a sharing of whatever wealth was available, an obviously important device for people on a subsistence level, whether surviving on game as in the past or on welfare as in the present.

The kinship terminology of present-day Lower Brule has changed, reflecting the changing conditions. English terms are commonly used; and when speaking English, relatives are defined in the same way white Americans define them. But the Siouan language is still very important to the Lower Brule, and most of them understand it, even those who cannot speak it. The major characteristic of the old system, as described in the first chapter, was that a person's mother and mother's sister were both called *ina* while the father's sister was *towin*.[3] Likewise the father and father's brother were one, *ate*, while mother's brother was different, *lekshi*. This type of grouping of relatives is familiar to anthropologists because it is so commonplace around the world. One consequence of grouping mother and her sisters together is that all the children of sisters are like siblings to each other. The children of brothers are also siblings to each other. In other words, a Dakota recognized only his mother's brothers' children and his father's sisters' children as cousins. His mother's sisters' children and father's brothers' children were his brothers and sisters. Today most Lower Brule have expanded the system so that the mother's brother is now also recognized as *ate* or "father" and the father's sister as *ina* or "mother." If asked who now is *towin* or *lekshi,* a Lower Brule may respond, "You use those terms for anyone older who you think is related to you. It's the polite thing to do. And, we're all related here."

The present terminology is not as accurate an index of kin obligations as the original one, but it is a reflection that the kin network is now coterminous with the community. Lower Brule now feel they are all interrelated, whereas in the past they did not and probably were not related because of shifting summer alliances and a greater degree of community exogamy. Indeed, elsewhere it is almost certain that endogamy, or marriage within a group, has led to kinship terminologies like that of the contemporary Lower Brule.[4] It is a system that provides a variety of kin links to others so that one is not bound strictly to another person by only one specific relationship.

The flexibility of the kinship system is not matched by Lower Brule's economic organization because of the considerable restraint imposed on them by the dominant society. In the past, the Dakota have made some radical economic adjustments as in the change to hunting bison and to mastering a horse technology. The later incorporation of fur trading is still more evidence of ready adaptability. Even more remarkable as an adaptation was the Dakota ability to escape infectious illness by scattering over the Plains during the early epidemics of new diseases introduced by whites.

However, as the Lower Brule settled more and more permanently along the Missouri River, a growing dependence upon white goods began to encroach upon their range of options. Their rights to hunting lands dwindled as the Upper Brule and Oglala continually utilized the territory in the headwaters of the White and Cheyenne Rivers. Traders and government agents began supplying enough food to the Lower Brule to keep them close to the posts on the Missouri River. The government agents in particular followed a deliberate policy of tying the Indians to the agency in order to exert authority and influence. In time the annuities and other payments made by the United States for rights to Indian lands expired, but these supplies were replaced by issues of rations necessary to sustain the Indians.

The Dakota must have assumed that the rations were the same as the annuities. The white man had taken the land; in return he would have to guarantee the support of the Indian. Of course whites had an entirely different view. Once final payment was made, according to treaty stipulation, the Indian was supposed to be ready for independence and self-support. When the government found it was in a position where it was forced to continue the dependence it had fostered, Washington attempted to assume full authority over political as well as economic matters on the premise that people not capable of feeding themselves must also be incapable of political management.

At the local level, agents vacillated considerably in their relation to the camp leaders among the Lower Brule. At first a few of the leaders openly defied some agents' orders; later, they found it more expedient simply to evade them. At one time an agent might try to elevate one chief over all the others; later, no chiefs would be recognized. Such a state of affairs continued until the 1930s when the tribal council was formed and recognized as a governing body under the Indian Reorganization Act.

Most tribal councils resemble in form the governing bodies or town councils of small white communities. In 1960 the Lower Brule elected six members to the council and chose one of the members to be tribal chairman. The council operates much like its white counterpart with the chairman more or less following familiar parliamentary procedure. Minutes are kept by a tribal secretary, members receive a per diem allowance, motions are offered, seconded, and voted along with resolutions. Even some informal joking among the council members reminds one strongly of white governing bodies.

At the first meetings I attended, I was impressed with the importance of tribal business especially because I had been told that tribal councils had no power. Yet I saw the body making decisions about buying and selling land that involved tens of thousands of dollars. Still, the council members showed about the same amount of gravity and concern later when they had to decide how to allocate a small amount for baseball uniforms and seeds for gardens. Indeed the matter of baseball uniforms caused more discussion than most of the land transactions. More important, much of the discussion focused on whether the superintendent of the Bureau of Indian Affairs would approve the purchase rather than upon the merits of a baseball team or its uniforms. Likewise, garden purchases had been quickly assented to on the basis of an argument that they had been approved in previous years. These actions served as clues that I should investigate the land transactions in more detail. I soon found that the Bureau of Indian Affairs had developed a land consolidation program for Lower Brule which consisted of building up Indian ownership in some areas of the reservation at the expense of others. The policy was a sound one to cattle-ranching experts and agricultural economists. The BIA had instituted it some years prior to 1960, and the Lower Brule well understood that as long as they had funds they could buy any available land in the consolidation areas and sell other land outside those areas. In short, the decisions that had impressed me with the power of the tribal council were actually ones that had already been made by the Bureau of Indian Affairs. The Lower Brule were simply voting to implement standing BIA policy.

Since three of the councilmen, including the chairman, were ranchers and believed ranching to be the reservation's mainstay, it is likely they fully supported the policy. But it would be a mistake to credit them with making significant decisions about which tracts of land to buy or sell. Such decisions had been made under the general policy which the council was only following when it voted on the impressive expenditures.

What little power the council does seem to hold lies in doing nothing. This approach may be self-defeating as illustrated by the following event. Shortly before I arrived on the reservation, the Public Health Service had drilled several wells for the Lower Brule. Ordinarily the Indians haul their drinking water from the Missouri River or a distant spring. Some water was available from artesian wells but had an unusual taste. It was fit only for white men. Since the Lower Brule had drunk river water all their lives, they knew that it was safe; yet they recognized that other people did get sick from it and that their own babies sometimes suffered from its effects. Sentiment was strong for a new source of water, and there was interest in the wells.

The Public Health Service, however, was operating under a motto of "Help others to help themselves," and under their terms they would only finish the wells if the Lower Brule cooperated in the project. It was the understanding of the local Public Health Officer that the tribal council previously had agreed to provide a small sum of money and labor for capping the wells properly; in turn the Public Health Service would cooperate by furnishing the more expensive drilling operation. The drilling had been accomplished, but the wells had not been capped. The Public Health Service would not allow the water to be used, arguing that the wells would become contaminated. Most of the people in the community who were complaining loudest directed their anger at the Public Health Service because it had ended up prohibiting use of the water for no apparent reason.

Meanwhile the tribal council debated approval of money for capping the wells at four successive monthly meetings without reaching a conclusion. Debate centered on minor technical matters and was incomprehensible to me until I began to realize that council members could show resentment about lack of important decision-making by taking no action at all in a case such as this one. I was not able to determine if the Public Health Service policy was truly more benevolent paternalism than cooperation, but even if it was the latter, the council could have been reacting to the general paternalistic stance of the government as evidenced by the Bureau of Indian Affairs.[5]

The lack of power of the tribal council is reflected in Indian attitudes toward it. Seldom is there much competition in the elections for office. When two candidates do vie for office, debates are strongly personal rather than issue-oriented.[6] Likewise, candidates gather support largely along kinship lines or personal appeals. Once in office, council members receive little support from their constituents. The Lower Brule who are not apathetic toward the council are almost always critical. A common view is that councilmen are only interested in the $10 per diem allowance or that they are advancing their own personal causes. This view of the electorate can cancel much action.

For example, most Lower Brule men argued strongly that a bar should be opened on the reservation. They understood that its establishment would keep money in the community, but they made the more important point that the chance of auto accidents would be greatly reduced if the long drive back from present bars was eliminated. Yet these same men were strongly opposed to the council chairman, who supported the appropriate legislation because they felt he wanted to open a bar to further his own interests. When they thought he might be the proprietor, they advanced many of the outdated ideas of whites supporting prohibition. A tavern was finally established in the confusion following resettlement above the new reservoir.

Of course, most of the time the Lower Brule clearly realize that the council is without power, and they know of no good reason why they should support it. Final decisions will always be made by the Bureau of Indian Affairs. Yet the council is the only political body of the community; the Lower Brule must turn to it whenever they have any hope for a political decision.[7] Furthermore, councilmen are personally known to individuals, and in some way obligated to them. Frequently these people expect that the tribal council will take some action favorable to them because of the obligations of kinship. Unfortunately power simply does not reside in the tribal council.

It is difficult to convince Indians, as well as many others, that the Bureau of Indian Affairs did not intentionally retain virtually all economic and political power over reservation life. I have argued elsewhere that government policy, since 1934 at least, has been to transfer power to the Indian communities and to make them as self-governing as any other American community.[8] Such a transfer has not been accomplished because the structure of the relationship between tribes and the federal government determines that power will reside and can only reside in the BIA. Even terminating the relationship between a tribe and the federal government, however, is no guarantee of self-government. If an Indian community is not also economically independent, then state or local governments or even other agencies simply replace the BIA as the source of power.[9]

It seems to me that some Lower Brule clearly recognized this situation in making their initial request for termination. Thus their plans pointed up the possibility that if the government doubled the funds compensating them for the land lost to Fort Randall Dam, they could invest this sum in land acquisition and cattle operations which would make the community economically independent. At that stage they could then be politically independent and ready to be severed from the Bureau of Indian Affairs.[10] The plan must have appealed to many congressmen because it stressed investment of funds rather than per capita distribution.[11] Even so the plan met much opposition in Washington when I began fieldwork. Among tribal members I found either opposition or apathy.

The BIA must have been pleased to receive the Lower Brule's request for termination even though it was conditional on receiving another million dollars for development. The Klamath and Menominee, scheduled for termination, were bitterly opposing it, and most other tribes throughout the nation had joined the opposition. The National Congress of American Indians was at its peak in organization because of nearly universal support from the tribes, and it was speaking most effectively against the measure. It is possible that termination had become such a controversial issue that the BIA had temporarily weakened its support for the appropriate legislation for the Lower Brule bill. Even congressmen who generally favored a termination policy failed to speak strongly for the Lower Brule. As a result the bill languished. The Lower Brule remained unpaid for their lost lands years after neighboring whites had received compensation for their inundated property. In addition, the Army Corps of Engineers was beginning a dam that would flood tens of thousands of acres even before a settlement had been made for the 8000 acres lost to the Fort Randall Dam.

Opposition to termination on the reservation stemmed from a variety of reasons. First, the Lower Brule have experienced numerous governmental plans, often contradicting each other. No plan has ever changed the economy substantially, and none has ever been controlled by the local community. Therefore Indians are logically skeptical of any government program regardless of its merits on the surface.

Second, the reservation population is divided approximately equally between mixed-bloods and full-bloods. Full-bloods occasionally will express the belief that their problems would be solved if they could "kick the half-breeds off the reservation." Mixed-bloods will sometimes complain that it is the "backward full-bloods" who prevent progress. Much of this hostility surely arises from the frustration of a community that lacks self-determination. The factionalism makes little sense otherwise. In 1958 factional disputes were minimal because the two factions had aligned against another group—the "outsiders." The outsiders were Lower Brule who are legally enrolled in the tribe but live off the reservation. According to the tribal rolls, more than half the Lower Brule are living away from the reservation. Although some of the non-residents had thoroughly severed their tribal ties and took no interest in tribal matters, a sizable group in Pierre and other South Dakota towns consistently maintained that they should receive their share of benefits for lost reservation land. They could receive compensation only through per capita payments, an unpopular measure in Congress but one also favored by full-bloods who desperately needed the funds. On the other hand, the mixed-bloods had convinced many full-bloods that Congress would not approve per capita payments; moreover investment or development of the reservation would mean that all funds remained within the reservation. Thus full-bloods and mixed-bloods had united temporarily to retain the compensation.[12]

The relationship between mixed-bloods and full-bloods is a complicated one. Although overtly one group is generally hostile to the other, there seem to be covert feelings of mutual dependence. Mixed-bloods may feel that the special rights they have as Indians accrue to them because of the full-bloods on the reservation. Full-blood dependence seems to be based on a belief that the mixed-bloods are necessary mediators with the white world. More than a hundred years ago, the Dakota tolerated mixed-bloods because they were literally translators; today the mixed-bloods are important as translators figuratively. Ironically, one neutral Dakota term for them is translator's sons. Thus feelings between the factions are markedly ambivalent. A similar ambivalence toward the federal government was a third factor in creating apathy and opposition toward the termination plan of the tribal council. This ambivalence was once vividly described to me by a wise old Lower Brule who had stopped his wagon to chat briefly. I had asked how he felt about a recent visit from a BIA representative:

The government has had control of us so long we're just like these horses. Only we don't even know what "whoa" means. The government keeps changing their minds what they're going to tell us to do. So my idea is only about an inch long. I only think of today or tomorrow. The White man's idea is about a yard long. You think of what you'll be doing in thirty or forty years. We don't have the same

*ideas. You know why? The government has taken care of the Indian so
long he can't get along without him.*

Most often Indians are sharply critical of the BIA, which
represents the federal government and is the obvious symbol
of dependency. Yet Indians also covertly fear ending the dreaded relationship partly because of obvious advantages in the
present situation, and partly because the Lower Brule seldom
have had the opportunity to prove to themselves that they are
capable of managing their own affairs. Probably some new legal
mechanisms can maintain the advantages while ending the dependency. But providing the opportunity to learn self-confi-
dence may be more difficult. Both these aspects need to be
examined in some depth because they are major forms of re-
striction over an otherwise flexible people.

The advantages of the Indian's special relation with the
federal government consist first of tax-free lands. Legally tribal
and individual land held in trust belongs to the United States
government and cannot be taxed by state governments. As a
result, the states do not provide their usual services, such as
education, so that local control over such services is made impossible. Instead the BIA operates the schools. Teachers are
civil service employees along with the rest of the staff, and all
other expenditures as well become the responsibility of the
secretary of the interior. In short, a Lower Brule Board of Education could only be superfluous. Likewise road-building, law
and order, sewage or water supply maintenance, and other public services come under jurisdiction of the BIA rather than the
tribal council at Lower Brule. Thus the tribal council is also
virtually superfluous.

Since the Lower Brule could raise little money even if they
would tax themselves, it seems only logical that the federal
government must continue to provide essential public services.
For the near future it indeed seems likely that the community
will be unable to finance public operations at their present level
and that federal support will continue to be necessary. Yet it is
equally logical to assume that the support need not necessarily

The new Lower Brule school constructed after the building of Big Bend Dam. The Bureau of Indian Affairs provides good facilities and teachers but excludes Indians from any control over education. (1970)

be through the BIA. Tribal councils could directly administer the funds necessary to maintain the community if legislation were approved making them the responsible bodies rather than the Bureau of Indian Affairs.

Such suggestions are generally welcomed by Indians, but the Lower Brule also have some trepidation about taking such steps. Perhaps they feel that they have been under the harness too long and cannot do without a guiding hand. Even on the rare occasions when they do manage an event solely and successfully, whites provide rationalizations which take credit away from the Indians. The Episcopal Convocation of 1958 at Lower Brule vividly illustrated such an outcome for me.

Traditionally, yearly convocations are hosted by the different Episcopal congregations throughout South Dakota. A church plays host about once a decade to several thousand visitors for a three-day weekend. Plans for the 1958 convocation had just begun when I arrived; I grew more and more skeptical that the Lower Brule could ever manage one as the months of planning passed.

First, the young Episcopal priest was just out of seminary. Although he had never experienced a convocation, he had assumed direction of the planning, and as summer began, he developed serious attacks of asthma. He had appointed numerous committees to perform a variety of tasks, but Indians shifted their membership while committee chairmen fluctuated rapidly. To add to the confusion, an older full-blood had secured the priest's permission to schedule Indian dancing. Some mixed-bloods opposed the step and convinced the priest to rescind his permission. As the confusion mounted, I tried to remain on the sidelines so as not to be associated with what I thought was an approaching disaster.

But about a month before the convocation was to convene, I began to reevaluate events. I had been helping with the construction of a large shade and platform for the outside ceremonies. I was most impressed at how mixed-bloods had secured cooperation from neighboring whites in supplying a huge water tank, an extended power line, and materials for a well-constructed stage. All of us, but especially the full-bloods, had joined in the manual labor. The structure was almost complete except for the leafy branches which could not be cut until a few days before they were needed. At a meeting called by the priest, committee chairmen were asked to report. The chairman of the Shade Committee, a young full-blood, reported "Doksha," usually translated as "later" but also meaning "okay." Anyone attending the meeting would have to agree with the report because he had to pass the shade which was obviously okay. Yet after the meeting, the priest confided to me that the convocation would be a failure without the shade. It struck me that the priest was depending more upon the oral report of a chairman than the physical evidence of the construction before his eyes.

It was part of white culture to be reassured by formal reporting of progress, a step totally unnecessary to the Indians, who had built the shade and knew it would be complete when necessary. Soon afterwards, without assurance of a chairman's report, the priest went into a hospital for an extended treatment of his asthma.

Meanwhile the Lower Brule continued to collect funds to purchase food; to establish a pure water supply for their guests; to form a patrol to keep order at night; to dig half a dozen privies and clean off a campground; to paint the church and parsonage; and to carry out a dozen other tasks that should have been too much for a people who cannot manage their own affairs. Not until the convocation ended did I realize what an unusual feat had been accomplished. Fewer than a hundred Indian church members had raised over $3000 to feed several thousand guests nine hot meals with typical Dakota hospitality. A complex division of labor had occurred with full-bloods doing the things that could be managed within the reservation while mixed-bloods negotiated with whites and performed similar services. A notorious troublemaker had served as law and order chairman; not one incident had occurred under his jurisdiction. One young full-blood male with a reputation for being wild had supervised each breakfast and luncheon with great success. A number of young girls who "never did anything but run around" had done much of the cooking. It was obvious the Lower Brule knew much about their potential as well as how to fulfill it. That they were totally responsible is beyond doubt since the priest was hospitalized up until the opening day of the convocation, and the Bureau of Indian Affairs remained aloof from a church activity.

Yet proof that Indians had not managed successfully was soon forthcoming. At the end of the convocation, the young manager of the cooking had taken his girl friend with him to Chamberlain where he concluded some convocation business and bought a bottle of wine. He was living with the girl at her parents' house with their approval, but she was only sixteen. On their return to the reservation, a BIA law officer from Pierre arrested the man and charged him with contributing to the delinquency of a minor. In later conversations with the officer, it was apparent that he had suspected there would be trouble with such a large gathering of Indians and had been looking hard for the chance to confirm his prejudgment. The arrest suddenly negated all the hard, responsible work the Indian had performed. Likewise the general convocation chairman, who had spent much of six months in preparation, had much of his work denied. He was to appear on local television at the end of the convocation to describe the event. When he failed to keep the appointment, he was accused of drinking instead. If a white man had celebrated the conclusion of a successful event in such a way, he would simply be doing what was expected of him. But in this case the instance was used to negate the remarkable organizing responsibility of the chairman in order to confirm the stereotype of irresponsible Indian.

If anyone had failed in his duty, it struck me that it was clearly the white priest, even though his failure might be excused because of medical reasons. Yet he was explicitly congratulated by the visiting white bishop, and others at Lower Brule were soon giving him much credit. I, too, was thanked over and over by Indians for all my help when actually I had been more of a hindrance than a helper. Soon it seemed to me that the Lower Brule, as well as neighboring whites and BIA bureaucrats, were crediting others for their own notable accomplishment. When I attempted to emphasize to the Indians that they had really done practically everything, they would exaggerate the ease of their performance noting that they or their parents had done it all before. Of course, that is why they are also capable of managing their own political life.

Their ability and responsibility in organizing the convocation should have demonstrated to the Episcopal hierarchy that the Lower Brule were capable of managing their own church affairs. I have argued before that the mission bodies are in a position to turn over budgets to Indian congregations.[13]

Should they choose to do so, perhaps missions could demonstrate to the BIA that economic dependence need not be linked to political dependency. As yet, however, no national mission boards have been willing to delegate fiscal responsibility to the Dakota churches.

The Episcopal Church at Lower Brule. Although missionaries have devoted more than a century of work to the reservation, the churches lack any independence because of their mission status. (1970)

Still, the churches generally have allowed more leeway in management. They have been especially active in recruiting Dakota to serve as priests or ministers, and Dakota comprise their own Presbyteries, boards of elders, and so forth. Although not encouraged by the churches to do so, the Indians have also been able to incorporate some of their former religious beliefs with the fundamentals of Christianity. At Lower Brule the use of Lakota (the native language) in hymns, some ritual, and even sermons allows an expression of belief that combines Christianity with former values. In fact, some individuals retained very much of the old religion interpreting it as compatible with Christian doctrine. For instance, one full-blood Episcopalian, who sometimes spoke from the pulpit with the confidence of the priest, also sought visions and consulted with *yuwipi*. One mixed-blood argued that the old Sun Dance pole was a kind of cross, and he was convinced that God must have favored his Indian forebears with religion just as he had the white man. Even an Indian lay priest was convinced that a medicine man held spiritual powers that could not be accounted for by Christianity.

Much of this latitude in belief must be the result of a cultural value that ascribes major responsibility to individuals. Dorothy Lee describes the situation as one in which individuals are seen so fully as responsible that one could not delegate responsibility. To be, is to be responsible. In her words:

> *The Dakota were responsible for all things, because they were at one with all things. In one way, this meant that all behavior had to be responsible, since its effect always went beyond the individual. In another way, it meant that an individual had to, was responsible to, increase, intensify, spread, recognize, experience this relationship. To grow in manliness, in humanness, in holiness, meant to plunge purposively deeper into the relatedness of all things. A Dakota never assumed responsibility, because responsibility was had, was there always. Where we would say that a man assumed a new responsibility, they would consider that, in such a situation, a man made an autonomous decision to carry out this particular had responsibility; or perhaps, that at the moment he was able to recognize this responsibility, or to act responsibly. For the Dakota, to be was to be responsible; because to be was to be related; and to be related meant to be responsible.*[14]

Given such a viewpoint, it is doubly unfortunate that the Lower Brule and other Dakota should find themselves treated as an incompetent and irresponsible people. It seems they, too, are beginning to accept this view of themselves, and the opinion that they have been under harness so long as to lose their independence is often heard. Yet many Dakota parents continue to see their children as related to all things and therefore responsible. Such a value leads to the formation of a distinct Dakota personality, and this personality, combined with an adaptable social organization, guarantees that the Lower Brule community will persist into the foreseeable future. These Dakota may have been forgotten by the dominant society, but their existence is in no way threatened by such neglect.

Notes

Introduction

1. Ernest Schusky, "Cultural Change and Continuity in the Lower Brule Community," in *The Modern Sioux,* ed. Ethel Nurge (Lincoln: University of Nebraska Press, 1970), pp. 107–122.

2. Vine Deloria, *Custer Died for Your Sins* (New York: The Macmillan Company, 1969).

Chapter 1

1. Frances Densmore, *Teton Sioux Music* (Washington: Bureau of American Ethnology, 1918), Bulletin 61, pp. 63–66.

2. S. R. Riggs, "Mythology of the Dakotas," *American Antiquarian,* V (1883): 149.

3. Edwin S. Curtis, *The North American Indian,* Vol. 3 (1908; reprint ed., Johnson Reprint Corp., 1970), p. 4.

4. Nancy Ossenberg. Paper presented at the Plains Conference, Winnipeg, Ontario, October, 1971.

5. C. F. Voegelin, "Internal Relationships of Siouan Languages," *American Anthropologist,* 43 (Spring 1941): 249.

6. John R. Swanton, "Early History of the Eastern Siouan Tribes," in *Essays in Anthropology Presented to A. L. Kroeber* (Berkeley: University of California Press, 1936), pp. 371–381.

7. John Swanton, "Siouan Tribes and the Ohio Valley," *American Anthropologist,* 45 (Winter 1943): 49–66

8. Ibid., p. 50.

9. Alice Fletcher and Francis La Flesche, *The Omaha Tribe* (Washington: Bureau of American Ethnology, 1905), 27th Annual Report, p. 36.

10. Ibid., p. 70.

11. George Catlin, *North American Indians,* Vol. I (London: Henry G. Bohn, 1851), p. 206.

12. George Catlin, *North American Indians,* Vol. II (London: Henry G. Bohn, 1851), pp. 527–561.

13. Horatio Hale, "The Tutelo Indians," *Proceedings of the American Philosophical Society,* 21 (1883): 1–47

14. James Griffin, "On the Historic Location of the Tutelo and the Mohetan in the Ohio Valley," *American Anthropologist,* 44 (Spring 1942): 275–280.

15. Swanton, "Siouan Tribes and the Ohio Valley," pp. 49–66.

16. Doane Robinson, *A History of the Dakota or Sioux Indians* (Pierre: South Dakota State Historical Society, 1904), pp. 19–24.

17. James Howard, "The Cultural Position of the Dakota: A Reassessment," in *Essays in the Science of Culture,* ed. Gertrude Dole and Robert Carneiro (New York: Crowell, 1960), pp. 249–268.

18. Albert Jenks. *The Wild Rice Gatherers of the Upper Lakes* (Washington: Bureau of American Ethnology, 1897), 19th Annual Report, pp. 1043–1047.

19. Ruth Landes, *The Mystic Lake Sioux* (Madison: University of Wisconsin Press, 1968).

20. Jenks, *The Wild Rice Gatherers of the Upper Lakes,* pp. 1056–1095.

21. John C. Ewers, *The Horse in Blackfoot Indian Culture* (Washington: Bureau of American Ethnology, 1955), Bulletin 159.

22. Robinson, *A History of the Dakota or Sioux Indians,* p. 29.

23. Catlin, *North American Indians,* Vol. I, p. 210.

24. Royal Hassrick, *The Sioux* (Norman: University of Oklahoma Press, 1964), p. 155.

25. Eldon Johnson, "The Tribes of the Great Plains," in *The Native Americans,* ed. Robert Spencer and Jesse Jennings (New York: Harper, 1965), p. 352.

26. John Anderson, *The Sioux of the Rosebud* (Norman: University of Oklahoma Press, 1971).

27. Gordon Macgregor, *Warriors Without Weapons* (Chicago: University of Chicago Press, 1946), p. 52.

28. Royal Hassrick, "Teton Dakota Kinship System," *American Anthropologist,* 46 (1944): 338–347.

29. J. Walker, "Oglala Kinship Terms," *American Anthropologist,* 16 (1914): 96–109.

30. Jeannette Mirsky, "The Dakota," in *Cooperation and Competition Among Primitive Peoples,* ed. Margaret Mead (New York: McGraw-Hill, 1937), pp. 390–394.

31. Clark Wissler, *Societies and Ceremonial Associations of the Oglala Division of the Teton-Dakota* (New York: American Museum of Natural History, Vol. XI, Part 1, 1912).

32. Robert Lowie, *Indians of the Plains* (New York: McGraw-Hill, 1954).

33. Stephen Feraca, "The Yuwipi Cult of the Oglala and Sicangu Teton Sioux, *Plains Anthropologist,* 6 (1961): 155–163.

34. Fieldwork notes of the author, 1958.

35. Robert Burnett and John Koster, *The Road to Wounded Knee* (New York: Bantam Books, 1974).

36. J. R. Walker, *The Sun Dance and Other Ceremonies of the Oglala Division of the Teton Dakota* (New York: American Museum of Natural History, Vol. XVI, 1917), pp. 51–221.

37. Densmore, *Teton Sioux Music.*

38. Stephen Feraca, "The Contemporary Teton Sun Dance." Unpublished master's thesis, Columbia University, 1957.

39. Dorothy Lee, *Freedom and Culture* (Englewood Cliffs: Prentice-Hall, 1959).

40. George Hyde, *Spotted Tail's Folk* (Norman: University of Oklahoma Press, 1961).

41. Hassrick, "Teton Dakota Kinship System."

Chapter 2

1. Robinson, *A History of the Dakota or Sioux Indian,* p. 26; George Hyde, *Spotted Tail's Folk* (Norman: University of Oklahoma Press, 1961), p. 5.

2. Hyde, *Spotted Tail's Folk,* p. 8, reports one trader at the mouth of White River as early as 1717, but trade did not become regular until late in the eighteenth century.

3. Battiste Good, a Brule, possessed a winter count calendar documented by William Corbusier. "The Corbusier Winter Counts" (Washington: Bureau of American Ethnology, 1882–83), Fourth Annual Report, pp. 127–146.

4. Nellis M. Crouse, *In Quest of the Western Ocean* (New York: Morrow and Co., 1928), pp. 379–405.

5. Annie H. Abel, ed., *Tabeau's Narrative of Loisel's Expedition to the Upper Missouri* (Norman: University of Oklahoma Press, 1939), pp. 3–52.

6. Corbusier, "The Corbusier Winter Counts." The use of American flags must surely mark the meeting with Lewis and Clark, but the present chronology indicates the 1805–1806 winter instead of 1804–1805.

7. Hyde, *Spotted Tail's Folk,* p. 17.

8. Abel, *Tabeau's Narrative of Loisel's Expedition to the Upper Missouri*, pp. 105–123.

9. Hiram M. Chittenden, *The American Fur Trade of the Far West* (New York: Francis P. Harper, 1902).

10. Doane Robinson, *Doane Robinson's Encyclopedia of South Dakota* (Pierre: the author, 1925), p. 259.

11. Hyde, *Spotted Tail's Folk*, p. 29.

12. Herbert Schell, *History of South Dakota* (Lincoln: University of Nebraska Press, 1968), pp. 61–64.

13. Richard Peters, *The Public Statutes at Large* (Boston: Little, Brown, 1846), p. 514.

14. Ernest Schusky, "The Upper Missouri Agency, 1819–1868," *The Missouri Historical Review*, LXV (April 1972): 249–69.

15. Russell Reid and Clell Gannon, eds., "Journal of the Atkinson-O'Fallon Expedition," *North Dakota Historical Quarterly*, IV (October 1929): 5–56.

16. Benjamin O'Fallon to William Clark, February 1824, National Archives and Record Service, Record Group 75, Microcopy 234, Roll 883, Records of the Bureau of Indian Affairs, Letters Received. All National Archives material cited in this book is from Record Group 75, Microcopy 234. A catalog of this Microcopy is available from the National Archives. Subsequent citation with be "NA 234."

17. John Dougherty to Senator Thomas H. Benton, January 1829, NA 234, Roll 883.

18. Pilcher's attempts to secure Dougherty's office took him to Washington in early 1832. Full details are in John Sunder, *Joshua Pilcher, Fur Trader and Indian Agent* (Norman: University of Oklahoma Press, 1968), pp. 85–90.

19. Joshua Pilcher to William Clark, February 27, 1838, NA 234, Roll 884.

20. Stella Drumm, *Dictionary of American Biography* (New York: Scribner, 1934), p. 41.

21. Lieutenant J. L. Gratton commanded the patrol that set out to punish the Dakota who had killed a cow. See Hyde, *Spotted Tail's Folk*, pp. 49–54.

22. Alfred Vaughn to Superintendent of Indian Affairs, July 1856, NA 234, Roll 885.

23. Ibid.

24. Ibid.

25. *The Weekly Dakotian,* Yankton, July 6, 1861, p. 2.

26. Ibid., September 7, 1861, p. 3.

27. Roy W. Meyer, *History of the Santee Sioux* (Lincoln: University of Nebraska Press, 1967), pp. 109–132.

28. *The Dakotian,* September 15, 1862, p. 1.

29. Ibid., September 30, 1862, p. 1.

30. Ibid., September 22, 1862, p. 1.

31. Ibid., January 27, 1863, p. 3. This editorial accompanies a front-page story that describes the hanging of thirty-eight Santee for the "Minnesota uprising."

32. Ibid., May 17, 1864, p. 3.

33. Frank Myers, *Soldiering in Dakota Among the Indians* (Huron: Huronite Printing House, 1888).

34. J. R. Drips, *Three Years Among the Indians* (Kimball, South Dakota: Brule Index, 1894).

35. Ibid., 33.

36. Ibid., 70.

37. Ibid., 112–113.

38. *The Dakota Union,* August 23, 1864, p. 1.

39. Mahlon Wilkinson to Commissioner of Indian Affairs, August 1865, NA 234, Roll 886.

40. Newton Edmunds to Commissioner of Indian Affairs, September 25, 1865, NA 234, Roll 886.

41. Major General Pope to Newton Edmunds, August 28, 1865, NA 234, Roll 886.

42. Alfred Sully to Commissioner of Indian Affairs, September 14, 1865, NA 234, Roll 886.

43. Harold Briggs, "The Settlement and Development of the Territory of Dakota, 1860–70," *North Dakota Historical Quarterly,* VII (1932): 114–149.

44. S. R. Curtis to Commissioner of Indian Affairs, May 30, 1866, NA 234, Roll 886.

45. Speeches reported by Newton Edmunds to Commissioner of Indian Affairs, April 9, 1866, NA 234, Roll 886.

46. J. R. Hanson to Commissioner of Indian Affairs, May 30, 1867, NA 234, Roll 887.

47. Hyde, *Spotted Tail's Folk,* pp. 123–125.

48. J. R. Hanson to Commissioner of Indian Affairs, February 27, 1867, NA 234, Roll 887.

49. George Hyde, *Red Cloud's Folk* (Norman: University of Oklahoma Press, 1937), pp. 162–184.

50. Macgregor, *Warriors Without Weapons,* p. 60.

51. Lee, *Freedom and Culture.*

52. J. R. Hanson to Governor Faulk, ex-officio Indian Superintendent, September 30, 1868, NA 234, Roll 887.

53. *The Union Dakotaian,* February 2, 1867, p. 2.

54. *Sioux City Register,* reprinted in *Union Dakotaian,* August 31. 1867, p. 2.

55. *Union Dakotaian,* September 7, 1867, p. 2.

56. James S. Foster, *Outlines of History of the Territory of Dakota* (Yankton: M'Intyre and Foster, Printers, 1870), p. 39.

Chapter 3

1. Ray Mattison, "The Indian Reservation System on the Upper Missouri, 1865–90," *Nebraska History,* 35 (1955): 141–174.

2. Hazel Hertzbert, *The Search for an American Indian Identity* (Syracuse: Syracuse University Press, 1971).

3. Francis A. Walker, *Report of the Commissioner of Indian Affairs* (Washington: U.S. Printing Office, 1873), pp. 391–401.

4. George A. Batchelder, *A Sketch of the History and Resources of Dakota Territory* (Yankton: Press Steam Power Printing Company, 1870), pp. 20–21.

5. DeWitt C. Poole, *Among the Sioux of South Dakota* (New York: Van Nostrand, 1881), p. 73.

6. Poole was the only eyewitness to the murder. Hyde, *Spotted Tail's Folk,* p. 153, shows the importance of his account by contrasting it with the many incorrect versions reported secondhand.

7. Hyde, *Spotted Tail's Folk,* p. 151.

8. Poole, *Among the Sioux of South Dakota,* p. 24.

9. Ibid., p. 100.

10. Ibid., p. 227.

11. Major General D. S. Stanley, August 1869, "Report" as an appendix in Poole, *Among the Sioux of South Dakota,* p. 233.

12. Colonel John Pattee to Newton Edmunds, March 23, 1866, NA 234, Roll 250.

13. Andrew J. Faulk to Commissioner of Indian Affairs, various months, 1868, NA 234, Roll 251.

14. J. R. Hanson, "Yearly Report for Crow Creek Agency," *Report of the Commissioner of Indian Affairs,* 1868.

15. *The Union Dakotaian,* October 28, 1868, p. 3.

16. *The Union Dakotaian,* May 29, 1869, p. 3.

17. J. R. Hanson to John Burbank, June 12, 1869, NA 234, Roll 251.

18. Ibid., June 29, 1869, NA 234, Roll 251.

19. *The Union Dakotaian,* March 13, 1869, p. 2.

20. John Burbank to William French, October 1869, NA 234, Roll 887.

21. William French to John Burbank, April 6, 1870, NA 234, Roll 888.

22. Ibid., April 24, 1870, NA 234, Roll 888.

23. David Krause to General O. D. Greene, July 31, 1870, NA 234, Roll 888.

24. William Welsh to Commissioner of Indian Affairs, November 28, 1871, NA 234, Roll 888.

25. Henry Livingstone to Commissioner of Indian Affairs, June 16, 1871, NA 234, Roll 249.

26. Commissioner of Indian Affairs, *Annual Report,* 1872, p. 263.

27. Henry Livingstone, diary entry October 13, 1873. Manuscript Collection of the Beinecke Library, Yale University. Diaries are preserved for the years 1866, 1867, 1868, 1869, 1870, 1873, 1874, 1875, 1876, 1877, 1878, 1879.

28. Brent Woodruff, "The Episcopal Mission to the Dakotas, 1860–1898," *South Dakota Historical Collections,* 17 (1934): 553–603.

29. Mark A. Howe, *The Life and Labors of Bishop Hare* (New York: Sturgis Walton, 1911).

30. Ibid., p. 46.

31. Felix Brunot to Commissioner of Indian Affairs, June 25, 1873, NA 234, Roll 252.

32. Secretary of the Interior to Commissioner of Indian Affairs, September 20, 1873, NA 234, Roll 252.

33. General D. S. Stanley to Department of Dakota, St. Paul, January 14, 1873, NA 234, Roll 252.

34. Captain J. De Russy to the Adjutant General, The Department of Dakota, September 16, 1874, NA 234, Roll 253.

35. Captain Joseph Bush to Adjutant General, Department of the Dakota, St. Paul, June 23, 1874, NA 234, Roll 888.

36. Howe, *Life and Labors of Bishop Hare,* p. 22.

37. Schell, *History of South Dakota,* p. 129.

38. Howe, *Life and Labors of Bishop Hare,* p. 123.

39. Attorneys Montory and Brownell, Chicago, to Commissioner of Indian Affairs, April 17, 1875, NA 234, Roll 254.

40. William Bounds, "The Ministry of the Reverend Samuel Dutton Hinman, Among the Sioux," *Historical Magazine of the Protestant Episcopal Church,* 38 (1969): 383–401.

41. Commissioner of Indian Affairs to W. B. Allison, et al., June 16, 1875, NA 234, Roll 254.

42. Hyde, *Red Cloud's Folk,* pp. 230–248; Schell, *History of South Dakota,* pp. 130–133.

43. Robert Mardock, *The Reformers and the American Indians* (Columbia: University of Missouri Press, 1971), pp. 150–167.

44. Hyde, *Red Cloud's Folk,* pp. 256–260.

45. For a variety of accounts see: Hyde, *Red Cloud's Folk,* pp. 277–293; James Howard, *The Warrior Who Killed Custer* (Lincoln: University of Nebraska Press, 1968); Robert Utley, *Custer and the Great Controversy* (Los Angeles: Westernlore Press, 1962); Don Russell, *Custer's Last* (Fort Worth: Amon Carter Museum, 1968).

46. Thomas Riley to Commissioner of Indian Affairs, July 28, 1876, NA 234, Roll 257.

47. Henry Livingstone to Commissioner of Indian Affairs, July 31, 1876, NA 234, Roll 257.

48. *Daily Press and Dakotaian,* July 8, 1876, p. 2.

49. Ibid., July 11, 1876, p. 2.

Chapter 4

1. Hazel Hertzberg, *The Search for an American Indian Identity* (Syracuse: Syracuse University Press, 1971), p. 20.

2. Frederic Bancroft, ed., *Speeches, Correspondence and Political Papers of Carl Schurz,* Vol. III. (New York: Putnam, 1913), p. 481.

3. Ibid., p. 487.

4. Henry Livingstone, diary entries March 21, 22, 23, 1878. Manuscript collection of the Beinecke Library, Yale University.

5. Record Book for Lower Brule Agency, 1879 (microfilm copy at South Dakota State Historical Society).

6. Records of these kinds for the Lower Brule Agency are deposited at the Federal Records Center, Kansas City.

7. *Lyman County Pioneers, 1885–1968* (Stickney, South Dakota: Lyman County Historical Society, 1968), p. 173.

8. Hyde, *A Sioux Chronicle.*

9. Commissioner of Indian Affairs, *Annual Report,* 1879, p. 33.

10. Ibid.

11. The dispute quickly subsided. Even before he was able to dispatch his report, the troubles had passed. Dougherty wrote: "P.S. Two days later. Called up all the chiefs and had a talk. They returned somewhat ashamed and humiliated and agreed to talk it over with the people. Perfect quiet. Rosebud Indians all gone." William Dougherty to Commissioner of Indian Affairs, March 24, 1879, NA 234, Roll 268.

12. Hyde, *A Sioux Chronicle,* pp. 40–42.

13. *Daily Press and Dakotaian,* July 1, 1879, p. 1.

14. Ibid., July 7, 1879, 1 and July 16, 1879, p. 4.

15. Ibid., December 22, 1879, p. 3.

16. Schell, *History of South Dakota,* pp. 161–165.

17. William Dougherty to Commissioner of Indian Affairs, February 4, 1879, NA 234, Roll 267.

18. William Dougherty to Commissioner of Indian Affairs, Annual Estimate for 1880, NA 234, Roll 267.

19. Commissioner of Indian Affairs, *Annual Report,* 1880, p. 34.

20. William Dougherty to Commissioner of Indian Affairs, February 20, 1879, NA 234, Roll 267.

21. Commissioner of Indian Affairs, *Annual Report,* 1880, p. 34.

22. William Dougherty to Carl Schurz, January 4, 1881. The original is in the National Archives but not on microfilm. The account sounds authentic to the author, as ethnographer. I know of no other Indian source that seems as reliable, and I judge it a better explanation than any of those provided by George Hyde in his histories of Rosebud and Pine Ridge.

23. Commissioner of Indian Affairs, *Annual Report,* 1881, p. 39.

24. Henry Pancost, *Impression of the Sioux Tribes in 1882* (Philadelphia: Press of Franklin Printing House, 1883), p. 17.

25. Herbert Welsh, *Report of a Visit to the Great Sioux Reserve, May and June 1883* (Philadelphia: Indian Rights Association, 1883), p. 10.

26. Report No. 283, Select Committee to Examine into the Condition of the Sioux and Crow Indians, U.S. Senate, 48th Congress, 1st Session, 1884.

27. Newton Edmunds to Secretary of the Interior, February 7, 1883, Letters Received, Records of the Bureau of Indian Affairs, Record Group 75, National Archives.

28. Hyde, *A Sioux Chronicle*, p. 134.

29. Welsh, *Report of a Visit to the Great Sioux Reserve, May and June, 1883*, p. 12.

30. Hyde, *A Sioux Chronicle*.

31. Report No. 283, Select Committee to Examine into the Condition of the Sioux and Crow Indians, U.S. Senate, 48th Congress, 1st Session, 1884.

32. Lower Brule chiefs and headmen to Commissioner of Indian Affairs, March 31, 1883, Letters Received, Records of the Bureau of Indian Affairs, Record Group 75, National Archives.

33. The men who petitioned signed themselves "Chiefs": Iron Nation, Medicine Bull, One Who Kills White Buffalo, Little Pheasant, Bullhead, Useful Heart, Shawalla, Long Claws, Standing Cloud, Knee, Black Dog, Big Mane, Handsome Elk, One Who Plays With.

34. Deadwood, *Daily and Weekly Pioneer*, August 1, 1884.

35. J. B. Harrison, *The Latest Studies on Indian Reservations* (Philadelphia: Indian Rights Association, 1887), p. 40.

36. Ibid., p. 41.

37. Ibid.

38. W. W. Anderson to Commissioner of Indian Affairs, March 25, 1886, Federal Records Center, Kansas City.

39. William Parsons to Commissioner of Indian Affairs. Depositions of W. W. Anderson, John Foster, U.S. Marshal; James B. White, farmer; Yellow Hawk, Captain of Police; Letters Received, Records of the Bureau of Indian Affairs, Record Group 75, National Archives, no date.

40. W. W. Anderson to Commissioner of Indian Affairs, September 11, 1886, Federal Records Center, Kansas City.

41. Henry Dawes, "Have We Failed the Indian?" *Atlantic Monthly*, 84 (1899): p. 281.

42. Hyde, *A Sioux Chronicle*, p. 152.

43. Chamberlain, *South Dakota Democrat*, August 8, 1889, p. 2.

44. Ernest Schusky, *The Right to Be Indian* (San Francisco: The Indian Historian Press, 1970).

45. *Pierre Daily Free Press*, April 12, 1890, p. 2.

46. Hyde, *A Sioux Chronicle*, pp. 202–228.

47. W. W. Anderson to Commissioner of Indian Affairs, August 5, 1889, Federal Records Center, Kansas City.

48. South Dakota Department of History, *Reports and Historical Collections, 33* (Pierre: State Publishing Company, 1966), p. 181, provides a biography of a wife of an early agency employee.

49. A. P. Dixon to Commissioner of Indian Affairs, November 25, 1890, Federal Records Center, Kansas City.

50. James Mooney, *The Ghost-Dance Religion* (Washington: Bureau of American Ethnology, 1896), 14th Annual Report, No. 2.

51. *South Dakota Democrat,* November 20, 1890, p. 2.

52. Ibid., December 4, 1890, p. 3.

53. Ibid., December 11, 1890, p. 2.

54. Ibid., December 18, 1890, p. 4.

55. Ibid., February 5, 1891, p. 2.

56. *Pierre Daily Free Press,* November 15, 1890, p. 2.

57. Ibid., November 17, 1890, p. 2.

58. Ibid., November 18, 1890, p. 3.

59. Ibid., November 20, 1890, p. 2.

60. Ibid., November 22, 1890, p. 1.

61. Ibid., November 29, 1890, p. 3.

62. Ibid., December 15, 1890, p. 3.

63. Ibid., December 16, 1890, p. 1.

64. Ibid., December 31, 1890, p. 2.

65. *The New York Times,* January 3, 1891, pp. 4–5.

66. Ibid.

67. *Pierre Daily Free Press,* January 15, 1891, p. 2.

68. Ibid., January 21, 1891, p. 1.

69. W. E. Dougherty, "The Recent Indian Craze," *Journal of the Military Service Institution of the United States,* 12 (1891), p. 576.

70. Ibid.

71. Robert Burnette and John Koster, *The Road to Wounded Knee* (New York: Bantam Books, 1974), pp. 10–11.

72. Ibid., p. 236.

73. A. P. Dixon to Commissioner of Indian Affairs, April 10, 1891, Federal Records Center, Kansas City.

Chapter 5

1. Commissioner of Indian Affairs, *Annual Report,* 1893, p. 439.

2. Ibid., p. 435.

3. Fred Treon to Office of Indian Affairs, November 1, 1893, Letters Received, Records of the Bureau of Indian Affairs, Record Group 75, Number 41281, National Archives.

4. Secretary of the Interior, *Annual Report,* 1893, p. 280.

5. Forwarded by Fred Treon to Commissioner of Indian Affairs, August 24, 1896, Letters Received, Records of the Bureau of Indian Affairs, Record Group 75, Number 33250, National Archives. As late as 1958 the Public Health Service was still trying without success to convince the Lower Brule to make use of artesian water.

6. J. M. Greene to W. A. Jones, Commissioner of Indian Affairs, August 22, 1898, Letters Received, Records of the Bureau of Indian Affairs, Record Group 75, Number 56116, National Archives.

7. B. C. Ash to Commissioner of Indian Affairs, *Annual Report of the Department of the Interior,* Part II, 1899, p. 248.

8. B. C. Ash to Commissioner of Indian Affairs, Ibid. Part I, 269.

9. Ernest Schusky, *Politics and Planning in a Dakota Indian Community* (Vermillion: Institute of Indian Studies, 1959), p. 43.

10. Schell, *History of South Dakota,* pp. 242–257.

11. Upton Sinclair, *The Jungle* (New York: Doubleday, 1906).

12. James McLaughlin to Secretary of the Interior, April 21, 1900, Letters Received, Records of the Bureau of Indian Affairs, Record Group 75, Number 21032, National Archives.

13. John DeSomette, Martin Black Elk, Matthew Big Mane to Commissioner of Indian Affairs, May 11, 1903, Letters Received, Records of the Bureau of Indian Affairs, Record Group 75, Number 31195, National Archives.

14. J. F. House to Commissioner of Indian Affairs, August 10, 1904, Letters Received, Records of the Bureau of Indian Affairs, Record Group 75, Number 552011, National Archives.

15. Ibid.

16. Francis E. Leupp, Commissioner of Indian Affairs, *Annual Report,* 1907, p. 16.

17. Edith Kohl, *Land of the Burnt Thigh* (New York: Funk and Wagnalls, 1938), pp. 51–52.

18. The process was similar for much of the Plains. John Bennett documents the process in detail for Western Canada in *The Plainsmen* (Chicago: Aldine Press, 1969).

19. Population figures and county boundaries are available in the U.S. Census Reports.

20. Commissioner of Indian Affairs, *Annual Report*, 1912, p. 5.

21. Jacob Levengood to Commissioner of Indian Affairs, Annual Report, 1910, Records of the Bureau of Indian Affairs, Record Group 75, National Archives.

22. Lower Brule Annual Report, 1913, p. 19, Records of the Bureau of Indian Affairs, Record Group 75, National Archives.

23. Lower Brule Annual Report, 1914, p. 8, Ibid.

24. Macgregor, *Warriors Without Weapons*, pp. 27–41.

25. Vernon Malan and Ernest Schusky, *The Dakota Indian Community* (Brookings, South Dakota: Agricultural Experiment Station, 1961).

26. Ruth Useem and Carl Eicher, "Rosebud Reservation Economy," in *The Modern Sioux*, ed. Ethel Nurge (Lincoln: University of Nebraska Press, 1970), pp. 3–34.

27. Dan Cushman, *Stay Away, Joe* (New York: Popular Library, 1953). The spirit of the novel is not fully captured in the Elvis Presley movie based on the book.

28. As late as 1918 the issue persisted in much the same form. At that time Superintendent Garber denied James Good Road's request to hold an Indian singing for the purpose of raising money to purchase Liberty Bonds. Commissioner Sells also objected to Good Road's attempts to revive "old injurious dances" under the guise of Red Cross meetings.

29. Cato Sells to Small Waisted Bear, September 21, 1914, Letters of the Commissioner, Records of the Bureau of Indian Affairs, Record Group 75, Number 102460, National Archives.

30. E. B. Meritt to Frank Brandon, Superintendent, June 28, 1915, Records of the Bureau of Indian Affairs, Record Group 75, Number 72481, National Archives.

31. In 1942 a hard-core group of Iroquois met to declare war again on the Axis since they still refused to acknowledge citizenship. Some Iroquois argued against the move. In a compromise the Iroquois decided a declaration of war was unnecessary; the Nation had not made a Peace Treaty in 1918 and so was still at war with Germany.

32. Cato Sells to Superintendent of Lower Brule School, Telegram, April 9, 1917, Federal Records Center, Kansas City.

33. Robert Burnette, *The Tortured Americans* (Englewood Cliffs, New Jersey: Prentice-Hall, 1971), p. 19.

34. Department of the Interior, *Annual Report*, 1918, p. 18.

35. Ibid.

36. E. B. Meritt to E. M. Garber, August 23, 1917, Records of the Bureau of Indian Affairs, Record Group 75, Number 7718817, National Archives. The 1917 Committee consisted of Reuben Estes, Philip Councilor, Charles Fish, Thomas Small Jumper, officers. Members were John De Smett, Grass Rope, Boy Elk, Big Mane, Black Elk, High Elk, Lone Horn, Pretty Shield, Spotted Horse, Standing Cloud, Small Waisted Bear, Big Heart, Two Hawks and Daniel Small.

37. E. M. Garber to Commissioner of Indian Affairs, November 24, 1917, Letters Received, Records of the Bureau of Indian Affairs, Record Group 75, Number 108830, National Archives.

38. Report of C. M. Knight, August 6, 1917, Central Consolidated Files, 1907–39, Record Group 75, Number 77537, National Archives.

39. Laurence F. Schmeckebier, *The Office of Indian Affairs* (Baltimore: The Johns Hopkins Press, 1927), p. 247.

40. C. H. Gensler, Lower Brule Annual Report, 1920, 7, Records of the Bureau of Indian Affairs, Record Group 75, National Archives.

41. Deloria, *Custer Died for Your Sins.*

42. C. H. Gensler, Lower Brule Annual Report, 1920, p. 9, Records of the Bureau of Indian Affairs, Record Group 75, National Archives.

43. Ibid., 1921, Sec. IV.

44. Ibid., 1922, Sec. IV.

45. Some Indian rights must inevitably conflict with citizenship rights, but this problem was simply passed over in 1924. Cf. Schusky, *The Right to Be Indian.*

46. C. H. Gensler, Lower Brule Annual Report, 1921, Sec. III, Records of the Bureau of Indian Affairs, Record Group 75, National Archives.

47. G. E. Lindquist, *The Red Man in the United States* (New York: Doran, 1923), p. xiv.

48. Charles H. Burke, "Foreword" in G. E. Lindquist, *The Red Man in the United States,* p. v.

49. C. H. Gensler, Lower Brule Annual Report, 1923, p. 1, Records of the Bureau of Indian Affairs, Record Group 75, National Archives.

50. Ibid.

51. D. H. Lawrence entered the controversy, contributing a lengthy, romanticized version of what dancing meant to the Indians.

"Indians and Entertainment," *New York Times,* October 26, 1924, Section IV.

52. John Collier to *New York Times,* November 16, 1924, Section IX, p. 12.

Chapter 6

1. W. E. Duncan, Lower Brule Annual Report, 1925, p. 1, Records of the Bureau of Indian Affairs, Record Group 75, National Archives.

2. Ibid.

3. Peyote has an apparently random distribution among the Dakota reservations. It is seldom used at Lower Brule except by visitors; ritual of the Native American Church is practiced by a small group at Crow Creek. Further information is pointed up by Wesley Hurt, "Factors in the Persistence of Peyote in the Northern Plains," *Plains Anthropologist,* 5 (1960): 16–27.

4. W. E. Duncan, Lower Brule Annual Report, 1926, Section 4, Records of the Bureau of Indian Affairs, Record Group 75, National Archives.

5. W. E. Duncan, Lower Brule Annual Report, 1927, p. 17, Ibid.

6. E. J. Peacore, Lower Brule Annual Report, 1928, Section 4, Ibid.

7. E. B. Wright, Lower Brule Annual Report, Section V, Ibid.

8. Lewis Meriam and others, *The Problem of Indian Administration* (Baltimore: The Johns Hopkins Press, 1928), pp. 32–37; 424–429.

9. W. E. Duncan, Lower Brule Annual Report, 1925, p. 2, Records of the Bureau of Indian Affairs, Record Group 75, National Archives.

10. *The Chamberlain Democrat,* September 4, 1924, p. 8.

11. *New York Times,* June 21, 1927, p. 17.

12. Ibid., June 26, 1927, Section IX, p. 8.

13. H. E. Wright, Lower Brule Annual Report, 1930, Section IV, Records of the Bureau of Indian Affairs, Record Group 75, National Archives.

14. H. E. Wright, Lower Brule Annual Report, 1931, Section II, Ibid.

15. W. E. Duncan, Lower Brule Annual Report, 1926, Section IV.

16. Ibid., Section VII.

17. H. E. Wright, Lower Brule Annual Report, 1930, Section VI.

18. Schell, *History of South Dakota,* p. 279.

19. Meriam et al., *The Problem of Indian Administration.*

20. Ibid., pp. 449–456.

21. Alden Stevens, "Whither the American Indian?" *Survey Graphic*, 29 (1940): 168; reprinted in *American Indians*, ed. Walter Daniels (New York: H. W. Wilson, 1957), pp. 47–53.

22. Ibid., p. 52.

23. *Chamberlain Register*, November 7, 1935, p. 1.

24. Technical Cooperation, B.I.A., "Human Dependency and Economic Survey, Lower Brule Indian Reservation, South Dakota," 1938 (mimeo). In the Nebraska State Historical Society Library.

25. Burnette, *The Tortured Americans*, p. 18.

26. Schell, *History of South Dakota*, p. 282.

27. James Hyde, Lower Brule Annual Report, 1934, Section I, Records of the Bureau of Indian Affairs, Record Group 75, National Archives.

28. Technical Cooperation, B.I.A., "Human Dependency and Economic Survey, Lower Brule Sioux Reservation, South Dakota," p. 11.

29. Ibid., p. 2.

30. Ernest Schusky, "Contemporary Migration and Culture Change on Two Dakota Indian Reservations," *Plains Anthropologist*, 7 (1962): pp. 178–183.

31. Technical Cooperation, B.I.A., "Human Dependency and Economic Survey, Lower Brule Sioux Reservation, South Dakota," p. 10.

32. Edward Bruner, "Primary Group Experience and the Process of Acculturation," *American Anthropologist*, 58 (1956): 605.

33. Technical Cooperation, B.I.A., "Human Dependency and Economic Survey, Lower Brule Sioux Reservation, South Dakota," p. 11.

34. News item submitted by Reuben Estes in *Indians at Work*, 5, Number 11 (July 1938). (mimeo) In the Nebraska State Historical Society library.

35. *New York Times*, May 2, 1936, p. 6.

36. Ibid., May 4, 1936, p. 4.

37. Ibid., December 5, 1939, p. 6.

38. Ibid., December 6, 1939, p. 24.

39. William Brophy and Sophie Aberle, *The Indian: America's Unfinished Business* (Norman: University of Oklahoma Press, 1966), p. 108.

40. *New York Times,* September 16, 1945, p. 27.

41. Glen Emmons, "U.S. Aim: Give Indians a Chance," *Nation's Business,* 43 (July 1955): pp. 40–43.

42. Association on American Indian Affairs, "Statement on Indian Land Alienation," in *American Indians,* ed. Walter Daniels (New York: H. W. Wilson, 1957), pp. 111–113.

43. Ralph Nader, "American Indians: People Without a Future," *Harvard Law Record,* 36 (April 1956): pp. 2–6.

44. Dorothy Van de Mark, "Raid on the Reservations," *Harper's Magazine,* 212 (March 1956): pp. 48–53.

45. George Estes and Richard Loder, *Kul Wicasa Oyate* (Lower Brule: Lower Brule Sioux Tribe, 1971), pp. 69–71.

Chapter 7

1. Ernest Schusky, "Culture Change and Continuity in the Lower Brule Community," in *The Modern Sioux,* ed. Ethel Nurge (Lincoln: University of Nebraska Press, 1970), p. 114.

2. Murray Wax, Rosalie Wax and Robert Dumont, "Formal Education in an American Indian Community," *Social Problems* (Supplement) 11, No. 4 (1964).

3. Walker, "Oglala Kinship Terms."

4. Gertrude Dole, "Generation Kinship Nomenclature as an Adaptation to Endogamy," *Southwestern Journal of Anthropology,* 25 (1969): pp. 105–123.

5. When I left the reservation, the wells were still uncapped. Even if they were eventually capped, they soon were flooded over by the backwater of the Big Bend Dam.

6. Burnette, *The Tortured Americans.*

7. On other reservations some individual Indians have found they can influence a Congressman. If they persuade him on an issue and he contacts the Washington office of the B.I.A., local bureau action is often swift. Although this method has been dramatically effective for some individuals, it is difficult to see how whole communities could operate in such a way.

8. Schusky, *The Right to Be Indian.*

9. Nancy Lurie, "Menominee Termination," *The Indian Historian,* 4 (1971): pp. 31–45.

10. Schusky, *Politics and Planning in a Dakota Indian Community.*

11. Monies due Indian tribes in the past have often been distributed evenly among the individual members, who appear to have wasted the money. Much of such money is used simply to pay off debts, which can hardly be described as "waste," but to whites the disturbing fact is that the reservation economy remains at a subsistence level even after a large infusion of money. Thus almost any plans for "investment" have great appeal to white observers such as Congressmen.

12. An attempt to compromise was written into the plan providing for a small per capita payment. Some non-residents interpreted it only as an attempt to "buy off" some of their numbers.

13. Ernest Schusky, "Mission and Government Policy in Dakota Indian Communities," *Practical Anthropology,* 13 (1963): pp. 109–114.

14. Lee, *Freedom and Culture,* p. 61.

Bibliography

Abel, Annie, ed. *Tabeau's Narrative of Loisel's Expedition to the Upper Missouri*. Norman: University of Oklahoma Press, 1939.

Anderson, John. *The Sioux of the Rosebud*. Norman: University of Oklahoma Press, 1971.

Association on American Indian Affairs. "Statement on Indian Land Alienation," in *American Indians*, ed. Walter Daniels. New York: H. W. Wilson, 1957.

Bailey, Thomas. *The American Pageant*. Boston: Little, Brown, 1956.

Bancroft, Frederic, ed. *Speeches, Correspondence and Political Papers of Carl Schurz*. New York: G. P. Putnam, 1913.

Batchelder, George A. *A Sketch of the History and Resources of Dakota Territory*. Yankton: Steam Power Printing Company, 1870.

Bennett, John. *The Plainsmen*. Chicago: Aldine, 1969.

Bounds, William. "The Ministry of the Reverend Samuel Dutton Hinman Among the Sioux," *Historical Magazine of the Protestant Episcopal Church*, 38 (1969), pp. 383–401.

Briggs, Harold. "The Settlement and Development of the Territory of Dakota, 1860–70," *North Dakota Historical Quarterly*, VII (1932) pp. 114–149.

Brophy, William, and Sophie Aberle. *The Indian: America's Unfinished Business*. Norman: University of Oklahoma Press, 1966.

Bruner, Edward. "Primary Group Experience and the Process of Acculturation," *American Anthropologist*, 58 (1956), pp. 605–623.

Burnette, Robert. *The Tortured Americans*. Englewood Cliffs: Prentice-Hall, 1971.

_____and John Koster. *The Road to Wounded Knee*. New York: Bantam Books, 1974.

Catlin, George. *North American Indians*. London: Henry Bohn, 1851.

Chittenden, Hiram M. *The American Fur Trade of the Far West*. New York: Francis P. Harper, 1902.

Corbusier, William. "The Corbusier Winter Counts," *Bureau of American Ethnology, Fourth Annual Report* (1882–83), pp. 127–147.

Crouse, Nellis M. *In Quest of the Western Ocean.* New York: Wm. Morrow, 1928.

Curtis, Edwin. *The North American Indian,* Vol. 3. New York: the author, 1908, reprinted by Johnson Reprint Corporation, 1970.

Cushman, Dan. *Stay Away, Joe.* New York: Popular Library, 1953.

Daniels, Walter, ed. *American Indians.* New York: H. W. Wilson Company, 1957.

Dawes, Henry. "Have We Failed the Indian?" *Atlantic Monthly,* 84 (August, 1899), pp. 280–285.

Deloria, Vine. *Custer Died For Your Sins.* New York: The Macmillan Company, 1969.

Densmore, Francis. *Teton Sioux Music.* Washington: Bureau of American Ethnology, Bulletin 61, 1918.

Dole, Gertrude. "Generation Kinship Nomenclature as an Adaptation to Endogamy," *Southwestern Journal of Anthropology,* 25 (1969), pp. 105–123.

Dougherty, W. E. "The Recent Indian Craze," *Journal of the Military Service Institute of the United States,* 12 (1891), pp. 576–578.

Drips, J. R. *Three Years Among the Indians.* Kimball, South Dakota: Brule Index, 1894.

Drumm, Stella. "David Mitchell," *Dictionary of American Biography.* New York: Scribner, 1934.

Emmons, Glen. "U.S. Aim: Give Indians a Chance," *Nation's Business,* 43 (July, 1955), pp. 40–43.

Estes, George, and Richard Loder. *Kul Wicasa Oyate.* Lower Brule: Lower Brule Sioux Tribe, 1971.

Ewers, John C. *The Horse in Blackfoot Culture.* Washington: Bureau of American Ethnology, Bulletin 159, 1955.

Feraca, Stephen. "The Contemporary Teton Sun Dance," unpublished master's thesis, Columbia University, 1957.

_____. "The Yuwipi Cult of the Oglala and Sicangu Teton Sioux," *Plains Anthropologist* 6 (1961), pp. 155–63.

Fletcher, Alice, and Francis La Flesche. *The Omaha Tribe.* Washington Bureau of American Ethnology, 27th Annual Report, 1905.

Foster, James S. *Outlines of History of the Territory of Dakota.* Yankton: M'Intyre and Foster, 1870.

Griffin, James. "On the Historic Location of the Tutelo and the Mohetan in the Ohio Valley," *American Anthropologist,* 44 (1942), pp. 275–280.

Hale, Horatio. "The Tutelo Indians," *Proceedings of the American Philosophical Society,* 21 (1883), pp. 1–47.

Harrison, J. B. *The Latest Studies on Indian Reservations.* Philadelphia: The Indian Rights Association, 1887.

Hassrick, Royal. "Teton Dakota Kinship System," *American Anthropologist,* 46 (1944), pp. 338–347.

_____. *The Sioux.* Norman: University of Oklahoma Press, 1964.

Hertzberg, Hazel. *The Search for an American Indian Identity.* Syracuse: Syracuse University Press, 1971.

Howard, James. *The Warrior Who Killed Custer.* Lincoln: The University of Nebraska Press, 1968.

_____. "The Cultural Position of the Dakota: A Reassessment," in *Essays in the Science of Culture,* eds. Gertrude Dole and Robert Carneiro. New York: Crowell, 1960.

Howe, Mark A. *The Life and Labors of Bishop Hare.* New York: Sturgis Walton, 1911.

Hurt, Wesley. "Factors in the Persistence of Peyote in the Northern Plains," *Plains Anthropologist,* 5 (1960), pp. 16–27.

Hyde, George. *Red Cloud's Folk.* Norman: University of Oklahoma Press, 1937.

_____. *A Sioux Chronicle.* Norman: University of Oklahoma Press, 1956.

_____. *Spotted Tail's Folk.* Norman: University of Oklahoma Press, 1961.

Jenks, Albert. *The Wild Rice Gatherers of the Upper Lakes.* Washington: Bureau of American Ethnology, 19th Annual Report, 1897.

Johnson, Eldon. "The Tribes of the Great Plains," in *The Native Americans,* eds. Robert Spencer and Jesse Jennings. New York: Harper and Row, 1965.

Kohl, Edith. *Land of the Burnt Thigh.* New York: Funk and Wagnalls, 1938.

Landes, Ruth. *The Mystic Lake Sioux*. Madison: University of Wisconsin Press, 1968.

Lee, Dorothy. *Freedom and Culture*. Englewood Cliffs: Prentice-Hall, 1959.

Lindquist, G. E. *The Red Man in the United States*. New York: Doran, 1923.

Livingstone, Henry. Diaries between 1866 and 1879 in the manuscript collection of the Beinecke Library, Yale University.

Lowie, Robert. *Indians of the Plains*. New York: McGraw-Hill, 1954.

Lurie, Nancy O. "Menominee Termination," *The Indian Historian*, 4 (1971), pp. 31–45.

Lyman County Pioneers, 1885–1968. Stickney, South Dakota: Lyman County Historical Society, 1968.

Macgregor, Gordon. *Warriors Without Weapons*. Chicago: University of Chicago Press, 1946.

Malan, Vernon, and Ernest L. Schusky. *The Dakota Indian Community*. Brookings: The Agricultural Experiment Station, 1961.

Mardock, Robert W. *The Reformers and the American Indian*. Columbia: University of Missouri Press, 1971.

Mattison, Ray. "The Indian Reservation System on the Upper Missouri, 1865–90," *Nebraska History*, 35 (1955), pp. 141–174.

Meriam, Lewis, and others. *The Problem of Indian Administration*. Baltimore: Johns Hopkins, 1928.

Meyer, Roy W. *History of the Santee Sioux*. Lincoln: University of Nebraska Press, 1967.

Mirsky, Jeannette. "The Dakota," in *Cooperation and Competition Among Primitive Peoples*, ed. Margaret Mead. New York: McGraw-Hill, 1937.

Mooney, James. *The Ghost Dance Religion*. Washington: Bureau of American Ethnology, 14th Annual Report, 1896.

Myers, Frank. *Soldiering in Dakota Among the Indians*. Huron: Huronite Printing House, 1888.

Nader, Ralph. "American Indians: People Without a Future," *Harvard Law Record*, 36 (April 1956), pp. 2–6.

Nurge, Ethel, ed. *The Modern Sioux*. Lincoln: University of Nebraska Press, 1970.

Pancrost, Henry. *Impression of the Sioux Tribes in 1882*. Philadelphia: Press of Franklin Printing House, 1883.

Peters, Richard. *The Public Statutes at Large.* Boston: Little, Brown, 1846.

Poole, DeWitt C. *Among the Sioux of South Dakota.* New York: Van Nostrand, 1881.

Reid, Russell, and Clell Gannon, eds. "Journal of the Atkinson—O'Fallon Expeditions," *North Dakota Historical Quarterly,* 4 (October 1929), pp. 5–56.

Riggs, S. R. "Mythology of the Dakotas," *The American Antiquarian,* 5 (1883), p. 149.

Robinson, Doane. *Doane Robinson's Encyclopedia of South Dakota.* Pierre: the author, 1925.

———. *A History of the Dakota or Sioux Indians.* Minneapolis: Ross and Haines, 1904.

Russell, Don. *Custer's Last.* Fort Worth: Amon Carter Museum, 1968.

Schell, Herbert. *History of South Dakota.* Lincoln: University of Nebraska Press, 1968, 1st ed. 1961.

Schmeckebier, Laurence F. *The Office of Indian Affairs.* Baltimore: Johns Hopkins, 1927.

Schusky, Ernest L. *Politics and Planning in a Dakota Indian Community.* Vermillion: Institute of Indian Studies, 1959.

———. "Contemporary Migration and Culture Change on Two Dakota Indian Reservations," *Plains Anthropologist,* 7 (1962), pp. 178–183.

———. "Mission and Government Policy in Dakota Indian Communities," *Practical Anthropology,* 13 (1963), pp. 109–114.

———. "Culture Change and Continuity in the Lower Brule Community," in *The Modern Sioux,* ed. Ethel Nurge. Lincoln: University of Nebraska Press, 1970.

———. *The Right To Be Indian.* San Francisco: The Indian Historian Press, 1970.

———. "The Upper Missouri Indian Agency, 1819–1868," *The Missouri Historical Review,* 65 (April 1971), pp. 249–269.

Sinclair, Upton. *The Jungle.* New York: Doubleday, 1906.

South Dakota Department of History. *Reports and Historical Collections, 33.* Pierre: State Publishing Company, 1966.

Stevens, Alden. "Whither the American Indian?" *Survey Graphic,* 29 (1940), p. 168.

Sunder, John. *Joshua Pilcher, Fur Trader and Indian Agent.* Norman: University of Oklahoma Press, 1968.

Swanton, John R. "Early History of the Eastern Siouan Tribes," in *Essays in Anthropology Presented to A. L. Kroeber,* ed. Robert Lowie. Berkeley: University of California Press, 1936.

_____. "Siouan Tribes and the Ohio Valley," *American Anthropologist,* 45 (1943), pp. 49–66.

Technical Cooperation, Bureau of Indian Affairs. "Human Dependency and Economic Survey, Lower Brule Indian Reservation, South Dakota," 1938 (mimeo.), in the Nebraska State Historical Society, Lincoln.

Useem, Ruth and Carl Eicher. "Rosebud Reservation Economy," in *The Modern Sioux,* ed. Ethel Nurge. Lincoln: University of Nebraska Press, 1970.

Utley, Robert. *Custer and the Great Controversy.* Los Angeles: Westernlore Press, 1962.

Van de Mark, Dorothy. "Raid on the Reservations," *Harper's Magazine,* 212 (March 1956), pp. 48–53.

Voegelin, C. F. "Internal Relationships of Siouan Languages," *American Anthropologist,* 43 (1941), pp. 246–250.

Walker, Francis A. *Report of the Commissioner of Indian Affairs.* Washington: U.S. Printing Office, 1873.

Walker, J. R. "Oglala Kinship Terms," *American Anthropologist,* 16 (1914), pp. 96–109.

_____. *The Sun Dance and Other Ceremonies of the Oglala Division of the Teton Dakota.* New York: American Museum of National History, Vol. XVI, 1917.

Wax, Murray, Rosalie Wax, and Robert Dumont. "Formal Education in an American Indian Community," *Social Problems Supplement,* 11, No. 4 (1964).

Welsh, Herbert. *Report of a Visit to the Great Sioux Reserve, May and June 1883.* Philadelphia: Indian Rights Association, 1883.

Wissler, Clark. *Societies and Ceremonial Associations of the Oglala Division of the Teton—Dakota.* New York: American Museum of National History, Vol. XI, 1912.

Woodruff, Brent. "The Episcopal Mission to the Dakotas, 1860–1898," *South Dakota Historical Collections,* 17 (1934), pp. 553–603.

Newspapers

The Chamberlain Democrat.
Chamberlain Register.
Chamberlain *South Dakota Democrat.*
Deadwood *Daily and Weekly Pioneer.*
New York Times
Pierre Daily Free Press.
Sioux City Register.
Yankton *Daily Press and Dakotaian.*
Yankton *The Dakota Union.*
Yankton *The Dakotian.*
Yankton *The Union Dakotian.*
Yankton *The Weekly Dakotian.*

Government Reports

U.S. Department of the Interior. *Report of the Commissioner of Indian Affairs.* Washington: U.S. Printing Office, 1872, 1879, 1880, 1881, 1893, 1899, 1907, 1912, 1918.

Index

Vaughn, Alfred, 45
Vision Quest, 20, 28

Walker, Francis A., 67
Walker, Luke, 84, 105, 114, 115,
    117, 120, 129, 149, 155
War Relocation Authority, 203,
    206
Wells, for drinking water,
    224–25, 248n.5
Welsh, Herbert, 115, 178
Welsh, William, 81
Whetstone Reservation, 69, 70
White Buffalo Cow that Walks,
    60, 95
White River, 33, 36, 45, 56, 76,
    111, 114, 116, 130, 143,
    147, 221

White Stone Hill, battle of, 51
Wild rice gathering, 16
Wilkinson, Mahlon, 53, 54
Wilson, Peter, 39
Winter counts, 33, 35
Wissler, Clark, 202
Wounded Knee
    1890, 134–39
    1973, 137
Wounded Man, 60
Wright, E. B., 183
Wright, H. E., 187, 189

Yankton Reservation, 47, 107,
    116, 132, 147, 153, 190, 204
Yuwipi, xiv, 16, 21, 27, 28, 71,
    110, 235